SWINDON TOWN

SWINDON TOWN
The Lou Macari Years

DAVID WALLIS

First published by Pitch Publishing, 2025

1

Pitch Publishing
9 Donnington Park,
85 Birdham Road,
Chichester, West Sussex,
PO20 7AJ
www.pitchpublishing.co.uk
info@pitchpublishing.co.uk

© 2025, David Wallis

Every effort has been made to trace the copyright. Any oversight will be rectified in future editions at the earliest opportunity by the publisher.

All rights reserved. No part of this book may be reproduced, sold or utilised in any form or transmitted in any form or by any means, electronic or mechanical, including photocopying, recording or by any information storage and retrieval system, without prior permission in writing from the publisher.

A CIP catalogue record is available for this book from the British Library.

ISBN 978 1 80150 997 8

Typesetting and origination by Pitch Publishing

Printed and bound on FSC® certified paper in line with our continuing commitment to ethical business practices, sustainability and the environment.

Printed and bound in India by Thomson Press

Contents

About the Author 9
Foreword by David Hockaday 11
Acknowledgements 13
Introduction 17

1: 1979–1984: from 54th to 85th
   Swindon Town before Lou Macari 19

2: Lou Macari before Swindon Town 29

3: 1984/85: from 85th to 76th
   The beginning – and almost the end 38

4: 1985/86: from 76th to 69th
   The resurgence starts 62

5: 1986/87: from 69th to 47th
   The rise continues 92

6: 1987/88: from 47th to 33rd
   Consolidation 127

7: 1988/89: from 33rd to 26th
   On the brink of the top flight 162

8. 1989/90: from 26th to 24th
   Consequences 197

9: Lou's Views 209

10: Legacy 236

11: 87th
   The Summer of 2024 246

For Mel

By my side, every step of my journey

About the Author

MY FIRST trip to the County Ground to watch Swindon Town came in the autumn of 1969, at a time when the Robins had just won the League Cup. I'd missed that big day at Wembley the previous March, and I never forgave my parents for waiting six months too long to move my sister and I to Swindon.

I've since spent over half a century as a Swindon supporter, and almost 50 years as a season ticket holder, as I enjoyed the successes, suffered the failings, and hoped for good times at the County Ground.

So, back in 1969 Swindon were the League Cup holders. Fifty-five years later, in August 2024, they lost in the first round of the same competition. The result, the latest in a sequence of consecutive first-round League Cup eliminations, meant that Swindon had not won a League Cup match for a decade.

Did I mention the suffering?

Having spent my professional career in the electronics manufacturing industry, it has been writing about my football club, which has given me my greatest satisfactions, and it was telling the story of Lou Macari's time at Swindon Town back in the 1980s that nagged at the back of my mind for well over ten seasons.

I finally put fingers to keyboard and, with the help of Lou himself, you are holding the result.

I hope it's an accurate representation of a five-year period of constant success for a club that has occupied far too much of my time, thoughts and emotions to be healthy, and that it makes a worthwhile and enjoyable read.

As is often heard around the County Ground, COYR.

David Wallis

Foreword by David Hockaday

LOU MACARI became my manager at Swindon Town in 1984 and forged a golden period in the club's history. This proved to be my most enjoyable and successful time at any one club.

Lou didn't teach me how to play football, Lou taught me how to play football to win. He showed me what was needed to become a winner: the lifestyle, the sacrifices and dedication, required fitness levels and most importantly the mental resilience needed to grind out results and performances in the tough times.

It was difficult as a player then to see things as clearly as I do now looking back, why, when, how he did certain things. All of the 'tough love' was aimed at moulding a winning team and to constantly challenge us to be better, fitter, stronger, meaner both mentally and physically.

Lou brought great times to STFC, he gave our incredible supporters a team and a club to be proud of and he forged a nucleus of players and staff who had an unbelievable connection with the fans.

Lou has my utmost respect both as a winning manager and as a man and I (along with many, many others) will be for ever in his debt for showing me the way, the winning way, the Lou Macari way.

Thanks Gaffer.

David Hockaday
Swindon Town, 1983–1990

Acknowledgements

TOP OF the list of my thanks for their help producing this book must be the main man himself, Lou Macari.

Lou was very generous in his time, and our phone conversations became an enjoyable weekly interlude as he recounted his memories of his time at the County Ground. I hope my writings can accurately convey the integrity that Lou exudes and his respect for those who exhibit football professionalism.

But ahead of that I must express my gratitude to Lou Macari the Swindon Town manager for bringing about such great times and memories for a Robins supporter.

When David Hockaday agreed to pen a foreword for the book, I was extremely grateful to get the views of someone who knew Lou inside out, and of someone who had played a huge part in the success of the club in the 1980s. Someone who plainly values and respects his ex-boss as highly as I had learned to. Thank you, David.

Phil Leslie, a fellow Swindon-supporting sufferer, deserves my heartfelt thanks for volunteering to proofread the work as it grew. It was Phil's offer to cast his judgement over my feverish ramblings which motivated me to finally start telling the story of *Swindon Town: The Lou Macari Years*. It would have been understandable if he wondered what on earth he had let himself in for, while the summer of 2024 slipped through his fingers and he toiled, professionally critically but supportively, over my latest missive. Cheers Phil.

The two greatest sources of Swindon Town facts and figures are without doubt Paul Plowman and Richard Banyard. Without the data compiled by each, any compendium of Robins history would be immensely more difficult, and I thank them both for the work they have done, both online at www.townenders.com and in the printed media, in supplying such a valuable resource for this book.

Long-standing photographer Dave Evans was responsible for so many of the images that have been included, and I thank him for giving his blessing for their appearances within these pages. *Swindon Advertiser* editor Daniel Chipperfield helpfully supplied the authority to reproduce those which Dave had taken on behalf of the local newspaper, and I spent a very enjoyable few hours trawling through what would be photographic gold for any Town fan.

Peter Matthews, a man with a foot in each of the Robins' nests of Swindon and Cheltenham, was magnanimous in allowing a quote or two from his book, *John Trollope Record Breaker*. My thanks for that Peter, and also to Mike Berry, editor of *Backpass* magazine, who allowed references from a couple of pieces that featured in his excellent publication. Henry Port, media manager at

ACKNOWLEDGEMENTS

Swindon Town, also helpfully offered his agreement for me to use references from within the club's publications.

My thanks also go to the team at Pitch Publishing for their expertise in turning what was a long-term idea into such a professional presentation.

I hope this book is an accurate reflection of a momentous period of the Robins' history, and that it supplies an enjoyable read for anyone who feels the need to revisit a time when football seemed so much more understandable.

And thank you to you, the reader. I hope you enjoy it.

Introduction

IN THE summer of 1984, Manchester United midfielder Lou Macari was unveiled as the new player-manager of Fourth Division Swindon Town.

Macari's impeccable pedigree was faultless: winner of 24 Scottish caps; scorer of five international goals; holder of winners' medals for the Scottish League, Scottish FA Cup and Scottish League Cup; and in England, a Second Division champions' medal and one as an FA Cup winner.

The man who was for ever known as 'the diminutive Scot', 5ft 5in Lou, was ready for a new challenge at the age of 34.

Swindon's fortunes, meanwhile, were at an all-time low. Relegated to the basement division of the Football League for the first time in their history two seasons previously, there had been precious little to suggest that they were likely to reclaim a higher status any time soon.

With little money, dwindling attendances and constantly lowering expectations, Swindon were in need of a messiah.

The club and its supporters had just found one.

1

1979–1984: from 54th to 85th Swindon Town before Lou Macari

IT'S DIFFICULT to be sure when the rot set in, but as the 1970s turned into the 1980s things at Swindon Town had rarely looked rosier.

Led by manager Bob Smith, Town had cruised towards the top of the Third Division before August 1979 reached its end.

Smith, appointed boss in May 1978 when he was 34 years old, was lured from Port Vale and had been trusted to invest large sums of money in the playing staff. With £80,000 claiming the signature of striker Alan Mayes from Watford and a similar figure prising fellow frontman Andy Rowland from Bury, big money was being found to mount a promotion push, in an attempt to regain the Second Division place that had been surrendered in 1974.

Future national TV treasure Chris Kamara already graced the midfield, and before the turn of the decade a couple of club records were set when £150,000 was used to claim left-back David Peach from Southampton, with another £110,000 spent to bring midfielder Glenn Cockerill from Lincoln City.

Peach didn't enjoy the experience, saying in a *Backpass* magazine interview, 'Swindon had offered £150,000 for me and although I didn't want to go, [Southampton manager] Lawrie McMenemy thought it was too good an offer for a player approaching 30 to reject. They offered me a five-year contract on good money, but I should never have gone. It was a terrible move.'

Dropped almost as soon as he arrived and made to train with the youth team, Peach said, 'I don't know why. Money I would imagine. John Trollope took over from Smith and recalled me, but that didn't last for long and he put me back in the reserves.' Peach moved on to Orient on a free transfer after two years.

Cockerill also had an unhappy time, telling the same magazine, 'I suppose you could say it was a lot of money for a basement division player then, but it never really worked out for me at Swindon. Chris Kamara was there; Andy Rowland was scoring goals for fun and Bobby Smith the manager had been given a lot of dough to sign players. To be honest the manager had a nightmare, or at least the team did, and he was soon sacked. John Trollope took over, and I never really had a chance under him – but he'd take me to away games as 13th man, no bonuses, just to make my life difficult.'

Defender Colin Barrett arrived from Nottingham Forest on a free transfer, but surely on top wages, and there had even been a national story that Swindon were preparing a rumoured £250,000 bid for Wiltshire-born England striker Mick Channon to tempt the target man back to his home county from Southampton.

Never before had such sums and the name of Swindon Town been mentioned in the same sentence, and previous accusations that the board of directors lacked ambition were being disproved in astonishing manner.

And if it was a gamble, it was one that looked like paying off big time.

On 8 December 1979 Swindon crushed one of Smith's previous managerial charges, Bury, 8-0 at the County Ground to end the day in third place in the Third Division table. But incredibly that was not even half the story that week.

Because the previous Tuesday evening, an 84th-minute header from central defender Billy Tucker had given Town a 1-1 draw at Highbury, where Smith's men claimed a replay against Arsenal in a League Cup quarter-final. A week later, an unforgettable 4-3 win at the County Ground disposed of the Gunners and took Swindon into the League Cup semi-finals where they would meet Wolverhampton Wanderers to decide a place at Wembley.

It was an eight-day period that brought Town 13 goals, five of which were against First Division opposition. As weeks went, it's tempting to suggest that there had never been a better one for the County Ground club.

Paralleling their League Cup exploits, Town had also stormed through the early rounds of the FA Cup, and in the first month of 1980 they faced Tottenham Hotspur in round four. A goalless draw at the County Ground on 26 January was followed by a heartbreaking defeat at White Hart Lane, where a 55th-minute lead from a Ray McHale penalty was wiped out by two quick goals in the last few minutes and took the London team through to the fifth round.

All this cup activity did two things for Town's fortunes. One was to bring in vast sums of money via gate receipts. The two Arsenal games were watched by crowds totalling almost 60,000, the matches against Spurs by more than 72,000. The two home games alone were watched by over 47,000.

All very welcome, but short-term gains.

The second consequence was the huge backlog of Third Division fixtures that the total of 17 cup ties brought.

While the first seemed to justify the faith in extra playing staff expenditure, the overstretching of the budget could realistically be accused of scuppering that season, and perhaps many more to come.

As February reached mid-term, defeat at Molineux in the second leg of the League Cup semi-final saw the much-hoped for Wembley final place go to First Division Wolves, leaving Town drained, slipping down the league table and with up to five games in hand on their divisional peers.

Even the income of another 25,000-plus gate for the previous home leg with Wolves couldn't prepare the club for the exertions still required.

Perhaps this was the seminal moment when reality struck, and the consequence of extravagance commenced.

With 20 league games crammed into the last two and a half months of the season, the previous efforts took their toll. Town slipped out of the promotion running and a tenth-placed finish was far removed from what had been hoped for earlier.

And that was just about it. It wasn't evident at the time, but the dream had ended.

Five matches into the following season, Town had lost the lot, and despite the oh-so-close exploits of the previous campaign, confidence in Bob Smith in the boardroom was draining. The disastrous run of defeats abated but results still didn't justify the contract extension that Smith had recently signed.

The manager was elbowed on the first day of October, with Swindon just two places off the bottom of the Third Division table.

A new era beckoned, and it wasn't to be pretty.

In the second week of November, legendary Robins left-back John Trollope was promoted from youth team coach to first-team manager.

The perceived safe hands, his heartfelt love of the club, coupled with the undoubted support of the County Ground faithful, meant Trollope was an obvious choice. With John already on the payroll, it surely would have been hoped that fans would have overlooked the advantage of the financial prudence of promoting a man from within.

It's worth detailing just what makes John Trollope the legend he is within the history of Swindon Town.

John had played a total of 889 first-team games for Town and accepted the managerial reins four days after the last of them. Locally born, Trollope had spent his entire playing career at the County Ground, signing on as a professional in the summer of 1960.

One of the heroes of the 1969 League Cup Final win over Arsenal at Wembley and winner of two promotions with the club, Trollope only bled red because it was the colour of Swindon Town's shirts, but the Town legend was unable to stop the rot.

With his hands tied financially and with expensive signings departing to help balance the books, an increasing reliance on the youth team members, of whom Trollope had recently been in charge, was inevitable.

At the end of 1980/81, Town finished 17th in the Third Division, just one point above the drop zone to the Fourth Division, and with little hope of change the following season there was to be little respite.

Six victories in the first ten matches of 1981/82 took Town to the very top of the Third Division table, but things slipped away such that the next league win didn't come until the last day of January 1982. Victories remained elusive with just two in the next 15 matches, and four games from the end of the season, an always welcome win against Oxford United was the last three-point haul of the campaign.

The last game of 1981/82 brought a trip to Somerton Park, Newport, and only a Swindon win would suffice.

A 0-0 draw for Walsall at home to Doncaster the previous Saturday had finished the Saddlers' season in 20th place, and looking safe, on 53 points. Meanwhile Town, on 52 points, knew a draw wouldn't be enough to overhaul Walsall's superior goal difference, but a win would lift them to fifth from bottom and secure Third Division survival for another season.

Sadly for all those who travelled from Wiltshire to south Wales, it was not to be. Town midfielder Roy Carter handled the ball which gave Newport striker Tommy Tynan the opportunity to net an 81st-minute winner from the penalty spot. Town were relegated to the bottom division of the Football League for the first time in their history.

For such a dedicated Swindon man, the pain of relegation to the Fourth Division must have been as excruciating for John Trollope as it was for the travelling Town supporters.

Trollope remained in charge as Town commenced their first campaign in the basement division with hopes of an instant return to the higher status. By mid-December 1982 Town sat second in the table behind Bury, but just two wins in the next 17 attempts saw them drop 20 points behind the division's leaders.

On 19 March 1983 a 2-1 home defeat against Darlington, a team threatened with having to seek re-election, was witnessed by fewer than 3,000 supporters. The result left Town eighth in the Fourth Division table, but a significant 14 points off a promotion place having taken just one point from the previous seven games.

The following Monday brought the dismissal of John Trollope as manager. Contractually it had been agreed that he could return to youth coaching if it hadn't worked out.

In Peter Matthews' book, *John Trollope Record Breaker*, Trollope says about his managerial stint, 'I wish I hadn't done it! I really didn't enjoy dealing with senior players, I found having to keep them happy just too difficult. I didn't think I did badly, given the financial position I worked under.'

It's easy to sympathise with the much-loved left-back, that this was the poisoned chalice that he accepted when Town were desperate for a saviour. Such a dedicated Robins servant would surely have found it impossible to ignore the call from his only footballing love, when asked to give the County Ground outfit the new direction so desperately sought after the sacking of Bob Smith.

Charged with completing the last four games of the season was Ken Beamish, who had joined Town from Tranmere Rovers as player-coach in August 1981.

A striker as a player, Beamish had taken to the pitch during the relegation season, coming on as a substitute for Brian Williams in a home defeat to Burnley in February 1982 and starting in a draw at Reading a week later.

Beamish did his best to complete the season as boss as optimistically as possible, overseeing two wins and two defeats, but still the club finished the season in eighth place in the Fourth Division.

But in truth, as the summer gave way to the 1983/84 season, nothing had changed for the better at the

County Ground in three years. Still there was no money, supporters had become apathetic towards their team, and it wasn't unusual to hear laughter from the gathered few at some of the perceived ineptitude that they were witnessing on the pitch.

Attendances had dwindled to an average of 4,195 and expectation had plummeted, perhaps to its lowest depths so far.

Four games into the new season, Town were 20th in the table having lost three times already. By the beginning of December they had risen to the dizzy heights of ninth, the highest place to be achieved that campaign.

Tuesday, 17 April 1984 brought a new low for Swindon Town when just 1,681 witnessed a home win against Darlington, the lowest-ever Football League attendance at the County Ground.

One win in the last five games of the season then brought about the lowest-ever finish for a Swindon team in the club's Football League history. That was confirmed when a 2-1 defeat at Bury on Saturday, 12 May brought a 17th-placed finish in the Fourth Division.

That final placing, with a tally of 58 points, has become known as 'The Beamish Line'. Like its nautical namesake 'The Plimsoll Line', and similarly named after the man responsible for it, it was an indicator of just how low a vessel (this one carrying a cargo of hopes and dreams) could sink.

An all-time low in the history of Swindon Town.

Attendances had now dropped to an average of 3,344, but with little money available and so little optimism to offer supporters, Beamish was still offered a new 12-month contract to carry on for the following season. That was until 21 June when club sponsor Lowndes Lambert offered a significant cash injection, dependent on a new, high-profile player-manager being appointed.

As a result, the offer of a contract extension to Beamish was withdrawn unsigned, leaving Beamish to consider his future after leading the club to its worst-ever league finish.

The contrast between the optimism, financial profligacy and sheer excitement of the Bob Smith era, with the austerity and despondency of the three subsequent seasons, was stark. The conclusion that one undeniably led to the other seemed inevitable.

In little over three seasons, Swindon had dropped from just a few places below what would one day be rechristened the Championship, to only six places above the Alliance Premier League, the top echelons of non-league football.

Their league status had plummeted from 54th in the pecking order of English football, to 85th.

That John Trollope and Ken Beamish were victims of their circumstances is also undeniable. It took an upturn in opportunity, a cash injection from new sponsors and perhaps a celestial alignment of fate to offer the right man the chance to grab the opportunity.

Lou Macari was that man.

2

Lou Macari before Swindon Town

LUIGI MACARI'S father had an Italian family background but was born in Scotland. His mother was also born a Scot and Lou himself was born in Edinburgh.

So, any mistaken belief of Lou's apparently Italian derivation is brought about purely in the name he was given.

Born in June 1949 and an only child, Lou's life from the age of six months old was spent in England where his father took a cafe, and he remained in London until he was approaching ten. It was then that Macari senior took the opportunity to move the family back north across the border.

It's an intriguing thought to imagine Lou talking with Italian intonations or speaking with a south-east England, 'Cockney' accent, and Lou admits that the latter was developing nicely in his first decade. But in reality, such considerations are of little consequence. Lou Macari is a proud Scot through and through, and he is as Scottish as he sounds.

Scottish football supporters in the 1970s will have been relieved about that. If the association with Rome had been less tenuous, the winner of 24 caps and scorer of five international goals for their country might have represented the *Azzurri*, instead of gracing Hampden Park wearing a blue shirt of a darker hue.

But back in Scotland and settled at Kilwinning, a coastal town between Glasgow and Largs, Lou started attracting attention for his footballing prowess as Scottish international schoolboy honours followed.

Also came attention from potential football suitors, with Wolverhampton Wanderers being among those who showed an interest.

But Lou's real love was for Celtic, and when the Parkhead club invited him to train with them at the age of 14 the future took a predictable twist. An offer to become an apprentice followed, then came a graduation to the Scotland under-18 side.

Lou signed his first contract with Celtic at the age of 19 in 1968, earning the sum of £15 a week. His Scottish League debut came against Morton two years later on 29 August 1970, coinciding with a first professional contract on the increased wage of £50 a week.

Gaining a reputation as a hard-working goal scorer, Scottish under-23 honours followed soon after Lou made his debut for Celtic.

Celtic boss Jock Stein was renowned for his frugality along with his famous disciplinary strictness, and it would be this, coupled with Macari's increasing awareness of his own worth, that would eventually bring about the parting of the ways. Dissatisfied that the progression of his bank account wasn't matching his progress on the field and despite his huge respect for boss Stein, in April 1971 Lou submitted a written transfer request. A month later he withdrew the demand and signed a new five-year contract, but it only took until Christmas 1972 for Lou to re-file his request for a move.

Liverpool were known to be interested suitors and Lou was invited to Anfield to discuss terms. But then Manchester United boss Tommy Docherty made his move, matching Liverpool's £200,000 offer and giving Macari food for thought.

Docherty was at Anfield that day to watch his son Michael play for Burnley. Spotting Macari at the match he chatted to him, but with Celtic never publicising that Lou was looking to get away, the Doc was taken completely by surprise by Macari's availability. Without permission from Celtic to approach him he was unable to formally discuss his desire to sign the player.

Realising that Lou would be talking to Bill Shankly later and knowing that the Anfield boss would sing the praises of Liverpool, Docherty knew that Shanks would exert pressure on his target to sign there and then. But also knowing Macari as he did, the Doc felt that he would have misgivings about a manager who attempted to act without due consideration.

Docherty gained permission to speak to Macari the next day and his understanding of Lou's character was proven. Lou had not signed the previous evening;

Liverpool had withdrawn their offer, and the way was open for Macari to become a United player.

Lou's own recollection of the evening makes for interesting confirmation, 'Bill Shankly spoke with great enthusiasm of his ambitions for Liverpool and of the part he wanted me to play in the future success of the club. And when Bill Shankly is in full flow, he is a persuasive man. But somewhere in my make-up there is a mule-like streak of stubbornness, and I wasn't to be persuaded so easily.'

Shankly had offered Lou a contract of £180 a week, coupled with a £9,000 signing-on fee, a substantial increase on his salary back at Celtic Park. Docherty trumped that figure with a three-year contract of £200 a week and a £10,000 signing-on bonus – and won his fellow Scot's signature.

So, despite Liverpool's championship pretensions compared with United's First Division relegation battle, it was Docherty who won the day. Perhaps Macari's liking for a challenge had shown through.

By the time Lou left for Manchester United, he had played over 100 games for the Bhoys with some considerable success.

With a goal in a 2-1 victory over Rangers in the 1971 Scottish FA Cup Final, plus two more at the same stage of the tournament against Hibernian in 1972, each brought winners' medals. In addition, four Scottish League championships and a Scottish League Cup proved quite a haul for four seasons' professional endeavours.

European football experience had naturally accompanied this, with Celtic's regular participation in the European Cup offering Lou a dozen encounters against continental opponents.

It was Docherty who, as Scotland boss, first called Lou into the Scotland under-23 side while he was still a young Celtic player, and it seems obvious just how much mutual respect the pair had for each other.

Both were near-neighbours in Scotland for a while and occasional visitors to each other's houses, and with each contributing the preamble to the other's autobiography, it's striking how similarly each mirrors the character of the other.

Both are plainly single-minded. Docherty described Macari as a man who likes a joke; an independent spirit but someone who is very much a team man and talker on the field. A natural athlete who loves his football, and obviously not someone who suffers fools gladly. Certainly not a 'yes' man, he is wise enough to stop pursuing an argument when he realises that his is a lost cause.

Macari is well known to be a teetotaller, and a man who knows the benefit of hard work to any aspiring footballer. Lou once wrote, 'I have never claimed to be the world's most complete footballer, although I have my fair share of skills. Once I'm in the thick of the action I am not plagued by nerves.'

And perhaps tellingly, 'I thrive on the stimulus of a new challenge.'

Macari started on the path of becoming a legend in Manchester, just as he had in Glasgow. The drop was avoided at the end of 1972/73, but 12 months later came relegation and Lou was a Second Division player, playing in England.

While the spell in the Second Division was only of a year's duration it's fair to say that Manchester United were a club in transition, but Lou was to claim great credit for his part in their return to the top.

Not that it was all plain sailing, as would be expected of two independently minded individuals.

Docherty and Macari fell out when the boss dropped the player in October 1973, told him to train with the reserves and ordered him to play in a friendly. Macari was furious and let Docherty know, leading the Doc to tell him he would be fined, and transfer-listed.

The issue had arisen as a result of Macari's lack of success playing the striker's role that Docherty had envisaged him in, believing the Scot to be an out-and-out goalscorer.

When it was agreed that 5ft 5in tall Lou was better suited in the deeper role which he preferred and in which he could contribute more to all-round play, Docherty was magnanimous enough to accept that, peace was restored and the stage was set for Macari to participate in ten years of Manchester United achievement.

Starting with a Second Division champions' medal, Lou claimed an FA Cup winners' medal and a couple more runners-up medals in the same competition. Coupled with two League Cup runners-up gongs and two winning appearances in the Charity Shield, Macari's trophy haul was fewer in number than those gained back in Scotland, but each was won with the trademark effort that he made his own.

When Docherty left Old Trafford in 1977, Macari had made around 150 league appearances and recorded almost 40 goals, with another 18 in domestic cup competitions. Consistency was to follow over the three seasons of Dave Sexton's reign as boss at Old Trafford, but with the arrival of Ron Atkinson and with Lou now in his early 30s, appearances understandably started to seep away.

Macari made 37 outings in 1980/81, with his usual creditable strike record of a goal every fourth match, but over the following two seasons his position had been superseded in the first team by the inevitable team rebuilding of a new manager, and he took to the pitch on just a dozen occasions.

When he left Old Trafford for the last time as a Manchester United player, his record showed almost 100 goals across just over 400 appearances in all competitions, reflecting his 'one goal in four games' record admirably.

By this time, Lou Macari's career as a Scotland international midfielder had long since drawn to a close.

Following that under-23 debut call-up by Tommy Docherty in 1972, a second game at that level came against England.

Then, starting with a substitute's appearance against Wales in May 1972 when he replaced John O'Hare, Lou claimed a further five full international caps for his country while still a Celtic player. Two goals against Yugoslavia in his third match announced him as an international goalscorer.

In October 1973 he scored Scotland's first goal against Denmark in a 4-1 win in Copenhagen as the Scots commenced their successful qualifying campaign for the 1974 World Cup finals, but Lou failed to make Willie Ormond's squad to travel to West Germany.

Then, four years later, he appeared in Scotland's celebrated 2-0 qualifying win against Wales at Anfield in Liverpool, a result which took the national team to a second consecutive World Cup finals, this one in Argentina in 1978 where he appeared twice on the world stage under the managership of Ally MacLeod.

But in typical, perhaps his belligerent style, Lou ruffled feathers by contesting the perceived paltriness of the bonuses available to him and his playing colleagues should they be successful in winning the World Cup. Not something that ultimately troubled the Scottish FA's coffers, but another indication of Macari's readiness to fight his corner in the face of an apparent shortage of respect.

The tournament brought Lou's swansong on the international scene when the 1-1 draw with Iran in Córdoba on 7 June 1978 effectively ended the World Cup campaign. Then, on arrival back on British soil the Scottish FA had something to say.

Plainly stung by Macari's stance, they announced, 'The team manager, in selecting players in the future, is recommended to bear in mind the vehement complaints directed at the association and its arrangements by the player Lou Macari. He should give serious consideration to the advisability of subjecting the player again to these arrangements which he professes to find unsatisfactory.'

A sad way to culminate Macari's international career, but one brought about by another indication of the man's character and sense of right and wrong.

The Scottish FA had offered little support or sympathy to the additional pressure Macari would have felt, having tragically and suddenly lost his mother prior to leaving for Argentina.

All told, Macari made 24 appearances for his country, scoring five times, and graced the international stage with typical industry and endeavour.

All of this offers an interesting insight into his character.

Plainly a man of integrity, he demonstrated a spirit of determination and single-mindedness. Lou knew his own mind, showed a healthy cynicism for the patter of a salesman, and he was not a man to shirk a challenge.

Ten years after his earlier exchanges with Bill Shankly and Tommy Docherty, Macari would sit down with Swindon Town chairman Maurice Earle to discuss becoming manager of the Fourth Division club.

Whatever was said at the time, it seems Earle was more successful in selling an opportunity than the legendary Shanks.

And if Lou Macari was up for a challenge, he had certainly picked one.

3

1984/85: from 85th to 76th
The beginning – and almost the end

PRIOR TO Lou Macari's arrival there had been three years of stagnation at Swindon Town: two seasons of Fourth Division football, a level to which the club had never previously been subjected since formation 105 years previously; four years of decreasing financial status and a constant erosion of expectation, belief, and even hope for supporters.

So far, this story has consisted of two separate threads – of Swindon Town and Lou Macari. Now those two paths merge, as the summer of 1984 saw things in Wiltshire take an interesting turn for the better.

Macari arrived in Swindon to discuss the vacancy of player-manager in July. He had asked a friend to ring on his behalf to express his interest in the role to gauge Town's level of interest, and when the response appeared positive an interview was arranged.

Anyone who has undergone a job interview would know the sort of questions to expect. Lou was asked about his readiness to step down to the Fourth Division, the contrast of training facilities to that which he was accustomed and the travel arrangements for away games. Would all of this be a culture shock?

Asked about the likelihood of post-match meals of fish and chips on return bus journeys, Lou was unfazed. The experience reminded him of his early days at Celtic, and the interviewee was even the owner of a fish and chip shop near Old Trafford.

Making sure he said the things that he felt were important rather than just being led by the questions asked, Lou admits he spoke his mind, 'I did not tailor my answers according to what they wanted to hear, I just told it as I saw it, for better or worse. I left with no idea as to how I'd been received, but a couple of days later I got word that they were happy.'

Town chairman Maurice Earle, soon to resign and be replaced by vice-chairman Brian Hillier, was moved to comment, 'We didn't interview him. He interviewed us.'

The other man who had been in the frame for the job had been former Liverpool defender Phil Thompson, but after two interviews and a job offer, Thompson had turned it down, leaving the way open for Lou.

The very opportunity for a fresh managerial appointment had come about through a cash injection by club sponsors, insurance company Lowndes Lambert. Surely hoping for greater exposure for their involvement, the company had stumped up a fee believed to be between

£100,000 and £150,000 to finance the recruitment and salary of a new player-manager, one with a higher profile than Ken Beamish.

The money was to pave the way for the introduction of Lou Macari and his chosen deputy, Harry Gregg, a fellow Manchester United legend and also a survivor of the terrible Munich air crash of 1958.

Possibly not made plain to Lou at the time of discussion, he was not aware of just how fractured relations were between the board and the supporter base.

With the exception of the out-of-character extravagances of the Bob Smith era of 1979/80, finances were always to be sparse when set against the business interests of the board of directors. And with the County Ground owned by the local council and hence rent due, and interest payments of a loan used to build the comparatively recently constructed North Stand, an annual six-figure sum was required to service these needs alone.

The reduced attendances suffered since relegation to the Fourth Division had taken their toll, and the overdraft was mounting. It's not surprising just how welcome the involvement of Lowndes Lambert had been.

Lou Macari held Jock Stein, his first manager at Celtic, in great esteem. The Scot had constructed a Celtic team from apparently non-exceptional but success-hungry individual talent into such a formidable and cohesive unit that they won the European Cup in 1967.

Perhaps this was the inspiration behind the group of players he started assembling at Swindon in 1984,

THE BEGINNING – AND ALMOST THE END

although immediate progress in influencing the playing staff to his liking would have been tempered by the usual cashflow constraints, coupled with Lou's understandable need to evaluate the players already at his disposal.

But with a sparse playing staff headcount and the new season just weeks away, work would need to start quickly.

On the evening of 8 August 1984, a Town team took to the County Ground pitch for the first time under the tutelage of Lou Macari.

The occasion was a pre-season friendly against his old club, Manchester United, an arrangement made between Lou and the Red Devils with the express intention that it would bring some immediate and very welcome extra cash to Town's bank balance.

Lou's first programme notes as manager that evening make for an interesting read.

Starting by offering a 'hello' to the gathered supporters, he went on, 'I hope that the "marriage" between Harry Gregg and myself, and the players, staff and supporters of the club will be a long and happy one.'

A wish that would be prophetically correct in some respects but misplaced in one crucial detail.

Carrying on, Lou expressed, 'The message I wish to convey to you is that Lou Macari and Harry Gregg are not miracle workers. Our first task is to get the players to want to play for Swindon Town and to go out on a Saturday afternoon and give 100 per cent effort throughout each game. We will lose games, this is a fact of football, but I will be disappointed at the end of any game we have lost if anyone can point a finger and say the lads did not try.'

Exactly the sort of sentiment the supporters of any team want to hear from their new manager.

The result of this exhibition match was of course as insignificant as it was predictable, although it has been recorded that a 4-1 win for the away side was notable only for the two goals scored by United's Norman Whiteside. A third was recorded by young midfielder Mark Dempsey, who would spend a month on loan with Swindon at the beginning of 1985.

As player-manager, Macari started the game, but took himself off at half-time, perhaps in order to analyse the performance of his new charges from a more dispassionate position.

When he named his team for his first competitive fixture, against Wrexham on 25 August 1984, eight of his players had played in Beamish's last.

The only changes were the inclusion of Macari himself, winger/striker Garry Nelson – a Ken Beamish recruit a year earlier – and the returning Andy Rowland, who had missed the closing stages of the previous season when he lost his place to Jim Quinn.

Striker Quinn had departed for Blackburn Rovers in August but was fated to return to Wiltshire two years later and would one day occupy the same County Ground managerial office that Macari was just familiarising himself with.

The home match ended in a 2-1 win for Town. Macari himself scored the first goal of the campaign,

Alan Mayes grabbed the winner three minutes from time, and 3,591 witnessed the spectacle.

The squad had been further weakened under Beamish by the retirement of goalkeeper Jimmy Allan, a stalwart of 13 seasons and maker of over 430 appearances for the club over three divisions. A broken arm had forced his departure from the playing roster, and his presence would prove a loss that Macari would never reap the opportunity to name in his side.

Claiming the green shirt was Scott Endersby. Having already played 37 consecutive games under Beamish after Allan's injury, he brought a mix of relative youth and experience that no doubt Lou would have hoped to place faith in. By the end of the new manager's first season Endersby was to be ever-present and had taken his tally to well over 80 consecutive league appearances.

But Endersby drew criticism from his boss after the second match of the season, a 2-2 draw at Hartlepool United which Macari described as 'a complete disaster'. Further commenting, he said, 'We had three points in the bag and threw two of them away. We gave away a goal that Scott Endersby knows, without a doubt, he should have saved.'

Two wins arrived in the first seven league games, with the first of those being claimed in August and the second in September. It was not apparent at the time, but Town would go on to win just two league matches a month from October until March; the sort of return which virtually guarantees mid-table mediocrity.

The three league games that Swindon lost were all surrendered by a two-goal margin or greater, the last of the trio being a disappointing 3-0 home defeat to Hereford United.

Among the opening league fixtures had come a morale-sapping 5-1 home defeat to Bristol Rovers in the first round of the League Cup, and despite a win by a single goal in the away leg at Eastville, that was the end of Town's involvement in the tournament, of which they had once been winners and of which they had reached the semi-final just four seasons previously.

If this was to be a Lou Macari-led revolution, it looked like being a slow burner.

The new manager had added three names to the playing staff in the early days of his managerial tenure, all of whom would go on to be considered archetypal Macari signings.

The first was Peter Coyne, who signed for Town two days before the start of the season and came on as a substitute for Charlie Henry for his debut in the first game against Wrexham.

He had been one of the many saddled with the label 'The New George Best' when he was on the books of Manchester United as an apprentice, having scored a couple of hat-tricks as an England schoolboy international. Just two first-team appearances came at the Old Trafford club before he was released, but he had caught the eye of club-mate Macari.

A £5,000 fee drew him from non-league Hyde United where he arrived after a failed Football League resurrection with Crewe Alexandra, and he netted his first goal for Swindon in his second game, away at Hartlepool.

The signing of Colin Gordon bore startling similarities. The big striker had been plying his trade for Oldbury United when Swindon came calling; this time just £1,000 parted hands initially to make Gordon a professional footballer. The deal came after a week's trial, during which he scored his first Town goal, the winner at Rochdale on 3 November.

The arrivals of both from non-league teams were indicative of the sort of player who could be considered perfect Macari signings. The pair had encountered disappointment in their careers and as a result both had a point to prove.

Young enough to adapt, malleable enough to accept their illustrious boss's advice, and ready to adhere to the concept of hard work to attain what they may have feared they had lost in their career, could they be seen to be the very epitome of signings the great Jock Stein had used to forge a European Cup-winning team at Celtic? Town supporters could but hope.

The third signing was more of a known quantity.

Defender Chris Ramsey had played in the FA Cup Final as recently as 1983 in the colours of Brighton & Hove Albion. He arrived initially on loan, but as Macari said at the time, 'Let us hope that his stay here is a lot longer than the initial one-month loan period he is at present contracted for.' The boss's wishes were granted when Ramsey signed a permanent contract ten weeks later.

Through the course of the autumn, winter and into the spring, there was precious little indication that things were improving at the County Ground.

October began with Town in 11th place in the table on 11 points. November started with Swindon three places lower, and those were to be the two extremes of divisional position for four months.

Embarrassment ensued in the first round of the FA Cup in November when a respectable goalless draw at Alliance Premier League side Dagenham produced a replay at the County Ground which Town contrived to lose 2-1.

It is one of the greatest clichés in football that, now out of both cup competitions as early as three months into the season, Swindon could concentrate on the league. Could the new opportunity to focus be capitalised on?

Soon after the FA Cup exit by the Daggers, new chairman Brian Hiller alluded to the always-present financial considerations at the club.

Ongoing difficulties in maintaining the schedule of payment due to Thamesdown Borough Council through the construction of the North Stand were being addressed. The facility had been built over ten years previously, when Town's promotion to the Second Division had brought the need to accommodate higher match attendances.

A loan from the local council had facilitated the construction but also brought the millstone of a long-term debt, landing the club with a financial commitment for a structure which current attendances no longer justified.

'Our problem began back in 1982 when nobody foresaw that attendances would drop to their current low level,' explained Hillier.

The loss of cup revenue would not help.

October commenced with a 4-1 win over Blackpool which flattered to deceive but was a personal high for striker Alan Mayes. His hat-trick took his season's tally so far to six, and a further brace before the month's end could be considered the brightest light that Town supporters could see. Then a ligament injury severely interrupted Mayes's season and kept him out until April, an unfortunate circumstance which effectively heralded the end of his Swindon career.

The light at the end of the tunnel probably looked as far away as ever.

Town's top scorer had been one of those early Bob Smith signings and he scored a hat-trick on his debut at Rotherham. Tempted to Chelsea in the winter of 1980 by the waving of a £200,000 cheque, Mayes had become one of the sacrificial lambs of the cost-cutting exercise post-Smith.

When he returned to Wiltshire on a free transfer in July 1983 he was greeted like the returning of a prodigal son, and hopes were high that he and fellow strike partner Andy Rowland could be reunited with the form that had brought the pair a total of 56 goals between them in 1979/80.

Now, in November 1984, Swindon could ill afford to lose the goals that he was supplying if any progress could be hoped for.

When October concluded with the month's second four-goal tally, a 4-0 home win over Stockport County, Mayes grabbed his tenth of the season on what was to be his last Town appearance for some time.

His fellow forward Andy Rowland, meanwhile, having played the first game of the season in a striker's role, had been switched to the centre of defence where Macari hoped he could use his nous to stabilise a weak-looking back line. As successful as that might have been, there was the risk that it would deprive the forward line of goal potential, but the arrival of Colin Gordon certainly offset the loss.

The second day of December brought the highest gate that Town were to play in front of that season, and it was at an unlikely venue.

The Robins lost 1-0 at promotion-chasing Darlington in front of 6,099 people, an attendance that was far and away the highest number to watch Swindon on any matchday that campaign and double the average attendance that the County Ground could muster in 1984/85.

When 1985 broke with a New Year's Day fixture at home to Chesterfield, a new year brought new hope.

A brace of goals from Andy Rowland, his first strikes since the middle of September, and another pair from Colin Gordon gave Town the much-needed boost of a 4-0 win. All the more surprising in that the Spireites would go up as champions little over four months later.

If this upturn was hoped to indicate a turnaround in fortunes, hopes were dashed just four days later with a drubbing at Wrexham by the same scoreline.

Town were showing their ability to flicker into life unexpectedly and produce the sort of performance that could brighten the latter festivities of supporters, then crash and burn just as inexplicably soon after.

But even so, one consistency continued: the inability to win more than two matches a month.

February began with a 1-0 home win over Mansfield Town. Then Swindon lost by the same scoreline at Blackpool. A 2-1 victory against Rochdale was followed by a draw at Torquay.

Finally in March things showed signs of improvement when four victories came from the eight games played.

Something was subtly changing on the pitch, and it was a turn for the better that would not go unnoticed by supporters. Finally, there were glimmers of the end of the relentless cycle of one step forward, two steps back that those fans had suffered for years.

An injury forced Macari to step down as a player for the rest of the campaign and offered him the chance to view his team from the sidelines. How important that fresh perspective was is difficult to assess. Certainly, the workload of training and playing, managing the office requirements understood by a manager in any walk of life, and scouting new targets for potential recruitment was a heavy one.

Lou took to the field for the last time that season in a 2-0 defeat at Port Vale on 9 March. For the last two months he was able to concentrate solely on the task of shaping his team for success on the field of play, rather than worry about his contribution towards it. He was able to observe the performances of individuals and partnerships of groups, rather than be distracted with all the matchday clamour taking place around him.

The first game not involving Lou Macari the player was a midweek 1-0 home victory over Bury three days later. A Peter Coyne penalty settled the outcome and Lou was able to see things unfolding on the pitch in front of him for the first time.

The same player scored the goal which claimed a point at his previous employers Crewe the following weekend, then his single strike won the game at Peterborough a week later.

An emphatic 6-2 defeat in Lincolnshire at the hands of Scunthorpe could charitably be viewed as the exception which proved the rule, because when the month concluded with a 2-1 home victory over Hartlepool, Coyne had scored five times in less than three weeks and Town had won four games in a calendar month for the first time for two seasons.

When things went wrong, they were still capable of going wrong in spectacular style, but gradually perhaps more good things seemed to be happening than bad.

Lowndes Lambert's insistence on appointing a high-profile manager in a bid to increase the wider public's awareness of the club had certainly worked. Media coverage of the Robins had risen, and all reports began with the wording 'Lou Macari's Swindon Town'.

With this comes danger. There is a risk of the profile of the manager dominating that of the club itself, and it can serve a greater purpose for the boss than the team.

Successful implementation of such a strategy relies on the personality of the new manager engaging with supporters, so that it is understood on both sides that the important factor is the club, rather than the boss.

Lou Macari's persona was such that he was impressing with the lengths that he was going in order to bring about the rise of the status of Swindon Town. His consideration of future, more lucrative employment opportunities appeared way down his list of priorities, not something that was always seen in 1985, and something that is even more rarely encountered in football management in subsequent decades.

Supporters were also detecting an increased sense of their own worth to the arrangement. They were taking Macari to their hearts as they observed a display of passion from the boss as he seemed to understand just what they too were bringing to the party.

Fans were valuing the extra media coverage being afforded to Swindon, and the feeling that they were no longer just one of the forgotten clubs in the lower divisions of the country. No longer one to be ignored in the pursuit of the dominance that football was undergoing, and which would eventually bring about the formation of the self-serving Premier League.

It's never wise to view a club's supporters as a single entity, however. Each is an individual who makes his own evaluation of things going on at his or her club, and the persuasion of one does not automatically guarantee the acceptance of another. But there was enough groundswell of goodwill towards Macari among fans to indicate the boss was beginning to be seen as the man to bring about the progression to restore status and respect. It had been 15 years since Swindon's most recent promotion season, and two relegations had taken place since then.

The relationship between Macari and the fans was evolving, and that was about to become vitally important in the coming days.

With the expected spread of points gained across the teams in the table at this stage of the season, even the unusual occurrence of those four wins through March failed to lift Town higher than 11th as April began, the same position they had occupied six months earlier.

There was now a ten-point gap between Town and fourth-placed Blackpool, the last potential promotion place in these pre-play-off days.

But a bombshell behind the scenes was about to be detonated; April was to bring about one of the most traumatic weeks ever experienced at the County Ground. On 5 April as the Easter weekend approached, the club made an announcement which seemed to herald the end of all that Macari and Harry Gregg had been trying to do for six months.

Brian Hillier appeared on TV to state that both men had been sacked as a result of the deterioration of their working relationship. It was stated by sources in the know that the two would no longer even talk to each other. Youth team coach John Trollope was asked to steady the ship by taking the team's game against Southend United on Easter Saturday.

Supporters, who had started to believe in what was happening on the pitch, immediately organised a petition of 1,500 names, which included the signatures of various first-team players, calling for Macari's reinstatement. The match against Southend was interrupted by pitch invasions and chanting calling for Macari to be put back in charge, and the man himself was seen in the stands watching the game.

Showing immense professionalism, Town's players won 2-0 with goals from Garry Nelson and Colin Gordon.

As the story unfolded, it seems that Macari had found a series of notes that Gregg was making about his actions as Town manager and was understandably dismayed by the apparent lack of loyalty.

Tipped off that Gregg was trying hard to ingratiate himself with the club's directors at the expense of the boss, it appeared the assistant had his eyes on the top job. When Lou was asked to meet with the chairman to discuss the burgeoning dissent, Gregg gatecrashed the meeting and made sure his point of view could not be ignored.

Publicly, Hillier said that the problem between Macari and Gregg had been going on for some weeks, and that the board had felt they had no alternative but to relieve both men from their responsibilities.

Hillier seemed to pin the blame on Macari as the man in the senior position who was tasked to exercise his authority. It was implied that Macari had wanted to deal with the issue with Gregg, but had been unable, or at least unsuccessful, in doing so.

Macari's ability to manage was also called into question. Hillier appeared to feel Macari should have sacked his assistant, refusing to confirm or deny the existence of any diary.

As the story gained momentum on local TV, in an interview Macari said, 'I have three lads who had been fanatical Manchester United supporters and nine months later they are fanatical Swindon Town supporters. I didn't know how to tell them that their dad was no longer the manager or a player for Swindon. When I told them, it was me who started crying rather than them.'

Macari also denied that a clash of personalities with Gregg was to blame for the fracturing of the relationship between them, more a disagreement about who held ultimate decision-making authority. And he was upset at the insinuation that he had been too soft to take action to resolve the issue himself.

Via the TV crew Macari passed a message to the board of directors telling them that he wanted his job back. He had been very happy at the club and was upset to be sacked.

The whole club was in turmoil, and the supporters were making their dissatisfaction known.

Just five days later Brian Hillier made a new announcement on behalf of the board, saying, 'Having taken into consideration all the factors, the board have unanimously decided to reinstate Lou Macari.' The announcement came after a two-hour long meeting starting at 1pm on Wednesday, 10 April and made no reference to assistant Harry Gregg.

All ten board members were said to be involved, one of whom was a Lowndes Lambert representative who had been appointed as a result of the cash injection which paid the two sacked men's wages.

Lou's hope was that over the long term, everyone could move on and that the whole episode would bring the board, himself and the supporters closer together in support of Swindon Town.

It was interesting to hear Macari tell of the confusion the players had suffered as Gregg appeared to undermine his authority as manager.

Gregg was gone, Macari was back, and it left Lou needing to find a new assistant manager. He acted quickly to appoint John Trollope to the role.

As appointments go, the decision seemed almost inspired. If personality differences had contributed to the problems between Macari and Gregg, Trollope could hardly be more different.

Here was a man who was hardly likely to try to usurp Macari's authority – someone who had actively stated that he hadn't liked the responsibility of dealing with adult professional footballers and someone who had Swindon Town entwined in his DNA.

As youth team manager he was available immediately, and at the right price. He was loved by supporters and seemed the ideal choice to complement the growing affection that Lou Macari himself was engendering in the same people.

During Lou's brief absence Trollope had overseen two matches. The incident-packed win over Southend

United which had seen all the furore caused by Macari's dismissal, and a desperately close defeat at eventual champions Chesterfield, which had been surrendered to the only goal of the game in the last minute of the game.

John's comments in his biography about the time shed light on the events from a different perspective, 'I have to say, I found Harry Gregg a funny fellow. I didn't find him easy to get on with at all. Harry was always disagreeing with Lou about how things should be done, in public as well as in private, and the relationship went sour.'

Tellingly, John said, 'I'm not sure why Lou didn't just get rid of him.'

And he was pleased to be offered the chance to succeed Gregg, 'I was flattered to be asked because it was a sign of Lou's trust in me. I know he asked around football and the club about what I was like, and he must have liked what he heard. I did have to think about it for a while because I thought I was happiest working with younger players, but I decided to give it a go and I was very glad that I did because we had some great times.'

At the following game, against Northampton, punctuated by a spectacular overhead kick goal from Colin Gordon, there were unprecedented scenes of support for the boss. 'Without the support of fans, I wouldn't be back here today,' said Lou.

On the day, 3,457 of those supporters turned up to witness the return of the man they had started to invest their belief in and to see a 2-0 win against Northampton.

THE BEGINNING – AND ALMOST THE END

After the game Macari said, 'I can't describe the past week. It's been an event that I never dreamed would happen. We get a regular crowd of two and a half thousand. No one would have thought the TV cameras would be here, no one would have thought the press would have been here in the force they have been, and it's all been a new experience for everyone at the club and town.'

And to the TV gathering he said, 'The next time you are here, I hope it's for football reasons.'

The programme notes of the reinstated Lou Macari and chairman Brian Hillier attempted to draw a line under the events.

Macari wrote, 'A player or manager experiences many ups and downs during their footballing career. In the short time I have been here at Swindon Town there have been good times as well as bad. The events of the past week though have been an experience that I don't want to ever have to go through again. What should have been a happy working Easter for me was completely shattered on Good Friday, and for the next five days my spirits were very low. My family life totally disrupted.

'However, on Wednesday I felt ten feet tall again when I was asked by the board to return to Swindon Town as the manager – it was one of the greatest days of my life. I had no hesitation in accepting the offer and now look forward to continuing the challenge in front of me.

'I would appeal to all supporters to quickly put the events of the past week behind us and hope we can now all work together to the benefit of the club. The demonstrations last week were certainly not a victory for me even though I got my job back, or a defeat for the board.

'In my opinion they were a victory in the respect that they brought our supporters much closer to the football club. Finally, there are too many people to thank individually for their support during my hours of depression – I would from the bottom of my heart just like to say thank you to all of you.'

Meanwhile Hillier's thoughts were as follows, 'I am sure that it is unnecessary for me to describe the difficult time everyone at the club has experienced since the decision of the board taken a week ago last Thursday, the only decision that could have been taken after considering all the facts known to us. Nevertheless, the decision was a difficult one.

'Saturday's game was a very traumatic experience for everyone, but the feelings of very loyal and responsible supporters were made known to us. Following this match, I was contacted by Mr Macari who I met on Sunday evening when we had a very long and constructive discussion from which I felt that the board had an obligation to meet again to reconsider. The outcome of this meeting is now public knowledge, and we must all put behind us these events and look forward positively to the future.

'Although the players made their feelings known, no one can deny that in the games against Southend and Chesterfield they gave maximum effort. The match against Chesterfield was an exceptional one and we were indeed extremely unfortunate to be defeated in the last minute, but the players must be congratulated for the manner in which they dealt with their jobs despite all the distraction around them.'

If it had been hoped that Macari was to be a messiah when he joined the club in the summer, he had been cast aside at the beginning of Easter and resurrected five days later.

There were six games to go before the end of the season. Everyone drew breath and set about concentrating on football again. It may have been helpful that the next two matches were both away from home, allowing some of the emotion that had been aired over Easter to dissipate before crowds regathered at the County Ground.

Visits to Hereford and Aldershot produced consecutive wins over a four-day period. Colin Gordon scored all four goals and goalkeeper Scott Endersby kept two clean sheets.

When the last match of that month arrived with a home win over Darlington, as striker Alan Mayes scored his last goal for Swindon, the team which had been unable to win two matches in any calendar month until March had just won five in April.

Incredibly, and not without a huge level of irony, Lou Macari was presented with the Fourth Division Manager of the Month award for April. The irony was compounded that the teetotaller was presented with a gallon bottle of whisky.

Somewhere amid all the turmoil it had almost gone unnoticed that over the most recent 14 games, nine of them had produced three points. Returns of that nature over the course of 1984/85 would have had a significant, positive impact on Town's final Fourth Division placing.

There were now three games until the end of the season, and after such drama off the pitch had done so much to overshadow the action upon it, perhaps it's understandable if everyone with a love of Swindon Town was prepared to heave a sigh of relief and clear their minds over the forthcoming close season.

A 1-1 draw at Colchester United, followed by an incredible 4-4 draw at home to Chester City, came as a semblance of order started to be restored. Defeat at Halifax Town on 10 May brought the curtain down on a season which all were happy to see the back of.

There was now no doubt of the support that Macari had from fans, and it would be extremely unwise of the board of directors to risk demonstrating that they thought anything differently.

There would now be the usual three-month summer break during which all parties could reflect, and plan for the future.

Précised in retrospect, the first competitive game that Macari had overseen at the County Ground had ended in a 2-1 win. Macari himself scored the first goal of the campaign and 3,591 witnessed the spectacle.

Of his signings, by the end of Macari's first season Peter Coyne had scored 14 goals in 42 league appearances. Colin Gordon, meanwhile, had scored 17 times in 32 games. The only other Town goalscorer in double figures (in fact the only one on more than five) was Alan Mayes who had netted all but one of his goals by November.

Through the course of the campaign Macari had been player-manager, ex-player-manager, then player-manager again.

An eighth-placed finish in the Fourth Division was an improvement of nine positions on the all-time low of 12 months previous. Perhaps progress was not looking as swift as might have been hoped, but progress it was, and no one could have predicted the off-field difficulties that had to be overcome.

The average home attendance had actually reduced by over 300 from that achieved under Beamish, to 3,025 in Macari's first season.

But as Lou said back in July, he was not a miracle worker. Not yet at least.

After a false start, Lou Macari's reign as Swindon Town manager was about to take off.

4

1985/86: from 76th to 69th
The resurgence starts

'LET'S ALL enjoy ourselves.'

That was the message from Lou Macari in the club's pre-season brochure before the start of 1985/86, before he added, 'This club has financial problems that the club directors cannot put right in one season. There were problems when I arrived here and surely no one expects miracles and expects me to put these right overnight.'

But he continued more hopefully, 'Last season will have no bearing on this one, but we must make things happen.' And talking of his transfer dealings, he also said somewhat prophetically, 'If I found that I had made a bad signing they would soon be on their way, irrespective of whether they had signed a two-year contract.'

He continued, 'I have told my defenders that they are paid to defend. Last season they were not always doing that.'

Alluding to his commitment to Swindon, Lou commented that he had turned down an approach from a Second Division club in the summer but said, 'I want to stay at Swindon for a few years. This is our home and Swindon Town is my club.'

After a summer in which Swindon supporters drew breath, Macari had undertaken the daunting task of carrying on the rebuilding of his squad, and it must have seemed as though he was effectively starting again when he cast his eye around potential football recruitment targets.

He had enhanced his playing staff with the additions of goalkeeper Jake Findlay, and midfielders Tony Evans and Derek Hall, but it was probably the signing of David Moss which most caught the eye.

Witney lad Moss was a well-known and well-loved ex-Swindon winger who had left for Luton Town in 1978 after 230 Robins outings and 60 goals.

A similar number of appearances and even more goals came at Kenilworth Road, but on his return to Wiltshire an achilles tendon issue required surgery in September. Moss had played in all the first four games of Swindon's season, but that was the end of his second Town spell.

Liverpool-born Evans had arrived from Bolton Wanderers and had claimed the majority of his 230 appearances in one or other of the top two divisions with Cardiff City, Birmingham City, Crystal Palace, Wolverhampton Wanderers or Bolton Wanderers. Hall had started at Coventry City and moved on to Torquay United, but by the end of September both players' Swindon careers were effectively over.

Findlay's playing spell was the shortest of all, but his story takes the longest to relate.

All arrived with what seemed impressive pedigrees, and as such seemed departures from the type of signings for which Macari was already building a reputation.

Also coming in was striker Bryan Wade from Wiltshire neighbours Trowbridge Town. He was the first of Lou's additions and, it must be said, was more in the mould of the signings of Peter Coyne and Colin Gordon 12 months earlier. A player with improvements to make, and things to prove.

But what would prove to be the most influential recruit of this, and perhaps many seasons to come, arrived from Mansfield Town. Colin Calderwood joined for a tribunal-set fee of £27,500, a substantial saving from the £100,000 that Stags boss Ian Greaves had initially expected. Macari expressed being excited about the signing in a way that he didn't usually feel regarding defenders. He had just bagged himself a 20-year-old bargain.

Incredibly, when 1985/86 finally kicked off, things started every bit as badly as anyone could have feared.

Beginning with a single-goal defeat on the opening day at home to Wrexham, the fixture was a repeat of the one which began the previous season. But without the points.

A week later Town travelled to Hereford where four goals were conceded. They had equalised through a Colin Calderwood goal in the 65th minute but had conceded three times in the final 15 minutes to capitulate.

THE RESURGENCE STARTS

A question-and-answer session in a home matchday programme in the first week of September prompted some thought-provoking answers from Macari.

Asked whether supporters were correct to worry about the apparent lack of enthusiasm being shown by some of the players, Lou replied, 'They are right, and supporters are not as daft as some players might like to think they are. Some players do not enjoy the game the way they should.'

Also, asked about his attitude to discipline, he answered, 'I am watching a situation where I expect common sense to prevail.'

By the end of August, Town had lost two, drawn one, and grabbed a 2-1 win against Torquay. Four points and a worse start than had been managed the season before. And that was the good news. Because, by the end of September, they had lost five of the opening eight matches and sat fourth from bottom of the table.

Could supporters withstand another false dawn? This was not what they had hoped for when they had demonstrated for Lou Macari's reinstatement.

A 2-1 home win against Torquay was one of three games in 14 days in which the two teams would face each other. Before and after were the two legs of the first round of the League Cup.

Town claimed the upper hand between the two clubs by also winning through to the next round of the cup, 4-3 on aggregate, but as the Gulls were one of only three teams below them in the early Fourth Division table, it was hardly a ringing endorsement of progress.

By then injury was about to bring about the loss of David Moss, while Tony Evans and Derek Hall were on borrowed time. And one of the biggest-name signings of the summer, Jake Findlay, had by then already played his last game.

If there had previously been an intimation from chairman Brian Hillier that Macari lacked the strength of character to exert the required discipline upon his team to demonstrate his authority, that was about to be unequivocally disproved.

For a season that would develop into such a triumph it's interesting just how much trouble would come between the posts. All the drama was to play out over a two-month period, and it would be quite a story.

Scott Endersby had joined Town on a free transfer from Tranmere Rovers in the May of 1983 as a Ken Beamish signing. His elevation to the first team was hastened with the injury that ultimately ended Jimmy Allan's career the following October, and the ex-England youth keeper grasped the opportunity with relish.

He was so highly thought of he was voted as the player of the year at the end of that season, but after such a dismal campaign there was certainly a lack of competition for the honour. And there was a suspicion that sympathy for Scott, to be so exposed behind such a woeful defence, justified the award alone.

Nevertheless, Endersby was ever-present in Macari's first season at the County Ground and looked set to continue in the same vein in 1985/86. But he had blotted his copybook by declining a pay rise, leading to an understanding that he wished to leave, a situation that could only be resolved if another club made an approach for him.

Under those circumstances, at the end of July Macari had little choice but to pounce to sign Jake Findlay from Luton and subsequently played the new man in the opening games of the season. It would be understandable if Endersby felt snubbed, just as it was inevitable that the boss had to act to protect against the possibility of Endersby's departure.

Findlay's CV looked impressive and his acquisition on a free transfer, initially on a three-month contract, looked good business. He had been the subject of a £100,000 deal when Luton signed him from Aston Villa in 1978. He had made over 30 appearances for the Hatters as they clinched the Second Division title and promotion to the First Division in 1982 and had played almost 170 league games over six seasons before injury interrupted his career.

As he perused his signings in the summer, Macari had written, 'Jake Findlay is a challenge. He is on a three-month contract with the offer of a longer one if he proves himself,' and sympathising with Findlay's injury issues he also said, 'If he can acquire the necessary standard of fitness, we have a First Division goalkeeper on our books.'

Findlay took the number one shirt for the first four league games of the campaign, but the six goals conceded didn't inspire confidence. Macari acted by recalling Endersby for the away League Cup match with Torquay as September commenced, and he kept his place for the next two league games.

Then things took an extraordinary twist.

Impressed by the performance of Gulls keeper Kenny Allen in the games against his team, Macari signed Allen on a free transfer on 16 September and unexpectedly opened a whole can of worms.

Thrusting his third stopper of the embryonic campaign into the next match at Crewe Alexandra, Endersby was again discarded and was probably justifiably upset. He had been reduced to the third choice in a matter of weeks.

But on 21 September it was announced that Findlay's contract had been terminated, and there were some insinuations regarding the reasons.

Two national newspapers had headlined a story regarding the off-field behaviour of some of Town's players. 'I can't name a team until I have smelt their breath and looked into their eyes,' it was reported that Macari had said.

There was no substantiated evidence to indicate to whom Macari was referring, but the teetotaller had certainly stamped his authority.

What had appeared to be a statement signing in the summer had been proved to be an unmitigated disaster and Town were back to two goalkeepers.

In the now weekly question-and-answer sessions, as September entered its third week, Macari was asked again about his previous comments regarding player behaviour. He answered, 'The situation has now corrected itself.'

THE RESURGENCE STARTS

Just to add insult to injury, in November it was revealed that through a mix-up during his registration, Findlay had not been cleared to play in his first two games and the club were to be fined £500.

A week later brought a high-profile League Cup match at Sunderland, a fixture that was the result of defeating Torquay in round one, and it seemed to take everyone at Swindon by surprise that, having already played for Torquay against Swindon, Allen was cup-tied.

So, with Findlay gone and Allen unavailable, Endersby was again expected to step in between the posts and the disgruntled keeper would have been justified in feeling less than happy.

Swindon, and Endersby, made the long trip to Roker Park to face Second Division Sunderland, and a heroic display saw Town twice come back from a goal down before conceding the first leg of the tie in the 77th minute.

Endersby's reward was to be dropped in favour of Allen for the next three league matches, then recalled for the second leg against Sunderland on 8 October.

His mood had surely been tested, but a magnificent collective display against the Mackems saw Town triumph 3-1 after extra time to take the tie 4-3 on aggregate.

Well over 9,000 supporters had witnessed the spectacle and there was much rejoicing in the bars of Swindon that night. But one must wonder about the frame of mind of Scott Endersby. Four days later, Kenny Allen was back in goal at Burnley.

On 29 October came Swindon's prize for such an impressive win over Sunderland – they were to host First Division Sheffield Wednesday in round three.

But Scott Endersby's patience had run out. A week earlier, realising that he would be dropped again as soon as league competition resumed, he played the only card he felt he had available. He refused to play unless the club agreed to give him a free transfer.

Macari again demonstrated who was boss by refusing to sanction such a demand, but it left him in the unenviable position of having to source a keeper on loan at short notice, one who wasn't cup-tied and whose parent club didn't mind him becoming so.

Lou found such a man, a non-contracted goalkeeper at Brentford who had spent time at six clubs and made over 220 league appearances, the majority at Exeter City. Richard Key signed a month's deal on 28 September and made his debut against the top-flight Owls 24 hours later, having only met his team-mates that morning.

Town had named their fourth goalkeeper in 19 games.

The evening was set for another inspired Swindon performance, against the team who earlier that month had sat third in the First Division table, the same month that had seen Town 21st in the Fourth Division. That represented an enormous gap of 85 Football League places between the two teams.

A tenth-minute goal by Peter Coyne decided the game and over 12,000 supporters were at the County Ground to see it.

Post-match, the scorer described the moment, 'It was a great corner from Leigh Barnard and I could see they were all going to miss it. All I had to do was wait and let it hit me on the head. As it was, it ran down the side of my face, over the ear, down my neck, hit my shoulder and bounced over the line. A really great header.'

Technically exemplary it might not have been. Hugely important it certainly was, and very few at the match cared two hoots.

Key himself had a solid game, repelling the Wednesday attack and acquitting himself well. The local paper said, '[Key did] a magnificent job, his work was clean and tidy. He did not hesitate to punch balls when attempting to catch them might have been dangerous, and he seemed to form a very quick and good understanding with his defence.'

Key said after the game, 'I didn't really have time to think about things before the start and it's even harder to realise what has happened now.'

What more can a goalkeeper hope for than a clean sheet, against top-flight opposition and behind a defence of whom you don't know the names?

Macari, who was crowned Fourth Division Manager of the Month immediately afterwards, said he was delighted for Key, 'He was on a hiding to nothing really. He performed well on the night, and everyone went away as pleased for him as he was in his own performance.'

Perhaps unfairly considering his previous commitment, an almost inevitable refrain or two came from the gathered Town supporters. 'Are you watching

Endersby?' was heard and also, to the same tune of 'Bread of Heaven', 'We don't need you any more'.

A sad end to the Town career of a keeper who had played 100 games for the Robins, but who was now to be consigned to a footnote in club history.

Macari had the last word in the club programme, explaining Scott simply wanted more money as, 'In his opinion he is one of the best goalkeepers in the division, but no one was willing to pay £3,500 for him.'

Endersby departed for Carlisle in November, initially on loan but on a deal that was converted to a permanent arrangement in February. Macari, exhibiting his 'not to be messed with' persona, held out for a fee for between £4,000 and £6,000 depending on which source was to be believed. Whatever the price, there was no free transfer.

All this cup progression had to be seen in the context of the fight to get out of the Fourth Division. As had been seen under Bob Smith, cup success was nothing but a distraction if it ultimately cost promotion.

Happily, Macari was not a man to allow that to happen. Starting on 1 October and amid the League Cup shenanigans, Town launched into a run of five consecutive league wins. A loss at Port Vale on 26 October ended the sequence, then after the momentous cup win over Sheffield Wednesday, Town won the next three. Eight Fourth Division wins in nine matches.

The start of the run had seen the very last Football League outing of Lou Macari, who, having made eight starts and a couple of substitute appearances, called an end to his illustrious playing career to concentrate solely on managing his team.

Local rivals Bristol City then helpfully contributed to Town's Fourth Division focus by knocking them out of the FA Cup at the first-round stage, and then the 2-1 home win over Mansfield Town on 23 November hoisted the club to fourth in the table.

After the previous League Cup exploits, things in the competition had to come to an end eventually, and when they did, they did so in spectacular style.

A trip to Portman Road on 26 November paired the two Towns of First Division Ipswich and Fourth Division Swindon in round four to see who would progress to the quarter-finals.

There, the wheels finally came off the Robins' cup express when the Tractor Boys did for Macari's men, 6-1. Richard Key was again named as Swindon's goalkeeper, but this time there was to be no fairytale ending.

For those Town supporters who were there, the night would be memorable for the chant of 'Lou Macari's Red and White Army', which rang out across Portman Road for a continuous 20 minutes as the score increased to an inevitable, and profuse, loss. It was a show of defiance and pride, in glorious but honourable defeat to a side with far greater resources.

It had been exhilarating while it lasted but there were other, more important, fish to fry.

A single-goal defeat at Orient four days later, the last day of the month, might have been described as a hangover from elimination from the League Cup, but if it was it was to be proved to be heaven-sent.

Lou Macari's Swindon Town were about to begin a run that was to set so many club records that it would sweep all before them.

Appearing on the substitutes' bench for a home game with Halifax midway through December was a man who had a Swindon background of big repute. Chris Kamara had returned from Brentford back in August, re-signing for the club for whom he had made almost 200 appearances over a four-season span.

Still with a home in Swindon, Kamara later explained that, wanting to be away from Griffin Park, he ignored the manager's advice regarding preparation for pre-season training. As a result, a ruptured hamstring injury suffered in the very first day back in training meant that when Macari gambled a £12,500 fee on signing him, he arrived at the County Ground unable to take to the pitch until he regained fitness.

It took until mid-December for Kamara to prove his pitch-worthiness, and after a sensible easing into the heat of the action, he went on to be almost ever-present to the end of the campaign. That meant the Middlesbrough-born midfielder was right in the thick of things as Swindon at last launched a meaningful attack on promotion from the basement division.

After that loss at Orient on the last day of November, there were 27 Fourth Division matches to play to the end of the season. The first resulted in a convincing 4-1 home victory over Preston North End and was a personal success for a player who could genuinely be claimed by fans to be 'one of our own'. Charlie Henry had been an apprentice at the County Ground before making his first-team debut in 1980, and for his first 130 appearances he had been seen as a no-nonsense, reliable full-back.

Usually found at the right side of defence, Charlie occasionally ventured into a centre-back role, but Macari had spotted something about the man who was soon to be known as 'Charlie, Charlie Henry' on the terraces that suggested that there was more to his game.

Macari had already tried Henry in a more forward role, but his transformation during 1985/86 was to be nothing less than sensational and helped raise the loyal player's standing to cult status.

Switched to a permanent place at the front of midfield, Charlie had already opened his scoring account in the third game of the campaign, but much of the goalscoring attention had been focused on the pairing of Colin Gordon and Peter Coyne.

Henry had chipped in with important, point-claiming goals already, but when he struck a hat-trick against Preston it caused ripples among supporters. This was a man who they thought they knew well, performing heroics that they never thought were likely.

It's easy to see what attracted Macari to place his confidence in him. There was nothing pretentious about Charlie Henry. He offered honest endeavour and a high work rate. He never shirked a challenge, and he loved the club he played for. Macari, who once described Henry as 'built of granite', must have identified something of himself in him.

When the boss saw a predatory instinct supplementing his obvious other attributes, Lou pushed him forward and made a new player of him.

Taking his boss's fitness regime to his heart, Charlie, Macari and the fans all reaped the benefit.

It's been said many times that Lou Macari never asked a player to do what they couldn't. What he did was to inspire his players to believe they could achieve more than they initially thought they could. Henry had demonstrated a new aspect of his play which proved he could do something that previous managers had never even guessed possible.

After Charlie's goals against Preston, he played against Halifax and scored again. Then again against Hereford, and by the end of December, Town had won four games out of four and risen to the top of the Fourth Division.

Swindon had found a new goalscorer in Charlie Henry, and when his contribution was added to that of the output from Gordon and Coyne, there appeared to be a whole new dimension to Town's promotion push.

Charlie's goal tally didn't conclude at the end of 1985 either. He scored in every match in February, another three the following month and claimed another treble in the away game at Halifax in the penultimate game of the season. He was to finish the season with 18 goals, outscoring all of his, perhaps more highly valued team-mates, and ensuring his place in the folklore of Robins history.

But this was a Swindon Town team, the success of which would come from the sum of its parts.

January carried on as December had concluded, with a 2-1 home win over Colchester United on New Year's Day. Henry was absent from the scoresheet that day, but on the stroke of half-time, summer signing Bryan Wade added to centre-back David Cole's opener with the deciding strike.

Wade's cut-price arrival from Trowbridge Town in May had been overshadowed by higher-profile signings, but the 5ft 8in forward had set about quietly establishing himself in professional football. First hitting the net at home to Rochdale in October, Bath-born Wade continued to justify his elevation in status just days later with two very late goals that brought about the defeat of Sunderland.

Three goals followed in November, so by the time New Year's Day was drawing to a close, Wade had already notched seven times.

That's as healthy a return as any professional debutant could surely hope for, so to hit a round dozen by the season's end and add in a Football League Fourth Division champions' medal, hopefully exceeded all Wade's expectations.

By the end of January Swindon had won three games of the four played. After Wade's winner against Colchester, Town lost at Tranmere Rovers three days later, and incredibly that was the last game that they were to lose that season.

Eight straight victories accounted for a third of the teams playing in the Fourth Division that year.

Southend United, Wrexham, Northampton Town, Stockport County, Preston North End, Exeter City, Rochdale and Burnley all succumbed to the Macari-inspired tsunami.

Even more impressive, six of the wins came away from home. Swindon had gone from a team who had won just four away fixtures in the whole of the preceding season to winning six on the trot in a month and a half.

When Swindon faced, and beat, Burnley at the County Ground on 15 March it took the run of consecutive wins to a new club record. Charlie Henry, Dave Bamber and Colin Gordon inflicted the damage in the 3-1 victory, and it didn't go unnoticed by many of the gathered crowd that the scoreline reflected that of Swindon's greatest-ever day, on the same date: the famous win over Arsenal at Wembley in the League Cup Final of 1969. A nice link between the present-day optimism and the past success.

When that run eventually ended, 10,122 turned up at the County Ground to watch a 0-0 draw against Port Vale. That must have seemed like a damp squib in comparison.

It seems strange to suggest that Swindon were now entering the closing straight but were still sprinting for the line, but incredibly that was what was happening. After such a horrendous start, and with almost two months of the season still to run, the campaign was effectively a done deal.

Over the next five matches, Town took 11 points from the 15 available. Three wins and a couple of draws extended their lead at the top of the table and set the scene for a vitally important game at the County Ground on a Tuesday night in early April.

Early in the season the front-runners had included Colchester and Peterborough, but both had slipped out of the picture. Hartlepool United flirted with an interest and Port Vale would eventually claim fourth spot, but by far the most consistent challengers for Town's superiority had been Mansfield Town and Chester City.

The pair would claim promotion in May, and Town had still to face them both.

On 8 April, Swindon took on second-placed Chester at the County Ground. The match was the 39th of the league season and just one point would be enough to guarantee promotion with seven games to spare.

City had been the team who had pushed Town hardest all season for superiority in the Fourth Division, and had been the last team to deprive Macari's team top spot as February commenced. But by the time the two teams faced each other, the points gap between the two was in double digits in Swindon's favour. A crowd of 12,630 turned up in anticipation.

Chester drew first blood, but Dave Bamber headed home a leveller three minutes before the break. Macari would have been preparing his half-time talk when Town conceded again through a twice-taken penalty.

Six minutes into the second period, Bamber repeated his aerial contributions to again square the score.

Perhaps learning the lesson that scoring increased vulnerability, a minute later Bryan Wade dived to head home the goal which gave the Town the lead for the first time.

When Leigh Barnard scored their fourth in the 67th minute there was a feeling that celebrations were just minutes away. There was still time for Peter Coyne to have a penalty saved, but while the extra goal would have put further shine on the night's achievements, in truth the miss was not likely to detract too much from the feeling of elation among everyone connected with the club.

Promotion was guaranteed.

Perhaps there was also a tinge of relief from assistant manager John Trollope that Town were to be back in the Third Division, four years after surrendering the status under his charge. With promotion secured, John would soon happily revert to his first coaching love, that of dealing with the youth team and looking to produce the next crop of Charlie Henrys.

The brace of goals from Dave Bamber were his fifth and sixth of his Swindon career. He had spent a ten-match loan spell from Portsmouth beginning in November, and while not making the scoresheet then, the 6ft 3in striker had gained a reputation for producing the runs that seemed to result in Town penalties.

Back at the County Ground on a permanent deal in the middle of March, Dave was to strike eight times in 13 matches.

In contrast the scorer of Town's fourth of the evening had been with the club since July 1982, and at 5ft 8in tall he contrasted with Bamber in more ways than one.

THE RESURGENCE STARTS

Ever-present during 1982/83, Leigh Barnard had clocked up over 30 games a season since, and while contributing a goal here and there, none would have been as important or satisfying as putting Swindon's promotion beyond doubt that evening.

After the game against Chester, Charlie Henry supplied some words for the local newspaper. He was unsurprisingly happy with life, 'Tuesday night was a night I'll always remember. We needed to win to be sure of promotion and the people of the town had been waiting two and a half months for the game. The noise was unbelievable. When we were 2-1 down at half-time, we made the decision to try to steamroller them. With the fantastic support behind us we reckoned we must be in with a chance. And it worked. In the end we could have had five or six.'

Showing his personal satisfaction with the achievement he said, 'Promotion is something very special, and especially for me. I am the longest serving player at the club. John Trollope signed me as an apprentice, just before Andy Rowland came in.'

And again, identifying with everyone who loved the club as much as he did, he said, 'I can still recall that terrible night at Newport when we could have won and stayed in Division Three, but were relegated. I remember missing a reasonable chance in that game as well.'

Perhaps with one thought of what the boss might think, Henry added, 'The celebration didn't go on for too long. We have still got some important games coming up and we want to be as well prepared for them as we can be. The lads know that if we can win our next three games the title will be ours.'

As all supporters were becoming used to expecting, they were to do better than that.

It also hadn't gone unnoticed that the anniversary of the sacking and reinstatement of Lou Macari was imminent.

Andy Rowland, who had been one of the signatories to the petition for his recall, said, 'It would have been a tragedy had he not returned. As soon as he arrived you could see he wanted to do a proper job, not just use it as a stepping stone. I felt from the start that he would get us promotion and when he was sacked, I felt we were losing the man who would take us where we wanted to go.'

And Macari was also plainly delighted. 'What can you say after that?' he asked. 'To go a goal down in the opening minutes and then go behind again in the last minute of the half would have floored most sides. I was so disappointed as I walked off at half-time, I could have been sick. But I couldn't go into the dressing room and let the players know how I felt so I tried to look confident and told them to keep plugging away.'

Not necessarily the most memorable of team talks, but it had worked magnificently.

Four days after claiming promotion, Swindon faced Scunthorpe United at home, and drew 1-1. By the standards that Macari demanded, that would have been considered unacceptable and while there would be one more single-point haul, the undefeated run since 4 January would be maintained.

THE RESURGENCE STARTS

The three goals scored against Peterborough on 15 April put the wheels back on the record-breakers' wagon, setting the scene for a momentous Saturday afternoon in Nottinghamshire.

When Swindon travelled to Mansfield on 19 April, they were going there to take on one of the clubs that had held its own promotion aspirations since the start of the season. During most seasons, at this stage Mansfield might have expected to be pushing their opposition to the wire for a superior position. Instead, Swindon were all but out of sight.

But while the home team had their own reasons for maximum points to aid their own promotion push, this campaign had developed into anything but normal.

Mansfield were the club from whom Macari had signed Colin Calderwood, and the match would decide the destination of the Fourth Division trophy. Just a draw would be enough for Swindon to claim the title.

Estimates of the number of travelling fans vary, but there is no doubt that between 2,000 and 3,000 supporters arrived at Field Mill in the hope they would see their side lift their first Football League divisional championship trophy after 46 years of trying.

With the game ten minutes from the break, the historically named Neville Chamberlain appeared to be in an offside position when he struck the ball at Kenny Allen's goal. Allen manfully tried to block the effort, but it sneaked over the goal line while the fans in the away end hoped for a reaction from the referee. With no such undertaking forthcoming and the goal ruled to stand, for Town supporters this was certainly not 'peace in our time'.

But cometh the moment, cometh the man. Or at least the men.

A Bamber free kick produced an opportunity for Barnard, via a Bryan Wade touch, and the little, little and large combination culminated in Barnard stabbing the ball home to bring parity to the scoreline for the half-time team talks.

While there were still 45 minutes to play, and still four matches to conclude the season, the party could begin. With no further score at Field Mill, despite the Stags pushing hard for the extra points they needed to support their own promotion aspirations, Swindon were crowned champions of the Fourth Division.

It was perhaps only under circumstances such as these that Macari might have been prepared to accept something other than a win.

The decision to play Charlie Henry up front in place of Colin Gordon was heralded as a masterstroke, harrying and chivvying away at the normally well-drilled defence as he had.

That just left the little matter of finishing off the season in the manner to which everyone had become accustomed. And what everyone had become accustomed to was winning.

A trip to Aldershot four games from the end was won 4-2. The pre-match entrance was memorable for a very sporting demonstration by the home side. Taking to the pitch before the start, the Shots players lined up in a guard of honour as the Robins emerged on to the field of play, applauding them on as champions.

It seemed a genuine acknowledgement from an opposing team of just how the Wiltshire club had set about their business over the preceding months, and a display of respect that had rarely been seen before and took a long time to catch on in the English game.

But of course, as welcome as respect from your peers is, Macari's team set about professionally claiming all three points anyway.

If you can score four times away from home, you can do it at home. Orient were dispatched 4-1 the following Saturday, then Charlie Henry claimed his second hat-trick of the campaign in a 3-1 away win at Halifax Town.

That left the small matter of a last game, this one at home to Crewe Alexandra, after which Swindon were to be presented with the Fourth Division trophy.

A crowd of 10,976 entered the County Ground to witness the coronation of Lou Macari's champions, and a solitary Peter Coyne goal produced the 1-0 win that drew the curtain down on the 1985/86 season.

Alex's keeper Rob Powner, in only his third game since being spotted playing park football, gave an inspired display and threatened to spoil the party, but Coyne's 70th-minute left-footed volley gave Town their fourth consecutive victory to start the presentations and celebrations.

The win gave Swindon a total of 102 points, a Football League record.

In readiness the Town End had started to climb the perimeter fencing some minutes before the final whistle, and there was some nervousness that exuberance might impinge on the enormous feeling of excitement that the culmination of such a campaign had produced.

But the supporters stayed where they should, Swindon finished the job in the professional manner that their manager insisted, and the silverware could be handed over.

Colin Calderwood concluded his campaign by claiming the annual player of the year award.

Calderwood, well respected for his unflustered displays in the centre of defence, declared, 'Oh that's great news, I'm delighted. I honestly thought Charlie Henry would get the award.'

Asked about whether he was happy about what his move to Swindon had brought, he said, 'That's the understatement of the year. To come here and get a championship in my first year is wonderful. And to clinch the title in an away game at Mansfield, the club I left to join Swindon, is the icing on the cake.'

When Calderwood arrived from Mansfield on the first day of July, the Stranraer-born centre-back had already played a century of games for the Stags over the first three years of his playing career.

So highly regarded by manager Ian Greaves that the Stags boss slapped a six-figure sum on his head, Colin had made his debut in an away game at Crewe on 13 March 1982 and by the end of the following season had already appeared 30 times.

Almost ever-present from then on, there was disappointment among fans when he left Mansfield for Swindon, a disappointment that was compounded when the tribunal fixed the fee at a little over a quarter of Greaves's valuation.

Calderwood scored on his second match for Swindon and his only other goal that season was a late winner at home to Exeter City on the first day of October. That goal had arrived after a run of three defeats on the trot, and Swindon were not to lose more than that number of league games again before the triumphant end of the campaign.

Over the years that Lou Macari was with Swindon he would garner much appreciation, particularly in the boardroom, for his astuteness in the transfer market. The signing of Calderwood would rank as probably the best piece of business he would ever do.

And such were the outstanding individual performances that contributed to so many momentous occasions throughout the season, it seems that the usual, and almost expected, goal contributions of strikers Colin Gordon and Peter Coyne appear to have almost gone uncommented upon.

Gordon hit 16 while Coyne managed 14 in all competitions, and both continued to enjoy the elevation that Macari had spotted and nurtured.

They were among the four players who topped double figures. Bryan Wade was the third, and of course Charlie Henry outscored all comers.

No fewer than seven players made over 40 appearances during the campaign. This was surely an indication of the fitness that Macari was instilling in his squad, and the list included men who performed heroics in such an understated way that inclusion of their names had almost passed unnoticed.

Chris Ramsey missed just three league games and was the reliable, aggressive right-back that he had proved to be the season before. He had refused to attend a team bonding session at Grittleton House before the title-deciding game at Mansfield, and it cost him a brownie point with Macari that saw Paul Roberts appear on the right side of defence for three matches. That deprived Ramsey the honour of an ever-present campaign.

Centre-back David Cole had also gone about his business in the almost unnoticed manner that proves the competence of the performer. Missing just two outings, which added to his unbroken run of 20 the previous campaign, he had become as much of a mainstay of the defence as Calderwood.

Paul Roberts had joined the Macari revolution in September. He had been playing lower-league football in Finland and made his debut against Sunderland in the League Cup that week. A midfielder, he was switched to left-back when Nicky Coleman returned to Millwall.

Coleman had joined from Millwall for a two-month loan spell at the beginning of October. He steadied a troublesome left-back position with 13 league games and the historic League Cup ties in the autumn, and even chipped in with four goals, three from the penalty spot.

Stalwart David Hockaday made 43 appearances in all competitions. A free transfer signing from Blackpool back in June 1983 and originally a winger, Hockaday's versatility, like Charlie Henry's, had been spotted by Macari. He was in the midst of dropping further and further back, en route to taking the full-back shirt that Henry had vacated.

After the turmoil between the posts for the first three months, Kenny Allen emerged as the winner of the goalkeeping stakes and went on to play 40 league matches by the season's end.

After leaving Wiltshire, Scott Endersby went on to make over 50 appearances for the Cumbrians of Carlisle United then moved on to York City and another 35 outings. He appears to have hung up his gloves after a loan spell at Cardiff City produced a final four appearances.

Jake Findlay signed for Portsmouth, then moved to Coventry City, but doesn't appear to have ever taken to the pitch after those four games for Swindon.

As for Richard Key, the hero of the hour in the goalkeeping crisis during the autumn, it appears he played three further Third Division games in January 1986 after returning to his parent club Brentford, and then seems to have left the game. It might be believed that the highlight of his 230-match career came at the County Ground in a famous 1-0 victory over First Division Sheffield Wednesday in October 1985.

If so, thanks for the memories, Richard.

Altogether, 23 players had pulled on a Town shirt during the season. The goals were so well spread among the players that no fewer than 12 made the scoresheet in the league at least once. In fact, disregarding the multiple goalkeepers used and anyone making fewer than five appearances, only Tony Evans, Derek Hall, Paul Roberts, Andy Rowland and Macari himself didn't find the net.

Even among those who didn't score in the league, Moss and Rowland managed to do so in cup competition.

There was an incredible number of records set by the club in 1985/86:

- Longest unbeaten league sequence – 21
- Most consecutive away league games without defeat – 11
- Fewest defeats in a league season – 8
- Highest number of consecutive home league wins – 14
- Highest number of consecutive away league wins – 6
- Highest number of league wins in a season – 32
- Highest number of home league wins in a season – 20
- Highest number of away league wins in a season – 12
- Longest sequence of time without conceding a goal – 592 minutes
- Longest sequence of time without conceding an away goal – 516 minutes
- Fewest number of goals conceded away from home in a league season – 24
- Highest goal difference in a league season – +39
- Highest number of points gained in a league season – 102
- Highest number of points gained at home in a season – 62
- Highest number of points gained away from home in a season – 40

THE RESURGENCE STARTS

The thing about 1984/85 was that it had started in mediocrity and stayed that way for months, but in contrast, 1985/86 had started horrendously and then got better. And better.

By November, not only had supporters enjoyed a run that had taken Town to round four of the League Cup, but league form had also lifted them from 23rd in the Fourth Division, where they had resided after three matches, to fourth by the time the cup run ended towards the end of November.

The Robins had reached the very top of the table on New Year's Eve, and with one minor blip in February, they stayed there for over four months.

On five occasions crowds at the County Ground had topped five figures, bringing with them the necessary financial boost that had been missing for so long. Overall home league attendances had averaged 6,457, a doubling of the previous season's number.

Lou Macari had won four Manager of the Month awards throughout the season and concluded that with the Fourth Division Manager of the Year honour.

The much longed-for return to the Third Division had finally been achieved and what everyone hoped for, but no one could know, was the journey had many miles to run.

5

1986/87: from 69th to 47th
The rise continues

AS AUGUST 1986 drew towards its final week, Swindon Town kicked off a new season in the Third Division, back at the level which had been lost in May 1982.

The huge margin by which Swindon had claimed the Fourth Division title had not gone unnoticed by the footballing world, and expectations were perhaps higher than allowed for comfort at the County Ground.

In his first programme notes of the new campaign, Lou Macari commented, 'You are probably aware that many pundits have made Swindon Town clear favourites for promotion again. Obviously, we all hope their optimism is well founded, but I feel I must add a warning note. The Third Division will be a much tougher proposition, as I'm sure you will all see as the season unfolds.'

A good call for caution, added to a large streak of realism.

THE RISE CONTINUES

A trip to Malta helped the developing squad to bond and skipper Colin Calderwood said, 'The pre-season training this year seems to be a lot harder than last year. We had some disastrous early season results and the boss has been intent on counteracting that this year.'

Among the opponents that Swindon would face in the coming months were far larger clubs than had needed to be overcome the previous season.

Middlesbrough had dropped from the Second Division in May, as had Fulham, and Town's opening game was at Bolton Wanderers, a club perhaps experiencing leaner times than had been enjoyed in the past, but still not a challenge to be taken lightly.

If Macari had been trying to condition fans to temper their expectations, the opening-day 2-1 victory at Burnden Park might have been a little counterproductive.

Peter Coyne scored both goals and immediately demonstrated that there was life after Colin Gordon. That's because Macari had moved Gordon on to First Division Wimbledon on 3 July, and the club had pocketed a very useful £100,000 in the bargain. That was quite some profit to show for the four-figure outlay for Gordon's capture 18 months earlier, and even a small sell-on fee agreed with Oldbury United wouldn't have dampened new accountant Vince Farrar's spirits unduly.

Gordon's 33 goals in 80 appearances looked a tall order to replace, but by then striker Jimmy Gilligan had already arrived from Grimsby Town in June, setting the club back £30,000. Even with that expenditure, seen in the light of the income generated from the departure of Gordon, that still represented a £70,000 net gain for Town's bank account.

Gilligan's stay at Swindon would be a short one, bringing just 22 outings in a Town shirt for the tall Londoner. His six goals perhaps gave an indication of what might have been, but even with the departure of Gordon, and his aborted replacement of Gilligan, very few people would bemoan the loss of either come the end of the season.

When Macari assembled his team that won the Fourth Division championship the previous season, he did it all on a budget of next to nothing. Calderwood's signing had been funded by the sale of left-back Colin Bailie, and at £27,500 it was the highest fee invested in the playing staff that season.

The signature of Chris Kamara had been described as having cost Swindon around £12,500 and the main striking options of Colin Gordon, Bryan Wade and Peter Coyne had all been added to the playing roster for such a low combination of fees that the total outlay went almost unnoticed even by a board of directors accustomed to financial paucity.

Try-before-you-buy forward Dave Bamber had initially arrived on loan, and then cost just £15,000 to add to the roster.

Every other addition to Macari's all-conquering title-winning side had either arrived on loan or on a free transfer. Derek Hall was described as a nominal fee signing at the time, but details since seem to suggest another zero-cost addition.

Now, with one promotion under his belt, there may have been some justification in asking for a bigger recruitment fund, but it was to Macari's huge credit, and an indication of his realistic frugality and motivation skills, that the next stage of the Robins' progression journey carried on in the same, almost austere way.

The summer preparation had seen the arrival of five players after that of Gilligan, and three of them had been brought in for nothing.

Denny Mundee from Queens Park Rangers would never make the grade at Swindon, but the same could certainly not be said of the two other freebies. Both would go on to score play-off final goals for Town.

First was Chipping Sodbury-born Bristol Rovers striker Steve White, who arrived in July. Glorying in the wondrously predictable nickname of 'Chalkie', the sort of epigraph synonymous within football circles for generations, Town had just found themselves a new goalscoring hero.

White made his first appearance in a Swindon shirt when he entered the fray as an 80th-minute substitute for Peter Coyne at home to Notts County in the second game of the season. A minute from the end he scored his first goal. The County Ground crowd had seen the first demonstration of White's predatory goalscoring instinct.

The strike, however, couldn't prevent Swindon falling to their first league home defeat of the campaign at the very first Third Division opportunity.

Steve had started his career with Bristol Rovers and after three seasons a fee of £150,000 had taken the

West Country boy to Second Division Luton Town. Two seasons later, after 25 goals and after claiming a champions medal with promotion to the top flight with the Hatters, another six-figure fee was invested by Charlton Athletic.

It will remain a mystery why clubs were prepared to discard such a ready source of goals, but after another 12 in a season at The Valley, Steve was back in Bristol for another three goal-laden campaigns.

When the Gas decided to offload 27-year-old Steve again, Lou Macari was only too ready to offer him a home at newly promoted Swindon. His relationship with the club was to last eight seasons and would bring his Town goal tally to well over 100 across 250 appearances in total.

Midfielder Alan McLoughlin followed White six weeks later, having been released by Manchester United.

The only two signings that summer who justified a fee were that of Bristol Rovers centre-back Tim Parkin and Exeter City's midfielder Martin Ling, for a combined total of a little over £50,000. Thankfully there still seemed little chance of a Bob Smith-style reckless overspend under Macari.

The new season was under way. Two games in: one away win, one home loss, and the next two matches renewed some old rivalries.

A trip to Newport County was first up, with a repeat of the fixture that had last seen Swindon relegated to the Fourth Division, four seasons earlier. Bryan Wade scored a brace, but it was not enough to claim all three points. By the end of the season Newport were to finish bottom of the table and were on their own way to experiencing life in the basement division of the Football League.

Immediately afterwards, Swindon entertained Chester City, a club who had joined them in winning promotion the previous season. This time it was Steve White's turn to put his name on Town's goalscoring list, but the outcome was the same. Both matches ended in draws.

If a return of five points from four games and 12th place in the table seemed a fairly respectable return after entry to the Third Division, there was a rude awakening to come. The next visitors to the County Ground were Blackpool on the midweek evening of 16 September. It was to be a night that would bring anger, soul-searching and repercussions to all who took part.

A horrendous display saw the visitors take all three points, but much worse than that was the manner in which they were surrendered. When the whistle blew Town had lost the encounter 6-2.

With Blackpool four goals to the good at half-time, old Robins favourite Alan Mayes added to the embarrassment with a goal for the visitors in the second half. It was Swindon's biggest home defeat in 24 years.

Two goals from Leigh Barnard may have saved the midfielder from some of the ire of his manager, but the brace was of little consequence to the result. Martin Ling, withdrawn on 53 minutes, was not to appear under Lou Macari again.

Macari was furious and kept his team locked in the dressing room for an hour and a half after the final whistle. Launching a scathing attack on his players, the boss was to voice a thinly veiled criticism about the professionalism of some sportsmen, 'The manner in which we lost to Blackpool was not only disappointing but disturbing. Once again, I reiterate my views that if professional sportsmen do not live like professionals they will not perform like professionals. At Swindon Town we have lost just two matches in 30 because we have lived like professionals for the last year. Sadly, a slight drop in standard has a catastrophic effect if you meet a team who are prepared to keep themselves in check.'

Continuing his attack, he said, 'Blackpool are not six goals superior to Swindon Town and my players know that, but they were fitter and sharper and better prepared for that particular evening. You can be assured that the players in this club from now on will be prepared for each match as professionals.'

Town had lost badly, the boss felt let down and the issue would be addressed.

No names, no pack drill. But the pack drill was yet to come, because another example of Macari's disciplinarian streak and his method of dealing with the perceived problem was to take his players to a 'training camp' on Salisbury Plain, something that would become a trademark solution to whatever he saw as intolerable behaviour.

Perhaps no one was to experience the turning of the tide more sharply than central defender David Cole.

An unsung hero since his Town debut in February 1985, ironically in a defeat against Blackpool, Cole had remained ever-present to the end of that season and missed just two games in the promotion campaign that followed.

Taking the field in the first five matches of 1986/87, the Blackpool match was David's 69th appearance in 71 league games, but the disastrous capitulation against the Tangerines was in need of scapegoats, and he was never to appear in a Town shirt again.

The beneficiary of Cole's dramatic fall from grace would be summer signing Tim Parkin.

Hot on the heels of Bristol Rovers team-mate Steve White, Parkin had cost £27,500 a week after Chalkie's arrival. He was installed to partner Colin Calderwood at the back and made his debut in a 2-0 home win against Rotherham, making the position his own before the end of the year.

Whether Macari's tirade against his players was a catalyst to better times is difficult to be certain. They had been left in no doubt that performances such as that seen against Blackpool would not be tolerated, and aspersions had been cast upon their very professionalism, probably the biggest insult that Macari would consider was in his armoury.

On the last day of September Swindon travelled to Ayresome Park, Middlesbrough. Recently relegated Boro sat at the top of the table as they set about returning to the Second Division at the first attempt. The single-goal defeat against such strong opposition was by no means a disappointment and brought the curtain down on the first complete month of Third Division action for Town.

Swindon were finding their feet at the new level and the improvement that Macari demanded was on its way. And just as the previous season, Town were to enjoy success in cup competition interspersed with the regular league list of fixtures.

As the year before, Swindon's first opponents in the League Cup had been Torquay United in a two-legged first round tie.

Both legs were won, starting with a perfunctory 3-0 home victory in the last week of August. The job was completed with a 3-2 win at Plainmoor, after which the goalscorer details made for familiar reading. Dave Bamber scored a brace in each, with Bryan Wade adding the other in both games.

That set up an intriguing second-round encounter with First Division Southampton, with the victors again to be determined over two legs.

Swindon travelled to The Dell first and faced a team including England goalkeeper Peter Shilton between the posts. Scottish forward Joe Jordan was up front and a one-time Swindon man, the reborn Glenn Cockerill, took to the midfield alongside ex-Liverpool star Jimmy Case. Named at the back was an up-and-coming defender called Jon Gittens, who would be a Swindon player within a year.

Fresh from a home win over Liverpool, the Saints would be a challenge for any Third Division side and George Lawrence grabbed two goals, with Jordan also on the scoresheet as the higher-ranked team ran out 3-0 winners. All as per expectations in the world of football.

By the time the second leg took place at the County Ground two weeks later, goalkeeper Kenny Allen had not recovered from a sprained ankle incurred at The Dell. That had forced Lou Macari to approach Manchester United to enquire of his old club as to whether they had any keepers he might be able to borrow.

As a result, on 25 September a youngster by the name of Fraser Digby arrived at the County Ground on loan, and by the time Southampton pitched up in Wiltshire, he had already kept his first Swindon Town clean sheet in the 2-0 win over Rotherham.

A three-goal deficit against a First Division team would be a huge challenge to overturn, and by the end of the night it had proved as impossible as it appeared.

But with almost 9,500 inside the County Ground, Town gave it the best shot they possibly could. The game remained goalless throughout, but few who witnessed it could understand how. A missed penalty, taken by Chris Kamara in the 17th minute, hadn't helped.

Macari said soon after, 'I still find it difficult to understand how we failed to gain a convincing win here at the County Ground against Southampton in the second leg.

'Rarely can a team have dominated any match to the extent that we did and have nothing to show for their efforts. We hit the woodwork three times and numerous shots were blocked or cleared off the line and there is no way you can account for those happenings. Overall, I thought my players performed marvellously.'

Elsewhere he was quoted as describing the game as 'a goalless annihilation'.

This time the boss was happy.

The south coast-based press was equally impressed. The local Southampton paper proclaimed, 'Little Swindon Town were glorious in defeat last night. They hit Saints with everything but the kitchen sink, miraculously failing to cut back a three-goal deficit from the first leg. But for the brilliance of Peter Shilton and the woodwork surrounding his goal, Saints would have been out on their ears.'

It soon became clear that Kenny Allen's ankle injury was worse than had originally been thought. This allowed Digby to stake his claim to the regular first-team green shirt and in December Allen left on a free transfer back to Torquay, from whence he had arrived in Swindon. He never took to the pitch again after Fraser's arrival.

A month into Fraser's loan spell, the teenager, whose contract with Manchester United was due to run out the following summer, said in the programme, 'I still don't know what will happen to me. It's something I intend to speak to Lou Macari about. Of course, things could be different for me at Old Trafford now Alex Ferguson has taken over. I don't think I stood a lot of chance of progressing with Ron Atkinson in charge.

'I knew Lou at Old Trafford and I think he is a good manager, well-disciplined and that is something that players will always respect of any manager.'

If Fraser was choosing his words carefully, they were selected to impress his potential long-term boss, and two days before Christmas £32,000 changed hands to make Digby a permanent member of Swindon's playing staff.

Macari was happy and said, 'It would be a mistake to say we are settled in defence this season where I have had to make several changes due to loss of form or injuries. However, I'm sure you will agree that the acquisition of Fraser Digby is a move in the right direction. It did not take much persuasion on my part to convince Fraser that he should join Swindon Town. Two minutes flat!'

It was to prove to be another landmark signing that would provide dividends long after Macari's departure from Wiltshire.

Free of League Cup distractions and probably still smarting from the tongue-lashing they had recently received from the gaffer, October saw a resurgent Swindon set about climbing the league table.

Four successive wins against Wigan, Fulham, Chesterfield and Port Vale at last started to show the rest of the division the sort of form that Town had shown for so long in the Fourth Division. On 21 October, and after the 4-3 defeat of Vale, the Robins sat seventh in the table after 11 games.

Mid-month brought the end of Martin Ling's short spell at the County Ground. It had cost the club £25,000 to gain his registration from Exeter City in July and having been made one of the fall guys after the Blackpool debacle in September, it seemed his was no longer the desired presence it had been just three months earlier. Ling left for Southend United with £15,000 changing hands.

It was suggested that a sell-on clause, which would have netted Exeter 50 per cent of any profit made on a future sale, was something Macari didn't like. The boss saw no justification for another club to profit from the work he intended to invest in Ling to improve his worth. By selling at a loss, that was effectively mitigated.

Macari had admitted his mistake, corrected the situation to his and Ling's satisfaction, and recouped 60 per cent of his initial outlay. A typical example of his decisive action.

Some weeks later, Macari was to say, 'It is often the situation that people do not blend into the pattern of play adopted by some clubs. Factors which are not always apparent at the time of signing. Individuals can be disappointing and, as in the case of Martin Ling, it was too long for the club to wait for the individual.'

Perhaps Macari had already seen the possibility of Ling's incompatibility with his methods when he made a loan signing of Mark Jones from Oxford United in September.

Jones slotted immediately into first-team action and had already added his name to Town's list of scorers. On the day Ling departed for Southend, Jones made his move permanent in return for a fee of £30,000 to the Manor Ground club.

Jones was to play almost every game to the end of the season and take on the mantle of penalty taker, and to that end he contributed ten goals, six of which came from the spot.

But sadly, having made such an impact at the County Ground, he was to suffer a serious knee injury the following pre-season, an injury which was to suspend the midfielder's career for two whole seasons.

Over the course of the eight weeks from the last week of October until four days before Christmas Day, Swindon hit the sort of consistency which could have been viewed in one of two ways.

Did three wins, three draws and three losses indicate a consolidation of the club's newly elevated status, as their league position levelled out at a consistent fifth or sixth place in the table? Or did it indicate a plateauing of ambition on the pitch? Did it show that the players were feeling too comfortable with their achievements and demonstrating a readiness to rest on their laurels?

If the latter, it was a change in attitude that Macari was never going to accept. A red rag to a bull. Mid-run there would be another triggering of the boss's irritation that would shake players out of any comfort zone that they may have been settling into.

That came at Farnborough Town in the first round of the FA Cup in November, and an examination of the bare facts might not indicate any reason for the teacups to be rattling in the dressing room.

A 4-0 win brought Swindon's safe passage to round two. One strike each for Peter Coyne, Bryan Wade and Jimmy Gilligan was supplemented by a helpful own goal from Farnborough defender Keith Baker, and a potential upset by the non-league side had been carefully navigated.

But that wasn't enough for Macari who was about to show his ruthless streak once again.

Although a convincing victory, the manager was less impressed with the overall performance of some, 'I thought we were dreadful in certain areas and the scoreline flattered Swindon Town. Only their inability to find the net saved us from an embarrassing situation. I realise I must act swiftly to put some areas of the team right.'

And, of those who might be feeling vulnerable, he gave food for thought, 'Since I have arrived at the club, every player has been given an opportunity to prove his worth. It may be in the interest of some of the players on the staff at present to find another club.'

Perhaps Jimmy Gilligan may have been the man targeted by Macari for specific attention this time. If so, the treatment meted out appears slightly harsh.

Gilligan had taken to the pitch a dozen times by then, but perhaps significantly, seven of them had seen the striker either start the game on the bench or be replaced before 90 minutes were up. Even so, he had scored at Farnborough and would do so again a week later in an away win at Bury, but the forward's Swindon days were numbered.

After a home defeat inflicted by Bristol City in mid-December, Gilligan was first substituted, then excluded from the first team. The following February he was loaned out to Newport County, then sold on to

Lincoln City in March. In all he had scored six times in 22 appearances.

His final appearance in a Swindon shirt came when he took to the pitch as a substitute in the last match of 1986, and if there had been any doubt that the writing was on the wall, that was dispelled when the man who gave way to him that day turned out to be his long-term replacement.

On 19 December, five days after Gilligan's last start, Macari had moved to sign ex-Swindon man Jim Quinn from Blackburn Rovers for £50,000.

And back to that win over Farnborough which had so dissatisfied the boss – five days later central defender Paul Franklin arrived on loan from Watford with a view to a permanent move.

Of the starters in the Farnborough tie, only two didn't make the starting line-up a week later. They were striker Peter Coyne and, perhaps more relevantly, centre-back Tim Parkin.

Franklin's stay in Wiltshire would last a month, spanning five League games and one in the Associate Members' Cup. Parkin meanwhile would not be seen in a Town shirt again until his replacement had left for Watford once more. An interview with Parkin at the time heard him say, 'No player likes to be left out of the team and it is my intention to recover my form and help the club to promotion.'

Returned to the line-up on Boxing Day, Parkin missed just one more match to the end of the season, and Franklin's continued presence was deemed unnecessary. Parkin was redeemed.

Had the team been chastised into renewed vigour after the Farnborough game? If so, the evidence was not immediate in coming.

Two days before the end of November, two things happened.

Firstly, Paul Franklin scored his one and only goal of his six-match loan spell from Watford. The strike, when added to one from Chris Kamara, gave Town a 2-0 home win over Carlisle United. But secondly, and more significantly, it hoisted the team to fifth in the table. Maintaining that position was to be more important this season than it had been in any preceding one.

The so-so results continued until Christmas when the scoring in a 2-0 home win over Brentford on Boxing Day commenced with a penalty from Mark Jones. Twenty-four hours later, Jones repeated the trick with a second spot-kick at Gillingham and Town had won two on the trot for the first time since October.

Even so, the six points left Swindon sixth in the table, and even a New Year's Day 1-0 defeat at the home of eventual title winners Bournemouth didn't dislodge them.

As 1987 began there were exactly half a season's worth of fixtures to complete, and Swindon were about to set off on a run which would see them lose just two. It would culminate in participation in a new footballing fiesta called the 'play-offs'.

At the beginning of the season, the Football League had announced the introduction of a 'new' format to determine promotion and relegation issues. It was decided that a series of matches to decide one last promotion place would pit some of those teams who previously would have gained automatic promotion against some of those who previously wouldn't have.

The concept was not actually that new as it had first been used in 1893 when they were dubbed 'test matches'. Six seasons later the idea was abandoned, but now it seemed it was thought that the original idea had been a good one all along.

The principle had been (re)introduced as part of a package of measures designed to systematically reduce the number of clubs competing in the First Division from 22 to 20. A move of dubious advantage, which was seen as vital to the self-serving needs of the top clubs in the country, and indicative of the thinking that would soon bring about the formation of the Premier League.

A side issue, and one which in lower-league clubs might have felt they had received less consideration, was that the number of teams in the Second Division would be increased from 22 to 24, surely another indication that the power of the biggest clubs would soon become relentless.

Another aim was to introduce automatic promotion and relegation between the Football League and the now established, and credible, top division of non-league football, the Conference.

And as part of the 'blue sky thinking', the opportunity for extra meddling and change for change's sake was too good to miss. It was decided that the play-offs were to be established at the end of the 1986/87 season.

As far as it specifically affected Swindon, the team finishing third would have to compete alongside the teams finishing fourth and fifth in the Third Division to justify their right to promotion all over again. Also included for this first, experimental, and expected temporary jamboree, were the team who finished third from bottom of the Second Division, who would need to prove their worthiness of retaining their status.

The unfairness of this contest was overlooked through its expected financial lucrativeness, and once this had been proved, and regardless of the completion of the other aims, the play-offs would be here to stay.

For the first time in living memory, the race was on to finish fifth. And with Town hovering between fifth and sixth it was suddenly crucial that they finished the season on the right side of the wire.

A 2-2 draw at Doncaster Rovers dropped Swindon to sixth, then two wins on the trot over Christmas helped with the re-escalation. By the time 1987 dawned with the loss at Bournemouth it was obvious that, with the correct application, Swindon could at least be expected to participate in these new-fangled play-offs.

Two days later, a 1-0 home win over Bury was the first in a run of ten matches without defeat. Two matches after that Town were back in fifth place, and by the time Steve White scored the only goal of the match against top-of-the-table Middlesbrough on 28 February, they were sitting fourth in the Third Division.

There were still 18 games to go, but Swindon would not occupy a place lower than that again that season.

Town had already embarked on a run of seven wins on the trot, a sequence that along with the 21 points on offer was distinguished by five clean sheets for young Fraser Digby. The 14 goals scored were shared between six players. Recent signing Jim Quinn was filling his boots in front of goal, while Steve White and Dave Bamber were adding their names to the scoresheet.

A narrow 3-2 loss at Wigan Athletic brought the run to an end in the last match of March and was a portent of things to come in May. When April Fool's Day brought a two-goal defeat at Chester, Town had suffered their last wobble of the regular season.

There were 11 games to go and each would add to Swindon's points haul.

Three goals without reply accounted for Mansfield at the County Ground, then a unique fixture saw Town travel to Ashton Gate, Bristol, but to take on Rovers, rather than City.

With the Gas forced out of their historic home at Eastville, their home fixtures were usually being played at Twerton Park, home of Bath City. The doubling of the workload on the pitch had though taken its toll, and the surface was declared unplayable ahead of the local derby.

An arrangement was reached between the two Bristol clubs for Rovers, in the bottom four of the table and in need of the points to avoid the drop, to host Swindon at the home of their greatest rivals.

The game was a goal-fest.

Gary Penrice pounced on a Digby parry 21 minutes in to knock in the first. Then Robbie Turner scrambled in the second after a corner found him on the far post just six minutes later. Not to be outdone, Rovers old boy Steve White scored for Swindon half an hour in.

A stiff wind gave the hosts the advantage in the first half, but Peter Coyne's far-post ball on to Quinn's head levelled four minutes after the interval.

Then Rovers took the lead again. David Hockaday was judged to have fouled Phil Purnell for a penalty, and Purnell drilled the resultant spot-kick past Digby's dive to the right to regain their lead.

The best goal of the game came from Dave Bamber on 62 minutes. The big man showed great control to bring the ball down on the edge of the box, turn and find the top corner to equalise again.

Just one minute later, Quinn struck for the second time, this time using his left foot from 12 yards out, bringing down a poorly headed clearance from a corner and dispatching to give Town all three points in a 4-3 victory.

Talking of the win, Lou Macari said, 'I did not intend for my players to commit Hari Kari, gift the opposition goals and then try to obtain a result. That is sheer lunacy. We gave one of the worst defensive performances that I have seen in my career. I do not excuse any of my defenders and they must take collective responsibility. Any more wretched displays in defence like that and we can forget any ideas we have of promotion.'

He continued using words such as, 'sloppiness, indecisive, ill-disciplined, suicidal motions', and all this to the side who were now second in the table.

Motivational or just raw emotion?

The result lifted Town above Middlesbrough into second on goal difference, and with it came hopes that they could grab an automatic promotion place rather than face the lottery of the play-offs.

Amid all the hullabaloo of the fight for promotion, there had of course been other cup action during the season as well.

The FA Cup first round victory over Farnborough back in November had brought a second-round tie with Conference side Enfield, an obstacle which was surmounted with a functional 3-0 win. This took Swindon through to the third round where they faced a trip to fellow Third Division club Fulham.

This looked a more significant challenge, with Fulham relegated only the previous May and now occupying a mid-table position some ten places below Swindon. In the end, a single 38th-minute goal from Bamber settled the outcome and led to a fourth-round tie hosting Leeds United.

This was a different kettle of fish. Second Division Leeds were challenging for promotion to the top flight, several seasons after relinquishing that status.

Bamber was again on target to give Swindon a 12th-minute lead with a towering header. Then Quinn added his name to the list of Town scorers 13 minutes before the break, but it was through an uncharacteristic mistake.

His own goal as he attempted to clear a near-post corner saw the ball diverted across goal and drop perfectly (at least from a Leeds perspective) inside Digby's far post, bringing Billy Bremner's team level for the half-time interval.

Just before the hour mark Ian Baird grabbed Leeds' second of the match, with a strike that looked to have taken a deflection off Colin Calderwood, and Town's FA Cup interest was over for another season.

Beginning in December, the other cup competition in which they participated was the Freight Rover Trophy, a tournament designed solely for members of the third and fourth tiers.

As clubs at this level were designated as just 'associate members' of the Football League, the competition had initially been launched with the less than snazzy, but more than adequate moniker, the Associate Members' Cup. A series of sponsorship deals over many years would subsequently cloud the issue of whether it was the same contest at all.

Starting with a multiple number of sets of three teams, and arranged on a geographical basis, each would play one home and one away game, with only the team finishing bottom of what might be loosely viewed as a qualifying group being eliminated. The arrangement was at best convoluted.

With Orient being determined as the worst team in the group, superior Swindon had an official first-round tie with Bournemouth, which took penalties to settle in their favour.

A 4-2 home win over Hereford United was next, by which time Town were deemed to be in the somewhat more grandly named but still considered rather insignificant southern area semi-final against Third Division rivals Aldershot.

By now, with a potential Wembley appearance on the horizon, interest in the competition had gathered a little, and almost 8,500 people gathered at the County Ground to watch the action.

And strange action it was.

On 43 minutes a harmless-looking header nodded forward by Peter Coyne found Steve White, whose own looping goal-bound header squirmed under the Shots' keeper and inside the post to give Swindon the lead.

White turned architect three minutes into the second half when he latched on to a long ball and raced at Aldershot's goal. His shot/pass found Quinn who had charged forward looking for any opportunity that might come his way. He drilled the ball home from the edge of the six-yard box and Town looked home and dry.

But with his team two goals to the good, Digby raced out of his box and brought down Shots' Martin Foyle, and referee Alan Gunn had little option but to dismiss the custodian. In these days before multiple substitution options allowed a replacement keeper on the bench, scorer Quinn replaced Digby in goal.

Six minutes after Digby's departure, Quinn did well to parry a shot, but the loose ball was finished by future Town manager Andy King for the visitors. Despite further manful goalkeeping work from Quinn, a long-range shot from Mike Ring 20 minutes from time made its way past the stand-in keeper and the scores were level.

And just as it looked as if extra time would beckon, Steve Wignall scored a last-minute goal at the back post after an Aldershot corner to seal the match for the Hampshire side.

Three cup competitions, some victories, some heroic failures, and some glorious defeats, but Swindon could do without the distraction that each had brought throughout the campaign. Now came the important business of securing back-to-back promotions.

After the league win at Bristol City against Bristol Rovers, a draw with champions-elect Bournemouth dropped Town back to third, where they remained until the end of the season. The stalemate was to be notable for a collector's item of a goal from stalwart defender David Hockaday.

His first of the season, it was followed by his second, and last, just four days later with a strike which settled a 1-0 win over Darlington. Singlehandedly, Hockaday had won his side three extra points with his unexpected goal contributions.

From then on, although victorious only three more times in the remaining eight games, it was perhaps just as crucial that none were lost. Alternating between draws and wins through the four games to the end of April, May began with a 3-0 success at Carlisle.

Keen observers may have spotted that of the nine goals scored between 20 April and 2 May, seven of them had come in the last 15 minutes of the game. Surely an indication of the superior fitness that Macari's team held over much of the opposition.

And perhaps most tellingly, two goals in the last 12 minutes at Notts County had helped to ensure a 3-2 win. That sort of resilience was soon to prove vital, replicated as it would be after the end of the regular season.

Perhaps because of the realisation that a top-two finish, and automatic promotion, was out of reach, but that a top-five and play-off place was confirmed, the last three games of the regular Third Division season ended in draws.

It was not known at the time but a 1-1 home draw with Gillingham, when May the fourth was with us, was the first of four meetings between the two sides in little over three weeks. The series might not have had the longevity of the *Star Wars* franchise, but it would still qualify as epic.

That draw against the Kent club had left Town five points behind second-placed Middlesbrough with six points to play for. Bournemouth, who had just one game left, were home and dry with a nine-point lead and promotion in the bag. Only Middlesbrough could deny them the title.

By the time Swindon's last game of the season arrived, they were already guaranteed a third-placed finish, safely inside the new play-off zone by 11 points, five behind second, but four above fourth-placed Wigan Athletic.

So, it could be considered that there was little for Town to play for on 9 May as team and supporters travelled to Ashton Gate to face Bristol City. For the Bristol Robins though, going into the match while in the play-off zone by just a one-point margin, there was more than just West Country pride to play for.

A 66th-minute Peter Coyne equaliser squared the score after City's Trevor Morgan's 12th-minute opener, and the 1-1 result did more damage to City than it did good for Swindon. The draw meant that they had been overtaken by Gillingham, who claimed the last play-off place in the Third Division.

Town's points tally of 87, and a goal difference of +30, would have seen them promoted in every one of the preceding five seasons, when three points for a win had been introduced, but there were few complaints that they hadn't made automatic promotion.

Middlesbrough in second had finished seven points ahead of Swindon, while champions Bournemouth had exceeded their total by a ten-point margin. And if all that seemed fair, Swindon had finished two points above Wigan who had claimed 85. Meanwhile, fifth-place Gillingham had amassed just 78.

This season though it would be necessary for Lou Macari's team to again prove that they were worthy of the points haul superiority already gained over the preceding nine months. Despite having already shared the points evenly with Wigan, and having taken four out of six off Gillingham, Swindon would need to prove they were the better side of the three all over again.

Macari had previously spoken of the potential play-offs participation and appealing to supporters he said, 'Collectively we can make the Second Division. I recall what a shambles this club was in when I first arrived here, not enough players, little pride, and virtually no hope. In three seasons that has all changed. Swindon Town have won more matches in the last two seasons than Liverpool. The Anfield club have won 48, while Swindon Town have won 55.'

And alluding to his continued commitment to the club, Macari said, 'You have had plenty to cheer in the last season or so, and it isn't over yet, whether this season or next. See you at the next game, whenever that is.'

Play-off protocol dictated that third-placed Swindon should be matched with fourth-placed Wigan in a two-legged semi-final. Meanwhile, fifth-placed Gillingham would face Sunderland, who had finished third from bottom of the Second Division. The winners of each semi-final would face each other in another two-legged affair to complete the composition of the following season's Second Division.

It must be said that Wigan were not the team in 1984 that they were to become. Only elected to the Football League in 1978 when they replaced Southport, games took place at Springfield Park under manager Ray Mathias and in front of average attendances of 3,000 to 4,000.

Dreams of top-flight football, FA Cup glory or European competition were to be a long time consummating for Wigan supporters.

In a fashion that Swindon fans would have identified with 18 months earlier, Wigan had lost their first four matches of the season but steadily climbed the table almost one place at a time. Eleventh in December, their home win over Swindon near the end of March left them seventh, and a subtle push from then on secured fourth place for the last four weeks of the regular season.

The teams were to meet in Wigan on 14 May, and if any Town fan was to be asked to identify a single match that epitomised the very spirit of a Lou Macari Swindon team, they would be hard-pressed to find a better example.

Two goals down inside 20 minutes, Swindon's entire campaign was in danger of fizzling out into a damp squib.

Just two minutes in, Chris Thompson fired in past Fraser Digby from 20 yards to rock Swindon right at the start. Little more than quarter of an hour later, a Bobby Campbell free kick from distance was parried by Digby, who uncharacteristically let the ball spill from his grasp. David Lowe swooped to net and double the hosts' lead.

This wasn't what Swindon supporters had grown accustomed to witnessing, but if the battle was looking lost at half-time, by full time the war was back on.

As time wore on in the second half it was becoming clear that Wigan's dominance was beginning to be tested by Swindon's determination. With 18 minutes of the first leg remaining Jim Quinn raced on to a Peter Coyne pass. Wigan goalkeeper Roy Tunks, who had charged out to meet him, stopped his shot but Dave Bamber followed up to net into the vacant goal.

Eight minutes later, Steve Berry's free kick dropped on to Quinn's head and the ball found its way past Tunks and into the net off a post for an equaliser. Then ex-Wigan man Coyne nodded past the hapless Tunks with just two minutes remaining as the game came to a breathless conclusion.

Town had turned around a two-goal deficit, and instead of going into the second leg at home hoping to overturn a losing position, they would instead hold the upper hand in the race for the play-off final. Their performance had demonstrated the fight and resolution that was a microcosm of everything that the Robins under Lou Macari were becoming.

The second leg just three days later was an altogether less fraught affair, and few Swindon supporters in the 12,485 crowd would have been overly disappointed with that. A 0-0 draw was all that was needed for Town to progress to the final, and that's what they got.

Meanwhile, Gillingham were perhaps unexpectedly overcoming Sunderland in the other semi-final, setting up a winner-takes-all, two-legged meeting to determine promotion to the Second Division. The action would take place over the late May bank holiday weekend.

The first leg, at Priestfield on the evening of Friday, 22 May, was decided by a single strike from David Smith nine minutes from time. The game was not a classic, and there were various opportunities for Swindon to have added their own entries to the scoreboard, but there was a feeling that their chances of ultimate promotion were far from over.

The following Monday the two teams reconvened at the County Ground in the match that was supposed to define the season of each. Swindon fans' optimism was high, even if nerves were palpable.

Town started on the front foot and Steve White and Jim Quinn engineered successive, if unsuccessful, opportunities, so when Karl Elsey struck a stunning 25-yard volley to draw first blood for the visitors, the jubilation from the Gills' supporters was matched by funereal silence from the remaining members of the 14,300 home crowd.

Not for the first time in these inaugural play-off fixtures, Swindon had a two-goal deficit to overcome.

White hit the Gills' crossbar and continued in a similarly determined vein in the second half. Bamber's downward header lacked the accuracy to dent Gillingham's lead, Coyne's header went the same way and Leigh Barnard was then next to hit the woodwork.

After all the missed chances there began to be a feeling that the season could even now come to nothing, but rather than petering out, it was Peter and in. Peter Coyne finally rose to the goalscoring challenge, striking a scrappy left-footed finish from just inside the penalty box as the hour mark passed.

Then came the moment of salvation that levelled the aggregate score, and it came from someone for whom it would mean every bit as much as it did to every Town supporter watching.

Charlie Henry had come on as a 46th-minute substitute to replace Chris Kamara, and with ten minutes remaining it was his left foot that supplied an unstoppable shot past keeper Phil Kite, giving Town the lead on the day, and a 2-2 draw over the two legs.

With the score locked that way to the end, the marathon season still had more to come; a single-leg play-off final on the neutral ground of Crystal Palace's Selhurst Park would be necessary.

There was at least one attendee of the game who, when asked some days later, 'Did the away goals rule not apply?', thanked his lucky stars that it hadn't occurred to him to wonder that during the match.

This time everything really did rest on the outcome of the one last match, the play-off final at Selhurst between Swindon and Gillingham on the evening of Friday, 29 May.

If the Robins had gained a reputation for persevering to the death and steamrollering the opposition to defeat by sheer fitness, this time they decided to do things the other way around.

Despite some very early pressure from Gillingham and with the match just two minutes old, White collected a flick-on from Charlie Henry after a long free kick. He outpaced Les Berry in the Gills' defence and poked the ball, right-footed, past Kite to give Town an early lead. It was their fastest goal of the season and helped to settle a few supporters' nerves.

That's the way things stayed for over an hour until a long ball from Swindon's Steve Berry reached Bamber. He used his strength to win the bouncing ball, held up play and it was Berry again who had made up the ground to collect Bamber's pass and push it further forward.

And there was White again, whose own persistence saw him win a ball that he appeared second-best for. On the edge of the six-yard box he shrugged off a challenge from Les Berry and pushed the ball past Kite for his and Town's second goal.

Gillingham undeniably had opportunities to reduce the arrears and over the course of the 90 minutes acquitted themselves well, but Swindon held firm.

After 46 games and five play-off matches, Swindon had claimed the final promotion spot to gain entry to the following season's Second Division campaign and as such could consider themselves among the top 44 teams in the country.

Lou Macari addressed the experience as being 'like a fairytale, I just couldn't describe how I'm feeling', helpfully continuing, 'It's the greatest feeling of triumph in my career,' as he described it anyway. 'Much better than an FA Cup Final at Wembley as a player,' he continued.

But he also said, 'I never want to experience a night like that again. The people who organise these things should scrap the play-offs straight away.' Showing compassion for his fellow professionals he said, 'There is no money in the world that can compensate for the disappointment in the Gillingham dressing room.'

During the course of the season, skipper Colin Calderwood had acquired the nickname 'The Fridge'. Suggestions vary for the reason for this. Some say it was due to his coolness under pressure as he coordinated Town's defensive rearguard. Other inside sources indicate it may have been for his propensity to enjoy his food.

But as nicknames go, it was substantially more original than Steve White's equivalent of 'Chalkie'.

The Fridge's assessment was, 'The Fourth Division championship was inevitable for us last season, and we had a long period to contemplate its arrival. Friday night's accomplishment was totally different. It was sudden death, there was no time to contemplate whether we would go up or not, a relief on the night and suddenly you are there. It was not cut and dried this time and sudden death was much more exciting.'

There was one member of the team through all this play-off drama who had a strangely fleeting role to play and whose contribution, and perhaps name, has since passed many by.

Midfielder Steve Berry had cost £12,500 from Newport County just before transfer deadline day in March 1987. He was 24 years old and had previously had a spell with Sunderland.

He made his Town debut in the last game of the regular season in the 1-1 draw at Bristol City, providing the cross for Peter Coyne to score.

He then went on to play in all five play-off matches, crossing for Jim Quinn to equalise at Wigan, and was a key contributor to Steve White's second goal against Gillingham at Selhurst Park which started the promotion party in earnest.

But then, after just four matches of the following campaign, Steve departed again, this time to Aldershot. A very strange cameo to play in a tumultuously successful few weeks.

When the dust had settled on 1986/87, it could be seen that over the previous two seasons Swindon had amassed a huge 189 points, and it was calculated that Lou Macari's total transfer activity over that time, offsetting fees paid against those incoming from sales, had balanced out at just £22,000.

The home attendances for the 23 league matches had seen an average 7,715 click the turnstiles each game.

The season ended with two players sharing the glory of top scorer. Dave Bamber and Steve White had scored 21 goals over all competitions and no fewer than another three had finished level on 12 each.

Unsurprisingly, once the Football League's objective of reducing the number of teams in the First Division to 20 had been achieved, five seasons later it was returned to 22 again. Indecisive action demonstrated by the Football League there then. But of course, the money-generating play-offs remained.

A Robins official assessed the impact that Lou Macari, who had received the Third Division Manager of the Month award in March, had had on the club thus, 'Lou is not God or an angel. There is no real secret to his powers, just an astute understanding of human nature, of making players respond with all the powers within their capabilities. He is, to a great extent, a loner, but has a mischievous sense of humour. It is fair comment that so much depends on Lou Macari remaining at the County Ground. Those who work alongside him are convinced he will remain with Swindon in the foreseeable future, and, if so, the club will continue to make further progress.'

6

1987/88: from 47th to 33rd Consolidation

LOU MACARI spent the summer of 1987 preparing his squad for a campaign of Second Division football, a level that Swindon Town fans hadn't experienced since 1973/74. Multiple challenges ahead could be expected.

The consistency of goalkeeper Fraser Digby who had been called into the England under-21 squad the season before, had seen him play an incredible 54 matches in 1986/87. He had missed just a couple in March when fellow England under-21 keeper Tim Flowers had been borrowed from Southampton to fill in during Digby's suspension after being sent off against Aldershot.

But without a recognised senior deputy to understudy Digby, the position was seriously exposed. Coming in during June to provide cover for the number one shirt was Nicky Hammond, who had been released by Arsenal. Midfielder Steve Foley, who was to be christened 'Stigger' during his Town career, cost £40,000 from Sheffield United, and fellow midfielder John Kelly arrived from Chester City.

Southampton central defender Jon Gittens, who had impressed Town's boss in the previous season's League Cup games against the Saints, arrived for £40,000 in July. Also incoming was midfielder Kieran O'Regan who arrived from Brighton & Hove Albion.

Right-back Chris Ramsey moved on to Southend United after three seasons and two promotions, and that concluded the summer transfer activity.

It had been a long time coming, but as members of the Second Division, Swindon could now seriously claim to be 'The Best in The West' at last, although contenders for the title were fewer than they would become.

The Bristol clubs of City and Rovers were both competing in the division below. Cheltenham Town were toiling away in the Conference and wouldn't make the Football League until the last year of the millennium, while Yeovil Town were 12 months away from promotion from the Isthmian League, at the time the second level of non-league football in England.

The Glovers would have to wait until 2003 to gain their own Football League status, while in their present form, the name Forest Green Rovers was little more than a glint in the eye of the residents of Nailsworth. The most serious contenders to swell the West Country numbers within the Football League were Bath City, who had finished one place above Cheltenham in the Conference.

CONSOLIDATION

The progress made by Swindon since the arrival of Lou Macari really had restored pride to anyone who called themself a Robins supporter.

After the meteoric rise through the divisions over the last two years, surely a campaign of consolidation was not only expected, but necessary.

Among the teams that Swindon would face on level terms over the next nine months were relatively recent European Cup winners Aston Villa, Leeds United who were soon to be winners of the last First Division title in the old format before the advent of the Premier League, Blackburn Rovers, who would be crowned champions in the third season of the Premier League, Leicester City who would also be future Premier League winners, and Manchester City, one day to be winners of everything.

And throughout 1987/88 Town were to take points off all but one of them.

With no disrespect meant to the likes of Darlington, Hartlepool and Rochdale, the forthcoming campaign looked a significantly greater challenge than had been faced over recent seasons.

It began with defeat at Bradford City, but that would be the only loss in the first five Second Division fixtures.

With away wins at West Bromwich Albion and Middlesbrough, coupled with three points at home to Sheffield United, newly promoted Swindon sat in fifth place in the table after five games.

Striker Jim Quinn had already hit three league goals and another four players had also registered. One of those was John Kelly who had struck Town's opener in the 2-1 win at The Hawthorns to overcome West Bromwich Albion.

It was Kelly's third start since signing in the summer, and it would be his last. Kelly would appear just four more times, coming off the bench in each, then he moved on to Oldham Athletic in November as the midfielder became the latest in a growing list of players who fell short of Macari's demanding expectations. His playing career at the County Ground had lasted fewer than two months, with his departure preceded by his dismissal for comments he made to the referee at the end of an away defeat at Ipswich Town.

Macari had this to say about the incident, 'The match at Ipswich was marred by the fact that John Kelly was sent off for an unnecessary action. When the final whistle blows the game is finished for players and being an experienced professional, he should have known better. We will now lose his services for a period.'

While that would have been disappointing for Kelly, the season's start had generally been as productive as could have been hoped, and first impressions of the Second Division looked as though Town would be more than capable of holding their own.

Coupled with a satisfying 5-3 aggregate win in the League Cup over neighbours Bristol City, there appeared to be reason for supporters to be optimistic for the developing campaign. Quinn hit a hat-trick in a 20-minute period in the home leg to open up a three-goal lead.

CONSOLIDATION

The away leg at Ashton Gate didn't come without its worrying moments though, and a missed penalty for the home side was also a missed opportunity for City to level the aggregate score, having already pulled two goals back. Dave Bamber calmed nerves when he grabbed his first of the season, and Steve Berry converted a penalty in what was his penultimate appearance in a Swindon shirt. In mid-October he moved to Aldershot on loan, a deal that was made permanent four days later.

At many clubs that may have seemed a strangely premature end to a club career, but with Kelly also on the move after a matter of months, coupled with the previous speedy in-out spells for Jake Findlay, Martin Ling and Jimmy Gilligan, such swift turnarounds were now nothing out of the ordinary at the County Ground.

Now into September, Town settled down into a pattern which indicated their confidence in their new status, and come the start of October, fifth place had been maintained.

Not only that, but First Division Portsmouth had been eliminated from the League Cup with a 3-1 Town win in each leg. Quinn struck his second hat-trick of the competition in the home meeting, then a Bamber pair, and a Steve White single repeated the scoreline at Fratton Park.

After the away game it was reported that Macari had actually thrown a punch at one of his own players. At the time he retorted, 'I don't want to comment on it,' but three days later he said in a TV interview, 'I was supposed to have hit one of my players, which I did. He was out of order. I would have done a little bit more, and I'd tell him that to his face. But it was about discipline, the sort of thing that, when I was playing, I wouldn't have dreamed of. It came natural to me not to say or do things. Over the last ten years that has deteriorated.'

The highly principled Macari had clearly let his emotions get the better of him. Was this the same man whose chairman had once doubted his strength of character when dealing with the Harry Gregg issue?

The victory over Pompey led to a home tie against more First Division opposition, this time Watford, when a Quinn penalty secured a 1-1 draw in front of a huge County Ground crowd of 13,833. These were days that were far removed from those home gates of 2,000 or fewer.

The replay at Vicarage Road was lost 4-2, but again Quinn was on the scoresheet, incredibly with his 16th goal of the season, after less than three months of action.

That was the sort of return that was guaranteed to attract attention from other clubs.

Swindon were proving that they belonged in the Second Division, but more than that, they were now regularly demonstrating that they were more than a match against opposition from the division above as well. Fans of no more than three years' standing could have been forgiven for pinching themselves in disbelief.

Not that everything in the garden was rosy and a 2-0 defeat at home to Birmingham City had Macari declaring the performance 'the worst in my three

CONSOLIDATION

years at the club'. An army training camp session was to follow.

The biggest margin of victory in September had come against Reading, who were now Town's closest rivals. Still at Elm Park, the Royals, who had ditched their less glamorous nickname of the Biscuitmen some years earlier, were defeated 4-0 at the County Ground as M4 rivalry now entailed a trip east, rather than west to Bristol.

Macari commented afterwards, 'What was most pleasing was that our attitude to the game was exactly right. Derby games are usually hard-fought affairs, and I expected this one to be like that. I would not have forecast either side winning 4-0.'

The win was attributed to the tactical decision of the boss to play Charlie Henry, who was now finding starting opportunities increasingly rare, up front between Quinn and Bamber. The move came about after Macari had watched Reading beat First Division Chelsea in the League Cup and spotted a vulnerability to exploit.

The highest home gate of the league campaign topped 10,000, and along with it came the welcome financial gains associated with it.

The win was the first in a run of five without defeat and on 10 October a 2-0 home win over Oldham lifted Town to fourth in the Second Division table. Interviewed on TV afterwards, BBC racing commentator and long-term Swindon supporter Julian Wilson assessed the boss, 'He has got terrific commitment, a great brain and is a hard demanding man, but most successful managers are.'

A 3-0 County Ground win over Stoke City ten days later meant that Swindon maintained their position of fourth, leaving them in the middle of the play-off zone and on target for a repeat of the previous season's dramatic end-of-season theatre.

Surely it wasn't possible for yet another promotion campaign for the third year running?

The lofty position had been achieved on the back of a five-match unbeaten run, but it was then followed by five without a win. That sequence of games was perhaps the most challenging set of fixtures Town would face all season.

An away defeat at Crystal Palace began the run. Steve White scored Town's only goal, but it was not to bring about such celebration as was seen after his most recent strike at Selhurst Park which had brought promotion the previous season.

Palace had grabbed the points with an 82nd-minute penalty which Macari described as 'the worst decision I've seen in my life'. Colin Calderwood was adjudged to have handled the ball by referee David Axcell after a Geoff Thomas free kick and the resultant spot-kick deprived Town of one of the points on offer.

Next came a home match with Manchester City, a much-anticipated meeting which epitomised the sort of game that supporters would have been licking their lips over when the fixture list had been published in the summer. The action would not disappoint.

In the pouring rain Jim Quinn hit the crossbar from a Dave Bamber cross, but Imre Varadi netted for the visitors from a corner in the 34th minute. Dave White then doubled the lead two minutes later as Nicky Hammond in goal allowed a shot to escape his grasp and trickle home. David Hockaday then produced the pass to allow new signing Bobby Barnes to slide in at the far post and reduce the arrears just before half-time.

In the second period Varadi broke down the right wing and squared into the six-yard box. Hammond did well to block the first shot, a follow-up hit the crossbar but Paul Simpson scored at the third attempt to restore City's two-goal advantage.

Bamber, who had recently been described as 'the most awkward customer in football' by Crystal Palace boss Steve Coppell, struck seven minutes into the second period to keep Town in contention but White, the City version, netted in the 68th minute to open up a two-goal cushion once again.

Pressing the opposition, as a Macari side was always expected to do, in the 74th minute Bobby Barnes collected a throw and ran across the face of the City penalty box. His pass found Steve Foley, who struck from the edge of the area past keeper Eric Nixon, but despite valiant efforts and an overhead attempt from Bamber, Swindon slipped to a thrilling 4-3 defeat. Over 11,500 watched the encounter.

Next came a narrow 3-2 loss at Filbert Street against Leicester City, and the proceedings that 1,000 travelling fans witnessed left them holding their heads in disbelief.

Barnes had given Town a ninth-minute lead after dancing his way past two defenders and striking accurately past goalkeeper Paul Cooper. Then Steve Foley, already booked for verbally abusing referee David Hutchinson, mistimed a tackle and was shown a red card with 43 minutes gone.

Undaunted, ten-man Town continued to stake their claim for the points. When Bamber executed a trademark piece of trickery, Steve Walsh tripped the striker in the penalty box and Hutchinson pointed to the spot. Quinn placed the ball and struck to Cooper's right, but the goalkeeper beat the ball away. The ball however didn't clear the danger area and Quinn raced in to tuck it over the goal line.

Town were 2-0 up and there were 23 minutes of the match remaining.

With just eight minutes left and with Swindon doggedly defending the two-goal lead, Hockaday appeared to be fouled by Leicester man Gary McAllister. The linesman thought so too, and waved for an infringement, but Hutchinson decided to overrule his assistant and waved play on. Surging forward and forcing a corner, substitute Paul Ramsey rifled past Hammond to halve Town's margin.

There were just 90 seconds remaining when the home team forced another corner, from which the ball was flicked across goal, and Walsh headed home at the far post. The home fans, who minutes earlier had been barracking their team, raised the volume and with the match well into added time, yet another corner found Mark Venus on the edge of the penalty box. His volley turned the result around for the Foxes.

CONSOLIDATION

Leading by two goals after 82 minutes and playing the entire second half with ten men, Town had been undone from three set pieces and left Leicestershire empty-handed. Macari described it as 'one of the worst ten minutes I've ever had in football' and, typically judgementally, he said of Steve Foley, 'He got himself sent off. There is no way I can defend him.'

After such tension had ultimately produced such disappointment, a 1-1 home draw with Plymouth Argyle a week later was certainly less dramatic, but at last produced Swindon's first point in three weeks of football. Barnes was on the mark for the third match on the trot a minute before half-time to equalise an 11th-minute opener from Stewart Evans.

Macari questioned his players' condition afterward, suggesting that perhaps they had lost their super-fitness and that some were carrying a little too much weight. An army camp was probably in the offing.

The game had featured future England international Tim Flowers lining up for Town as the Southampton goalkeeper arrived for his second spell on loan from The Dell. Fraser Digby had suffered a fractured thumb in the away loss at Crystal Palace, an injury that would keep him out of action until February.

Digby had initially been replaced by new understudy Nicky Hammond, but the more experienced Flowers would play five games over the course of a month. Then Nottingham Forest custodian Paul Crichton performed a similar role until Digby could be safely reintroduced to on-pitch business.

Things didn't get any easier for Swindon a week later with a trip to Elland Road to face Leeds United.

Starting as early as the third minute they went a goal down to a David Rennie goal. Bobby Davison doubled the margin, then Bob Taylor added a third. Barnes hit one for Town before the break and the winger struck again with 12 minutes of the match remaining to give the visitors hope of snatching some spoils.

But it was a goal from Leeds defender Peter Haddock which sealed the home team's 4-2 win, and again Swindon made a return to Wiltshire devoid of points.

Incredibly, over the five-match run Swindon had scored nine times and claimed just one point. The streak, with minimum rewards, had dropped them from fourth place to 13th.

That plainly wasn't in the script for a team hoping to chase for promotion for the third year running, but although it wouldn't have been known at the time, 13th place would be the lowest position that Swindon would occupy all season.

The lesson perhaps being that if you are looking to consolidate in a higher division, try to do it in the top half of the table.

The unproductive run finally came to an end at home to Bournemouth in the last match of November. Macari, probably dissatisfied with the points return, was off on a scouting mission and left managerial authority with his deputy John Trollope.

New star winger Bobby Barnes wasted little time adding his name to the scoresheet. Jim Quinn's drive struck the post of Gerry Peyton's goal and Barnes was first to the loose ball. His first strike was charged down but he had the presence of mind to slot home on the second attempt.

A minute later Steve White made it 2-0 when he latched on to a long kick from Flowers and left Peyton with no chance. Defensive marking was at fault to allow Bournemouth to pull a goal back, but Quinn followed up on a rebounded ball off the post after a White attempt nine minutes into the second half to add another to Swindon's tally.

Barnes's industry had tested the cool of Tom Heffernan all match, and the Bournemouth man was sent off for a foul on his tormentor soon after. Town left-back Phil King had a shot cleared off the line, but it was Bournemouth who struck next, David Puckett poking the ball home after yet further Swindon defensive frailty from a corner.

White settled the nerves among the home supporters with eight minutes to go and there was still time for the visitors to go down to nine men when Paul Morrell was sent off. Final score 4-2.

At the end, Trollope summed up, 'We were good going forward but I couldn't really be sure about winning until the final whistle. We looked in trouble at the back from every set piece.'

All those who had witnessed the capitulation from corners at Leicester at the beginning of the month would have identified with his comments, but he also said, 'The important thing is that we won. A few heads have been dropping in recent games but perhaps this will give us the boost we need.'

When Huddersfield Town came to the County Ground on the first day of December, Swindon scored four times again, and incredibly Barnes was on target once more as he recorded his seventh goal in six games.

Jamaica-born Barnes had arrived from Aldershot in mid-October in the deal which had seen unsettled Steve Berry move in the opposite direction. A fee of £50,000 also went on its way to Hampshire to seal the deal. Barnes had begun at West Ham United and was plainly finding life in Wiltshire very much to his liking.

A brace from White and yet another from Quinn completed the scoring for Town. This time they had won 4-1, and while two victories on the trot did little to elevate Swindon up the table, the welcome turnaround of form had restored some belief.

While all this league action had been going on, Swindon had been participating in a cup competition which brought a novel experience.

Just as the Associate Members' Cup had been designed to offer clubs from the bottom two tiers a route to a Wembley final, the ill-conceived Full Members' Cup did the same for the top two divisions, and this would be Swindon's first participation in the tournament. The short-lived competition was soon to be accused of unnecessarily cluttering the fixture list and was later scrapped, but this was during the days when the quaint idea of football clubs playing football was still considered a neat one.

CONSOLIDATION

Now with sponsorship, the first round of the Simod Cup took Town to Ewood Park in November to face fellow Second Division side Blackburn Rovers. Goals from defensive partnership Jon Gittens and Tim Parkin brought a 2-1 win and passage to round two.

Next came a stiffer test against First Division Derby County, who now featured England man Peter Shilton between the posts. Memories would have been stirred of the keeper's performance for Southampton, which had been instrumental in Swindon's elimination from the League Cup, a little over a year earlier.

Two days before Christmas Day, this time things would be different at the County Ground.

With the game goalless at half-time, Quinn spun and hooked a spectacular 20-yard opener over the fingers of Shilton ten minutes into the second period. The strike was already Quinn's 21st of the season with five months still to run.

Nicky Hammond's post came to the rescue for Town six minutes later, then Shilton proved his quality with an excellent stop from Dave Bamber. Substitute David Penney levelled with a header placed past Hammond, but Derby's reprieve was to be short-lived.

The visitors still seemed to be congratulating themselves on their fightback when David Hockaday scored what was surely his most memorable goal for the club.

Making a trademark surge down the right wing, the full-back whipped in a speculative cross into the box. Instead of finding a team-mate, the ball swung past a mesmerised Shilton, struck the far post and ended in the net. As the newspaper headline proclaimed the following day, 'Shilton proves human!'.

Hockaday explained afterwards, 'You see him off his line, you chip him, and everyone says it was a cross,' before admitting, 'It was a bit embarrassing.'

A 2-1 win over First Division opposition, passage to round three, and Town were to welcome more top-flight visitors in Chelsea to the County Ground in the new year.

But before that, consecutive Second Division away defeats at Aston Villa and Sheffield United in December continued to demonstrate that Swindon were still trying to find the consistency they needed following promotion. Villa were ultimately to be promoted at the end of the season, while the Blades were to drop down to the Third Division, but both games were lost by a one-goal margin and Town retained their mid-table status.

More satisfying though was the completion of a double over M4 rivals Reading when the trip to Berkshire on Boxing Day was decided by a single 76th-minute Jim Quinn strike. Only the third time the Robins had ever taken all the league points off Reading in a season, the result would have been good for local pride, and Swindon's new goalkeeper Paul Crichton had particular reason to be pleased.

He had signed on loan from Nottingham Forest on Christmas Eve and drew praise from his new boss Macari by his readiness to disrupt his festive planning to travel to Swindon at the drop of a hat, 'A lot of players would probably have wanted time to think about a move with Christmas so close, but he left his family to travel down on the night before the game. He did all right especially after being thrown in at the deep end.'

Crichton had made an important stop from the Royals' Martin Hicks with nine minutes to go when he parried a powerful header from a corner. He would play four games during his stay as he became the third goalkeeper to stand in for the injured Fraser Digby, leaving the club as Digby regained full fitness. Crichton did not leave the pitch as part of a defeated side during his spell at the County Ground.

A 4-2 home victory over Ipswich Town two days later was probably more meaningful.

No one would have been surprised to see Quinn's name on the scoresheet and, also somewhat expectedly, Dave Bamber grabbed the last, four minutes from time. Ipswich central defender Ian Cranson had helpfully opened Swindon's scoring by netting in his own goal in the 33rd minute, and despite the visitors fighting back to level in the second half, Phil King celebrated his 20th birthday by regaining Swindon's lead before Bamber settled the issue.

At this time a story emerged that would ultimately prove fruitless, but captured the imagination anyway.

Ex-Town striker Paul Rideout, a product of John Trollope's youth team efforts, had turned professional with Swindon in August 1981, and had left for Aston Villa two years later.

In between he'd scored 42 goals in little over 100 appearances. Despite such prolific marksmanship his goals couldn't prevent Town's continued descent, and £200,000 took the Bournemouth-born boy to the Midlands.

Having subsequently spent several seasons in Italy, a return to England was being mooted, and hopes were raised that Swindon could again feature in the 23-year-old's future.

With his destination still undecided in February, and genuine talks taking place between Rideout and the manager, the ex-Town hero was still answering the question of whether there was a chance of his return.

He said, 'Of course there is. I would not be wasting Lou Macari's time or mine talking about it if there was no chance of it happening. Neither would I bother if I thought Swindon had no ambition in reaching the First Division. But under this man they have. Since he's been here, he has transformed the club, and I would certainly play for him.'

It was well known that Rideout still had close links with Swindon, and the player plainly had a very high opinion of the man who was leading the club for ever upward.

One national paper commented that Macari seemed equally keen. 'Paul will cost anything between £300,000 and £400,000 but if you want to have a go, nothing is really beyond your scope. When he makes his move, the most important factor won't be finance but a location where he really wants to live,' Macari said.

The whole situation eventually brought a reality check for supporters. With Bari already considering

CONSOLIDATION

a bid of £1.5m from a fellow Italian club, contractual details suggested that Rideout could return to England for a lesser fee. That sum was eventually £430,000 and the lure of First Division Southampton would be far too attractive to ignore.

Swindon had made tremendous progress over the past few years. But not that much!

In financial contrast, their scorer against Ipswich, Phil King, had arrived for a fee more in keeping with County Ground budgetary expectations: £12,500 had secured the left-back's signature after a successful loan spell the previous February.

Bristol-born King had found his first professional home at Exeter City before moving on to Torquay United from whence he travelled north, but satisfyingly remained in the West Country, when he signed for Lou Macari's side.

King had settled in immediately in the Third Division and his arrival allowed David Hockaday to switch to a more natural right-back role. Ever-present to the end of the season, King had played a key part in promotion in 1986/87, and his goal against the Tractor Boys the following season was to be his only one of the campaign.

In January 1988 Swindon played six games. Just two of them were in the Second Division, with the remaining four either in the FA Cup or the Full Members' Cup.

Attendances broke the 12,000 barrier in each of the three home matches. In less than three weeks, the number of supporters who visited the County Ground was the equivalent of half a league season's worth of fixtures in Macari's first leadership season of 1984/85.

If anyone was still dismissive towards the progress that Swindon had made over the previous three seasons, the crowd figures throughout January would provide plenty of evidence to convince them otherwise.

The first of the half a dozen fixtures of January came on New Year's Day when West Bromwich Albion visited Wiltshire, and it wasn't without incident.

The fundamental statistic of the game was a 2-0 win for Town, with a couple of goals from Steve White, both inside the last six minutes. But the game was sparked into life with the 58th-minute dismissal of Bobby Barnes.

Barnes was adjudged to have used an abusive gesture after a goal was ruled out for offside by linesman John Roost. It was the second time that Roost had offered the referee advice which had denied Swindon a goal.

Showing the official two fingers to indicate the number of goals that he'd had disallowed, Barnes maintained the signal had been misinterpreted.

Photographic evidence would subsequently confirm the orientation of Barnes's digits in his favour, but the winger was sent to the dressing room by referee John Martin, leaving his side to play out more than half an hour with ten men.

A furious Barnes had to be manhandled from the pitch by his own team-mates, saying afterwards, 'I could not believe the referee's decision. I did not insult or swear at the linesman. I tried to persuade the referee to speak to the other players, but he had made up his mind.'

CONSOLIDATION

Macari was also not amused and chased Roost down the pitch demanding an explanation. He explained, 'At first, I couldn't understand why Barnes would not leave the pitch. Now I stand to lose one of my players for two matches. Normally we would accept the decision if a player deserves to be sent off, but there is no way we will accept this one. We will be appealing.'

Despite the feeling of injustice, Barnes would later serve a two-match ban.

Steve White had come on as part of a double substitution which saw Jim Quinn and Dave Bamber leave the pitch to be replaced by White and Charlie Henry. The effect was immediate, with White scoring his opener in his first minute on the pitch, and adding his second five minutes later.

It was Town's third consecutive win and started the new year well, by the number of points gained at least.

Twenty-four hours later, and perhaps inspired by the injustice of it all, Barnes's 75th-minute goal at St Andrew's helped Town to a 1-1 draw against Birmingham City. Appreciative of the response the estimated 1,000 travelling supporters gave him, Barnes said, 'I almost jumped over the fence into the crowd. The way they chanted my name really picked me up after what happened against West Brom.'

That concluded the Second Division football for Swindon for more than a month.

FA Cup action began a week later as the Robins enjoyed the luxury of beginning the competition in round three instead of round one, by dint of their newly won seniority as members of the Second Division.

First Division side Norwich City were the visitors, with the outcome a goalless draw, leading to a replay at Carrow Road four days later. It's possible that the Canaries thought that the hard work had been done. If so, they may have been well advised to have checked with Suffolk rivals Ipswich who had been beaten so convincingly by Swindon just two weeks prior.

On the Wednesday night in Norfolk, Dave Bamber was on the scoresheet twice, the first a powerful header from a David Hockaday corner halfway through the second half.

Before then the chances had been relatively evenly spread between the two teams. Mark Bowen had hit the bar for the home side, and a scramble from the rebound had seen two efforts desperately blocked.

Hockaday had fluffed a glorious chance after Norwich goalkeeper Bryan Gunn had been forced into an error by Bamber, and with just Dale Gordon between him and the net, the defender hit his shot into the midfielder's legs.

After Bamber's opener, Swindon looked hard to press home the advantage. Quinn twice went close, Hockaday brought the best out of Gunn with a diving header and the custodian did well again to deny Chris Kamara. At the other end Phil King blocked a shot on the line, and a handling offence by Kamara was judged to be just outside the penalty area as the travelling 500 supporters held their breath.

CONSOLIDATION

Finally, nerves were settled three minutes from time as Bamber struck again, this time with a header from a Quinn free kick.

The win brought a fourth-round tie at Newcastle United, scheduled for the end of the month. No one knew it then, but there would be many a restless night for anyone with a Swindon persuasion as a consequence.

After the win at Carrow Road, Macari said, 'Having Newcastle in the draw was a great incentive to win. There is no reason why we can't go there and do it again.'

Ahead of that though it was time for First Division Chelsea to visit the County Ground in the third round of the Full Members' Cup. By now the profile of the competition was beginning to be raised among supporters of the clubs still participating, with the potential of a Wembley final looming closer.

Chelsea fielded four full internationals in their side, and were considered to be at full strength, but within ten minutes of the start Town were two goals to the good.

Midfielder Kieran O'Regan slung a great cross into the Chelsea area, Bamber out-towered goalkeeper Roger Freestone and centre-back Tim Parkin dived in to head home. It was just six minutes after the kick-off.

Not to be outdone by a mere defender, striker Steve White added his own name to the scoresheet inside a further 60 seconds. Racing through on to a Hockaday ball, White evaded the offside trap and angled a lovely strike into the net to compound the visitors' discomfort.

Quinn nearly made it three with a volley just minutes later and Bamber did likewise with a curling shot almost immediately after that.

If Chelsea expected Swindon to be overawed by their illustrious opponents, they knew nothing about the mentality of a Lou Macari side.

O'Regan was again involved a minute before the break when his ball found White who approached the perhaps shell-shocked Freestone. Drawing the keeper out, White slipped the ball to Quinn who neatly finished to give Swindon a 3-0 half-time lead. Quinn was now up to 24 goals for the season.

The Blues, or the Pensioners as supporters of a certain age will always remember them, tried gallantly to redress the situation in the second half, but it all came to nought for the London team with just over an hour gone.

Bamber, chasing a Kamara through ball, was brought down by the desperate Freestone, but the big man slipped the ball out to White as he fell. Resisting the temptation to spoil things, referee Allan Gunn elected to play an advantage, and White netted his second of the match and Town's fourth without reply.

And so it stayed. Future Swindon duo Micky Hazard and Roy Wegerle could do little to stop the onslaught. The result took the Robins into the last eight of the competition, just two games from a trip to Wembley.

Macari's assessment afterwards was, 'Some of the players were saying we'll have to watch out for them, but I said, let's steamroller them. Let's get in amongst them. Let's show them who wants to win.'

CONSOLIDATION

Plainly Swindon did, and Chelsea less so. Those tactics seemed to have worked then, and the reward would be a third meeting of the season with Norwich in the quarter-final.

So on to the last Saturday of January, and back in the FA Cup, an exodus of supporters left Swindon bound for Newcastle to watch their Wiltshire heroes face the might of the top-flight Magpies. This was expected to be the toughest test that Macari's men had faced yet as they took on the side that sat halfway up the First Division table and had won the trophy no fewer than six times.

Over 27,000 people entered St James' Park, but this particular cup dream was about to run its course.

Scotland under-21 international Darren Jackson scored first for the home side, beating Nicky Hammond in the Town goal from 20 yards with 35 minutes gone.

Swindon had a chance to equalise when Steve Foley broke away and tried to find Jim Quinn. Anticipating the threat, the Newcastle defence smothered the opportunity mob-handed and staged a counterattack. Rising star Paul Gascoigne beat Hammond for the second of the match, and already the task had become significantly more challenging.

As the second half commenced Town had little option other than to press forward in search of goals, and United exploited the space left behind accordingly.

One penalty miss for the home side on the hour was followed by the third goal, when Michael O'Neill powered home a header, then Gascoigne took penalty responsibilities and netted his second goal of the match to make it four.

Brazilian Mirandinha supplied a cross which Phil King, who had previously hit a post at the other end, cleared. But the ball only reached striker Paul Goddard who struck a missile past Hammond from the edge of the box to finish the scoring at 5-0. It was Swindon's heaviest defeat in the FA Cup for 35 years.

Macari had thoughts for the travelling hordes, 'We were hoping at least to bring them back to Swindon but once we had gone two goals down the result was never going to be much of a shock. We wanted to try to get back into the game, so that meant throwing men forward. We eventually paid for it. We have a chance to rectify the situation with a good result against Norwich in the Simod Cup next week. I promise the supporters we will flog ourselves to death there.'

A whole month had passed since Swindon had last competed in a Second Division fixture and finally came a home match against Middlesbrough. Macari's team had been taught a lesson from one Tyneside giant, and now came the Teesside equivalent.

But the 1-1 draw saw Town take the fourth point of six from one of the sides who had risen from the Third Division with them just ten months earlier. In an entertaining game, 12 minutes in Chris Kamara played a one-two with Kieran O'Regan and when the ball fell to David Hockaday, his centre was met by Dave Bamber six yards out for his 11th goal of the season.

Fraser Digby, savouring his first match in over three months, needed to face half a dozen corners and had an escape or two, but could not prevent Tony Mowbray heading the equaliser in the 34th minute. Both teams went hammer and tongs for the win with Swindon opportunities for Tim Parkin, Bobby Barnes and O'Regan, and Digby denying Bernie Slaven and Gary Hamilton with a couple of excellent saves to celebrate his return.

And when that was followed by a 3-0 win at Huddersfield Town, Swindon had remained unbeaten in their last six Second Division matches.

O'Regan, scorer of the opener at Huddersfield, had participated in a trial match for Town while still on the books of Brighton & Hove Albion almost a year and a half before signing. Eventually captured by Macari in August 1987, he flitted in and out of the first team, but his first goal for the club would soon be followed by his second, and last, within a month.

The new year had broken with three consecutive Second Division victories, and as February turned into March three consecutive losses would perhaps start to herald the end of the dream of a third consecutive promotion. But before that, Swindon were still very much involved in a fight for a place at Wembley.

February's league action concluded with defeat at Shrewsbury Town and a narrow 1-0 loss at champions-elect Millwall which Colin Calderwood missed through suspension, but most of the attention would have been drawn to the home Full Members' Cup quarter-final with Norwich on 23 February.

With Macari having already promised flagellant endeavour in pursuit of a semi-final place, it remained to be seen whether the Canaries had learned from the lesson Swindon had dealt them in the FA Cup. But it was the Robins who appeared to have learned a lesson, and that lesson was how to do it again.

Chris Kamara was left out of the starting line-up, and with the midfielder's place taken by striker Steve White, the reduced headcount in the engine room in favour of additional men up front indicated that Town intended to go for the jugular.

White almost opened the scoring as early as the third minute, but his shot, set up by a Dave Bamber downward header, narrowly missed the target. The same man then saw Bryan Gunn parry a spectacular volley a quarter of an hour later.

The visitors rallied but Town's defensive pairing of Tim Parkin and Jon Gittens, with Calderwood unavailable, was more than capable of repelling the highly thought of, and highly valued, strike team of Robert Fleck and Kevin Drinkell.

Gunn claimed a Bamber effort, then Jim Quinn had a goal-bound shot fortuitously blocked by Mike Phelan. With the game goalless at half-time, Town grabbed the lead in the 64th minute through an unexpected source: City man Shaun Elliott attempted to intercept an O'Regan cross aimed for Bamber, but only managed to divert the ball into his own net.

Eight minutes later Bamber and then White got their heads to a cross from Phil King, and Steve Foley slammed home his sixth goal of the campaign to effectively end the encounter. A win for Swindon against First Division opposition for the sixth time that season.

Fleck almost had the last word with a chip over the advancing Digby, but his effort smacked against the crossbar and Town survived.

'We were just hoping that everything would go right tonight. I'm delighted for everyone that it did, especially for the fans who braved the cold to come and back us,' said Macari.

Those fans numbered 10,491, the seventh time that the County Ground crowd had broken the five-figure barrier since August.

Swindon were now just one match from a final at Wembley, and there would be precious little time for anyone to rest on their laurels: a semi-final at Luton Town awaited in just 14 days' time.

The two teams convened at Kenilworth Road on Tuesday, 8 March. The Hatters had already reached the final of the League Cup and sat ninth in the First Division. Swindon, comfortably nestled in mid-table in the Second Division, were still a whole division lower.

But the Wiltshire Town had proved they feared no one in cup competition, whatever their standing, reputation or benefit of a plastic pitch.

So, when Luton took the lead in the 29th minute courtesy of a Brian Stein header from a Tim Breacker cross, there was no panic within the Swindon ranks. Instead, efforts were doubled, and the home side were sometimes forced into desperate rearguard action.

Still a goal behind after the break, Hatters keeper Les Sealey punched a ball against Tim Parkin ten minutes after the restart. With the ball bound for the net, defender Mal Donaghy hacked it off the line.

Industrious Swindon continued to press and midway through the second half they were awarded a free kick 25 yards from goal. Jim Quinn found a way through the defensive wall with a powerful strike, one which Sealey failed to hold. Kieran O'Regan pounced on the loose ball and fired it home to bring the two teams level.

Two minutes later Swindon almost struck again when Phil King crossed for Bamber to run in on goal. Having avoided the potential of an offside decision he ran at Sealey, who was having an uncertain evening. But instead of leaving the hesitant goalkeeper with no chance, Bamber chose to try to chip the advanced Sealey, allowing him to desperately push the ball around a post.

Then it was the turn of Fraser Digby to face a 73rd-minute penalty when the referee decided that Ian Allinson had been tripped by Bobby Barnes. It seemed a harsh decision, but Digby came to the rescue, saving Mick Harford's powerful shot and keeping the night level. That was how the scores remained at the end of 90 minutes as extra time was needed to split the two sides.

More nip and tuck followed, but with the game still poised to swing either way and with the extra-time break looming, the chance fell to Foley to put Swindon in front.

His shot from distance banged against Sealey's post, rebounded against the custodian and rolled towards the net. Bamber rushed in to feed on the scraps, but Sealey managed to regain his composure and block the follow-up.

The incident would prove to be decisive.

Four minutes later Luton substitute Kingsley Black found a way past David Hockaday and sought out Harford with a cross. His header saw Mark Stein, brother of earlier scorer Brian, nod home from close range to seal the match.

It was the Town of Luton, rather than that of Swindon, who would grace the Wembley pitch on the last weekend of March.

Asked after the game how his players felt, Macari sarcastically announced, 'Oh, they're delighted,' but added, 'It was a night of disappointment. Our players battled well and at the end of the game they left me with no doubt, and I would think our fans, that they were a bit unfortunate not to be going to Wembley.'

Luton manager Ray Harford was praising in his assessment of the vanquished side, 'They are either ultra-fit or ultra-committed. At half-time I think we had played as well as I've seen us play. It's certainly the hardest game we've had for a long time.'

When defeat came at Luton, and with the realisation that Wembley would not feature in the list of 1987/88 activities, did a sense of satisfaction for all that had preceded replace a striving for more? Or did the exhaustion of having already played 46 competitive fixtures with more than a dozen still to play produce some lethargy?

If the former, such thoughts might be considered understandable. So much had been achieved over three seasons of unbridled success.

Whether this was an acceptable consideration or not, the 3-0 home win over Barnsley on 15 March, achieved with five first-team players either injured or suspended, was to be followed by just two more three-point hauls, before the season concluded on 7 May.

A 4-3 loss at Oldham was notable for Charlie Henry's only goal of the season in 15 starts, and at the end of the afternoon Town sat in 13th place in the Second Division. Enduring a snowstorm, Swindon were ahead twice but were still two goals behind in the final minute. It was typical of Henry's work ethic that he scored in the 90th minute, but even scoring three goals away from home could not, this time, claim any points.

While a run of five matches to the start of April saw Swindon undefeated, and while there were still significantly impressive results achieved, such as a draw at Maine Road against Manchester City and another point at home to Crystal Palace, the six points collected did little to improve their Second Division standing.

Even the 3-2 home win over Leicester City wasn't enough to elevate Town close enough to the promotion frame for the third season running, but they were still tenth in the Second Division table, a level which the club and supporters could only have dreamed about less than three years before.

Ahead of the televised home match with Blackburn on 25 April, and realistic that the season was at an end for his side, Macari said, 'We now have the fate of other teams in our hands. We have Blackburn, Aston Villa and Bournemouth still to play. From now to the end of the season there will be no slack moments from us. We had prepared for the reverse and to be in the driving seat but that has slipped away from us in the last month or so.'

Showing confidence in his side's attributes, the manager concluded, 'I'd prefer to be Blackburn up there at the top, but I know that if we were in their position, we'd win tonight.'

A goalless draw brought victory for neither side.

One last away win at Hull City in mid-April certainly didn't smack of lethargy. After going a goal down, Quinn and Bamber registered braces as Town ran out 4-1 winners. Nicky Hammond was back in goal while Fraser Digby was away on England under-21 duty and loan signing Roy Wegerle, who joined from Chelsea after the Blues' drubbing in the Full Members' Cup, featured in midfield.

Another recent recruit, Paul Bodin, who had signed in early March and who made his debut against Luton in the unsuccessful Full Members' Cup semi-final, came on as a substitute, but it was probably the goalscoring exploits of Messrs Quinn and Bamber that would have caught the eye of any visiting scouts.

Neither would be with Swindon by the start of the next season.

There were five games still to go to the end, but just one more goal would be scored, a 41st-minute strike by Quinn in a 2-1 loss at home to Leeds. In all competitions that was Quinn's 31st goal of the season. Bamber, the second-highest scorer, finished the campaign with 17.

Quinn had played 54 games since the season's start on 15 August. Bamber had played 55. Meanwhile, of course, the Football League was busy reducing the number of league fixtures that top-flight clubs would play to 38.

Three defeats and two draws lowered the curtain on 1987/88, leaving Swindon in 12th place in the Second Division.

There could be no arguments that Swindon were continuing to improve season by season. With just 21 teams in the First Division as the reduction of the clubs in the top tier progressed, only 32 teams finished with a league placing higher than the Robins. They could legitimately claim to be the 33rd-best club in the land.

If the first three seasons of Lou Macari's reign as manager had been defined by each finishing position, 1987/88 had not only continued that upwards trend but added a whole new dimension of knockout competition success to measure it by.

Town had played no fewer than 14 cup matches and 11 of them had been against First Division opposition. Just three had been lost.

The seven home ties alone had seen gates totalling almost 75,000. That was a higher number than those who had watched the entire home league programme in Macari's first year as boss. And with a matchday ticket in the Arkells Stand costing £5.50, over £400,000 would have been generated from cup action alone.

CONSOLIDATION

Meanwhile, the average attendance at the County Ground over the course of the 22 home league games was 9,541, over three times the average who had witnessed Macari's first campaign.

The large gates that Swindon were attracting would prove to be a double-edged sword. How could you reward players who were overachieving by such a large margin?

7

1988/89: from 33rd to 26th
On the brink of the top flight

ON 20 June, striker Jim Quinn left Swindon, bound for Leicester City. Despite the Robins finishing above the Foxes in the Second Division, this was still considered a step up for Quinn, an indictment of the tenuous nature of the football pecking order.

It was the end of Quinn's second spell at the County Ground, his first ending in August 1984, just days after Lou Macari's arrival in Wiltshire. His third was still to come. Over the course of his five seasons, he'd scored over 60 times across more than 120 appearances. A goal every other game is surely every striker's target.

Eight days after Quinn departed, Dave Bamber did likewise, with Watford his destination. Over his own three-season period, he'd scored a mere 45 times in more than 130 outings. At a rate closer to one goal in three games, Quinn might have been unimpressed.

The loss of the two men meant that Swindon had lost 48 goals from the team. In between the two departures,

£250,000 was invested to bring striker Duncan Shearer from Huddersfield Town. Typical of Macari's transfer dealings, the fee, which was the largest in the club's history, was more than balanced by the £315,000 which had been generated by the sales of Quinn and Bamber.

Macari had spent more than any previous Swindon manager on a single player, and over the course of a week the club were still in profit.

With the notable exceptions of the purchase of Shearer, and the arrival of Ross Maclaren from Derby County for £150,000 as August began, Town's squad preparation for 1988/89 was rather different from that of the previous few summers.

Professional contracts were offered for the first time to midfielder Fitzroy Simpson and central defender Adrian Viveash. Coupled with a youth contract for Eddie Murray, and added to that of Nicky Summerbee from the previous season, there was real reason to be optimistic that Swindon were beginning to see the fruits of the labours of John Trollope's efforts, as new talent ascended through the ranks once more.

There had been multiple departures on top of those of Quinn and Bamber. Chris Kamara had gained his independence by moving on to Stoke City on 4 July in return for £27,500, while fellow midfielder Kieran O'Regan travelled to Huddersfield Town on the same day and Bryan Wade joined Swansea City nearer the end of the month.

For the first time in three years Swindon kicked off at the same level as they had done 12 months earlier.

Two of the previous campaign's cup opponents, Watford and Portsmouth, had been relegated from the First Division and now were to face Swindon on level pegging. The third club to suffer the drop had been Oxford United and local derby status between the pair would be renewed. Meanwhile, up from the Third Division were Sunderland, Brighton & Hove Albion, and Walsall.

Due to unfinished work on the Stratton Bank end of the County Ground the match with Crystal Palace, which was planned to start the season, was rescheduled. That left Swindon facing two successive away fixtures to begin the new campaign, and their first home game, against Portsmouth, was not until Sunday, 11 September.

There had been plenty of speculation regarding Lou Macari's commitment to Swindon throughout the summer, and in his programme notes he stated, 'I am still manager of Swindon Town, so little took place. Chelsea approached me about a move to Stamford Bridge but I had never made up my mind to leave the County Ground.'

Macari had also said with some humour, 'I made my mind up some time back. When everyone started to pester me, I decide to play them along. If I could have dragged it on another three weeks I would have.'

Also referring to a backroom shuffle, it was made plain that Chic Bates would be taking a role with greater first-team involvement, while John Trollope and Andy Rowland would be tasked with more player scouting activities.

Over the coming months it would become obvious that Macari was committed to spending vast amounts of time traversing the country, searching for those elusive bargains which had become harder and harder to track down.

Macari made mention of the huge efforts required as the big kick-off approached, 'The transfer fees we have to pay for proven Second Division calibre are considerable compared to what this club has paid previously. The days of £10,000 to £20,000 transfers proving good enough for Swindon Town have almost disappeared if this club wishes to retain Second Division status and look towards the First Division.'

And predicting the campaign ahead, Lou said, 'This season will be a tough one. Swindon Town are no longer newcomers to the Second Division and other clubs are aware of our strengths and weaknesses.'

As if to emphasise the theme, Pompey, who had succumbed to Town twice in cup competition the previous season, left Wiltshire with a point from a 1-1 draw this time. Steve Foley scored his first goal of the season.

By then Steve White had already grabbed a couple of goals in the first two away fixtures. The first was an 86th-minute equaliser at Barnsley on the opening day, and the second was just seven minutes into the game at West Bromwich Albion the following weekend, a strike which sadly claimed no points.

White had exercised a high degree of patience the previous season. The prolific form of Quinn and Bamber had seen him relegated to third choice for much of the season, being named on the bench 18 times throughout the campaign.

But despite limited opportunities, White could still be relied on to contribute when given the chance. Eleven league goals had left the striker as the third-top scorer behind his two rivals, and with the departure of both, White was about to begin a new strike partnership with recent arrival Duncan Shearer.

A creditable goalless draw at Blackburn Rovers was followed by two successive three-point hauls, and when an impressive victory at Watford made that three on the trot on the first day of October, Town sat in seventh place in the table with seven games played. Swindon had thrown down a marker and demonstrated their intentions to mount another assault on a promotion season.

During the close season the Football League had tinkered once more, changing the play-off format after just three seasons. After decades of perceived intransigence, the Football League now seemed intent on change for change's sake.

Now four teams from the same division would play among themselves to determine promotion, rather than involving a club needing to prove they should avoid relegation.

That meant that the end of 1988/89 would see the play-offs involve the clubs finishing third to sixth in the Second Division, rather than third to fifth. That extra place would prove vital for Town's aspirations, but it meant that sitting seventh in the table would count for nothing when the campaign drew to a close.

Swindon had started well but would need to get better.

Straddling the end of September and start of October, Swindon faced Crystal Palace in a two-legged League Cup second round tie. Shearer scored his first Swindon goal in the home match, but it was not enough to avoid a 2-1 defeat. The Scotsman's tenth-minute strike had opened the scoring but Mark Bright and Ian Wright made the decisive contributions.

The build-up to Wright's goal had seen a linesman flagging the Palace man offside, but referee Paul Durkin had waved play on, and the soon-to-be England legend took advantage to score his side's second of the evening.

Midfielder Tom Jones, an £80,000 signing from Aberdeen a week earlier, had replaced Colin Calderwood with 16 minutes to go with the scores still level, and he immediately made a good impression on his new team-mates and supporters. One of the four goal attempts the new man made struck the bar and stayed out, and almost immediately Wright sealed the match with his controversial winner.

Then, when the away leg brought a 2-0 loss, Town were out of one of the cups in which they had performed so gallantly the season before.

Crystal Palace were to feature repeatedly in Swindon's strivings during the season.

Jones was to continue to make an impact as the matches followed thick and fast, grabbing the 71st-minute winner at Watford on his full debut. The game had also seen first-half goals for Shearer and Bobby Barnes as Town took on the recently relegated Hornets at Vicarage Road, and with the hosts on a run of three home victories without conceding a goal, they had dealt with the challenge magnificently.

In a 'too good to leave out' quote from the vastly respected – and sadly missed – *Swindon Advertiser* reporter Clive King, he said of Tom Jones's build-up to his goal, 'With a few hip movements which would have brought applause from his singing namesake, he almost turned the close marking [Kenny] Jackett into a three-piece suit.'

Next up was a match against another side who had descended from the top division the previous spring. A trip to the Manor Ground on 5 October brought the first league derby between Swindon Town and Oxford United since 1982, and it would be the perfect time for central defender Tim Parkin to claim his only goal of the season.

The home team had just taken the lead with fewer than 20 minutes remaining, when Parkin rose to head home a David Hockaday free kick to share the points. Scoring against your club's greatest rivals will always go down well with fans.

Acknowledging what such a point would mean to the travelling supporters, Lou Macari reflected, 'You've got to be pleased with any point away from home, especially in a needle derby game like this. You are screaming at them to go on and win it, but then you suddenly remember you are away from home, and playing a side who were in the First Division last season.'

Again, Jones almost stole the show with an 87th-minute drive which was deflected wide. Town's most recent signing was certainly making a good impression.

Any Swindon supporter who had looked at the fixtures when they were published may have viewed those in October with some trepidation. Having already won at Watford and taken a point at Oxford, there were another five fixtures to complete during the month, and they didn't appear any easier.

First came a home match with Chelsea, which brought a 1-1 draw against the team who would eventually finish champions by a huge 17-point margin. Duncan Shearer, who had picked up the nickname 'Postman Pat', was on the mark for Swindon as he continued to justify his £250,000 price tag.

He nodded home with five minutes remaining to equalise Kerry Dixon's opener for Chelsea, a result which had Macari saying afterwards, 'We were just too nice on the day. Had we got stuck into them a bit and put them under the kind of pressure we can apply, we would have won.'

A week later it was another home match, this time hosting Leeds United. Things continued to be as tough as they could get.

Another draw, the third on the trot and this one goalless, took Swindon's unbeaten run to eight. The game was as drab as the scoreline reflected and neither team deserved any more than each eventually achieved by the end of the Saturday afternoon.

But any Town fan of just a few seasons' standing may have been wise to consider the strides that had been made, that they might feel disappointed that their side had been unable to defeat Chelsea or Leeds.

If so, there was a rude awakening just around the corner when a trip to Sunderland resulted in a 4-0 thrashing at Roker Park.

They went behind in the 20th minute, the result of a calamitous mix-up involving David Hockaday, Jon Gittens and Fraser Digby which ended in the net. The defenders' blushes were spared that the goal was accredited to Gary Owers, as it could easily have been classified as an own goal.

Just minutes later Steve Foley was caught in possession, allowing Marco Gabbiadini to score the Rokermen's second. In the second half, Tim Parkin failed to return an easy ball to Digby and Billy Whitehurst stole in to place it wide of the keeper, before Gabbiadini completed his afternoon with Sunderland's fourth.

It was a performance not in keeping with those expected from a Lou Macari side and one which left the 200 travelling Town supporters with a long, sad journey home. And still there was time in October for Swindon to travel to Leicester City and return with a point from a 3-3 draw, then entertain Birmingham City and emerge with all three points from a 2-1 win.

The game at Filbert Street on a Wednesday night in the last week of the month could not have been more different to the capitulation at Roker Park four days earlier.

Out of the trap like whippets, Town were a goal to the good inside five minutes when Phil King rifled home after a free kick had seen multiple strikes at goal blocked. Little over 15 minutes later Steve White scored his fourth of the season, striking an unstoppable 25-yard volley past City keeper Paul Cooper after latching on to a long kick from Digby.

Then Charlie Henry, starting his first game of the season as a replacement for the injured Duncan Shearer, added the third in the 26th minute. He collected a pass from Bobby Barnes and left Cooper with no chance for the second time in four minutes.

Three goals to the good at half-time, Town had the game in the bag. The trip home for supporters would surely be shorter, and considerably more enjoyable, than that from Wearside. But then Steve Foley, who had been dismissed at Filbert Street in the corresponding fixture almost exactly 12 months earlier, was sent off again in the 52nd minute, and Swindon had to face over a third of the match with ten men.

A debatable decision gave the home side a penalty in the 64th minute, which was converted by Gary McAllister, then a nuisance run by Jim Quinn distracted Digby as he went to collect a cross. The ball ran loose and struck Phil King before ending in the net.

When McAllister scored his second of the night to draw the home side level, Swindon needed some strong rearguard action to protect their point. The task was to be made more difficult when referee Kelvin Morton decided the visitors would need to complete the game with their number reduced even further.

Tom Jones was adjudged to have unfairly blocked Leicester forward Peter Weir, and Jones would have been hoping that Foley had left some dry towels as he made his own trip for early ablutions.

Still, a draw at Filbert Street could hardly be seen as a failure, even if so much more had been promised at half-time, and three days later in the last game of October, Birmingham took to the County Ground pitch.

Steve White grabbed his fifth and sixth goals of the season, and City were dispatched 2-1. Town, while 12th in the table, just as they had finished the previous May, were only three points behind Manchester City who occupied the last play-off place.

In his programme notes, Lou Macari fielded speculation during the week with the following comment, 'I will not dwell too long on the various reports linking me with clubs in the First Division. I was approached by the Sheffield Wednesday chairman; I paid them the respect of considering their offer and respectfully declined his invitation. My family and I enjoy living in this part of the country. I am as ambitious as you are in your line of work but suffice to say I am not seeking any vacancy. Offers are made to me, and I have to be courteous, listen and consider.'

Macari's success at Swindon continued to attract attention from other envious clubs.

He'd just shown what was hoped to be his usual predatory skill in the transfer market, spending £40,000 to bring striker David Geddis from Shrewsbury Town. Geddis began his Swindon career serving a three-match suspension, carried over from his time at Gay Meadow, and made his debut in the win over Birmingham, but in truth his spell in Wiltshire wasn't to be considered a great success.

While grabbing three goals in six matches through December and into the new year, Geddis was to move on again in March 1990 with just those three strikes over 12 starts to his name.

November began with a trip to Boothferry Park to face Hull City, and while Town's travelling support had recently seen major drama at Leicester, this game continued to stretch the levels of incredulity.

Glaring opportunities were spurned by the visitors, starting when Steve Foley failed to connect as he slid on to a loose ball in the penalty box. The game was just six minutes old. Steve White then failed to trouble goalkeeper Tony Norman from just eight yards, and David Hockaday did likewise from twice the distance.

Next it was Charlie Henry's turn, when he couldn't make the most of a chance set up from a White header, but after all the early pressure, almost inevitably, Hull took the lead with a diving header from John Moore, scoring the only goal of the match after 25 minutes.

Barnes managed to head a glorious chance to equalise over the bar from a lovely chip delivered by Jones, Foley placed his own shot similarly skyward from six yards and Phil King had a fierce effort dealt with by Norman. Substitute Duncan Shearer missed his own chance, then King had his second opportunity to grab a point with four minutes left but found Norman sufficiently adept to deal with his powerful effort.

The season was a third of the way through, Swindon were mid-table, but the entertainment had been anything but mediocre.

Beaten semi-finalists in the Full Members' Cup the previous season, Swindon commenced the campaign in the same tournament with a trip to Norwich City, surely hoping to go one better. After all, Town had dealt with the challenge from the First Division Canaries admirably last time and should have little reason to be more overawed by a trip to Carrow Road than in 1987/88.

But plainly the Norfolk club had learned from the experience as well. Despite a goal from Steve White, the home side ran out 2-1 winners. Full Members' Cup action was completed after just the one game, and this season Swindon were making a habit of leaving knockout competitions early.

From Norfolk opposition to Suffolk and three days later the Tractor Boys left Ipswich to travel to Wiltshire as Second Division football recommenced.

A first, and only, goal of the season for central defender Jon Gittens, coupled with a second from Charlie Henry, gave Swindon a two-goal lead with half an hour to go.

Gittens's first-half opener came after a blocked King shot fell to the defender, and his powerful drive was deflected past goalkeeper Craig Forrest. Then Foley supplied the ball for Henry to run through and net on the hour mark.

That might have seemed enough to deal with the challenge from the visitors, but Ipswich's Dalian Atkinson, Jason Dozzell and Romeo Zondervan, who produced a last-minute winner, had other ideas, and all three points disappeared eastwards along the M4.

A post-match postmortem had the home side locked in the changing room for an hour as Chic Bates, increasingly taking first-team matchday responsibilities while Macari scouted talent, read the riot act.

Across league and cup action, the defeat was the third in seven days. It left a week to prepare for a trip to Stoke City, not a fixture that looked likely to offer the opportunity to end the longest run of consecutive losses Swindon had suffered all season.

So it proved, and as had already been seen several times, Town were at best architects of their own downfall, or at worst the victims of outrageous misfortune.

Referee Trevor West, in his first year at Second Division level, awarded a dubious penalty for the home side on the hour after an innocuous challenge by Jon Gittens on Simon Stainrod.

George Berry netted from 12 yards, then a scramble in the Stoke goalmouth was cleared from the danger area six minutes later. When the ball reached midfield man Tom Jones, his 25-yard rocket left City keeper Peter Fox with no chance and brought Town level at 1-1.

Five minutes later, the Potters' Peter Beagrie hit Fraser Digby's post with the ball bouncing away from danger, and then Steve White wasted a marvellous chance with a weak shot while Jones was far better placed to score.

That set the scene for the sort of events that Town supporters were getting used to.

Phil King was given the opportunity to clear the ball from danger but uncharacteristically dithered. Ex-Robins midfield favourite Chris Kamara was able to intercept for Stoke and find Beagrie. His far-post cross was met by Graham Shaw, and the diminutive substitute was able to head the winner ahead of much taller central defenders.

Town had slipped to defeat in the last five minutes of the game again, and in doing so suffered their fourth loss on the trot.

That left them 19th in the Second Division table. For the first time in several seasons, fans might have been forgiven for looking nervously towards the bottom of the table instead of the top when they picked up their Sunday newspaper.

So often in Lou Macari's earlier days at Swindon, his team had overpowered the opposition late in a match with sheer hard work and fitness. Now it seemed Town were falling prey to the same attributes demonstrated by their opposition and heading into its last week November had yet to bring a single Second Division point.

There was little to indicate that, when Walsall visited the County Ground four days before the end of the month, things were about to take another turn for the better. There were still 30 games of the Second Division season to go, Town were occupying the lowest position in the table that they had done since promotion to it, but their fortunes were about to burst into life again.

Walsall were to end the season in bottom place, but at the time were perched precariously outside the bottom three. Steve Foley, who had been gaining a reputation for earning cards from officials through his vocal remonstrations, scored the only goal of the game on the hour mark. This time he stayed on the pitch to the end, and the hoodoo of the losing run had been laid to rest.

Then the scoreline was repeated at the home of the other STFC three days into December as new signing David Geddis scored his first Swindon goal against his former employers Shrewsbury Town a few minutes before the break at Gay Meadow.

The six points helped to lift Swindon up the table and an impressive run had begun. Meanwhile, Lou Macari had observations to make in his matchday programme notes for the following game, 'Some people were becoming unduly dismayed at recent results. Since then, single-goal wins have given us six points and probably given our recent critics the best answer. After four successive defeats the players at the County Ground have responded in magnificent fashion. The matches against Walsall and Shrewsbury were "six pointers" and we took all of them.'

And answering queries regarding his recent absences from matches, Macari said, 'I have added to Chic Bates's responsibilities here at the County Ground, and his experience enables me to spend more time looking for players and sizing up forthcoming opposition.'

Five and a half months of the season remained, and Town had already faced most of the teams in the division. Only five of the last 28 games would be lost.

One of those came at eventual champions Chelsea, while two were against Manchester City, a team also destined for automatic promotion in May.

As December unfurled, Oldham Athletic travelled south to the County Ground and left with a point after a 2-2 draw. The much-appreciated local product Charlie Henry scored his last goal for the club before making a move to Aldershot in August, and the upward momentum was continuing. But Town had much to thank Oldham's Ian Marshall for, with his own goal six minutes from time gifting Swindon the equaliser.

Then the score was repeated at Bradford City a week later when it was David Geddis's turn to make the scoresheet along with Duncan Shearer, and if the point against Oldham a week earlier had an element of luck about it, this draw saw a return to the other type of luck that had dogged Town throughout the season.

Geddis hit the post within the first two minutes, but City took the lead shortly afterwards. Undeterred, within a minute Geddis powered home the equaliser from a Charlie Henry knockdown. But the best goal of the afternoon came 15 minutes before half-time when Tom Jones's determination in midfield culminated in an exquisite ball to the overlapping Phil King. The defender drew the goalkeeper out, then presented a cross from which Shearer added Town's second.

Seemingly in control of the match, Geddis and Shearer had chances to increase the margin of comfort, but from a 77th-minute Bradford corner Paul Jewell capitalised to power home what would prove to be the goal which shared the points.

A festive home double-header began on Boxing Day with a 1-0 home win over Plymouth Argyle, but New Year's Eve saw the first defeat in six weeks when Manchester City arrived and claimed the points at the County Ground with a 2-1 victory. Town's goal was scored by Steve White, but it might not have added to his 30th birthday celebrations appreciably.

The loss would prove to be the last of the season at home.

When 1989 started with a goal from Geddis, his third in six matches, and another from Shearer at Portsmouth, Town drew first blood in what was the first of three meetings between the teams in just eight days.

The 2-0 win was followed five days later with another trip to Fratton Park in the FA Cup, when Steve Foley scored two minutes from time to earn a replay. Determined not to fall foul of Swindon again, it took less than 30 seconds for Portsmouth's Mick Quinn to beat Fraser Digby at Fratton Park, but Foley's late show saved the Swindon day.

Three days later, and back at the County Ground again, Foley was on target once more against Pompey, and this time he didn't leave it so late. This time there were as many as nine minutes remaining when he struck the first goal of the encounter. Duncan Shearer calmed nerves six minutes after that to give Town a passage to round four where they were drawn to meet West Ham United.

And it was still January when the Hammers took to the M4 for Wiltshire, where a goalless stalemate in front of a huge crowd made another replay necessary. A single goal from Leroy Rosenior settled the tie at Upton Park and cup competition for Swindon was at an end for another season.

Attention could return to mounting a charge up the Second Division table with eyes set on promotion to the First Division, but the goalless home draw with Barnsley did little to instil confidence in the likelihood of success. A turgid display from both teams never threatened to offer value for money for the 10,000-plus crowd who had gathered to watch, and a planned fire drill to test evacuation procedures at the final whistle may have added to the supporters' frustration and offered more excitement in equal measures.

Perhaps catching the tone of the occasion, Chic Bates offered, 'We had no fire in midfield and no fire up front.' Lou Macari, also in attendance that afternoon, said, 'That is the poorest we have played at home, and unfortunately in front of a decent crowd.'

Perhaps the highlights were the displays of Alan McLoughlin and Paul Bodin, both of whom were making concerted attempts to claim a regular first-team shirt. McLoughlin in particular had begun in the right-back position and was not to relinquish a starting berth to the end of the season.

A week later Town travelled to Crystal Palace for the third meeting of the two teams that season, but the first in the Second Division.

Steve Foley netted six minutes from the break for what was his third goal since New Year's Day, a lead Town held until less than 20 minutes from the end. Then Mark Bright, whose goal had helped do for the Robins in the League Cup earlier in the season, did the business again.

First, he beat Colin Calderwood and Ross Maclaren to a high ball from Eddie McGoldrick and headed home powerfully past Fraser Digby with 19 minutes to go. Then just a minute later, he collected a header from Alan Pardew to volley the winner.

The defeat to the Eagles was the third time Town had failed to overcome the London-based team, and there would still be another three encounters to come.

The next trip to the capital came midway through February and it brought another of those extraordinary days that had peppered the season. Champions-elect Chelsea were the opposition, and after the game, defender Ross Maclaren offered, 'When people see we only lost 3-2 they will think it's quite a good result, but in reality, it's a bad one for us. We know we should have won.'

Sadly, it was Maclaren himself who was a major contributor to the away-day defeat.

A goal down after five minutes when Chelsea's Gordon Durie left Digby with no chance from the edge of the penalty box, it took just a further two for the score to worsen for Swindon as central defender Jon Gittens stuck a foot in the direction of a hopeful seventh-minute cross into the box and diverted the ball past his own goalkeeper to gift the home side a two-goal lead.

Still the game was less than 15 minutes old when Chelsea keeper Dave Beasant failed to collect a high ball into his box from Maclaren. Steve Foley claimed he was first to the ball to force it over the Chelsea goal line, and Blues defender Joe McLaughlin would have been happy to pass credit to the Town man rather than accept blame for the own goal.

Foley had the chance to level the score but couldn't take it, before Maclaren calmly back-headed a long ball to Digby, only to find his keeper nowhere near where he expected. With the ball neatly finding the top corner of the goal, Chelsea had scored once, but led 3-1.

The afternoon was not to be one for goalkeepers as Beasant was caught out of goal for Bodin to expertly lob home his first goal for the club and make the score 3-2 at the break.

There was one notable chance for the score to increase in the second half when Steve Clarke's backpass only just drifted past Beasant's post, but the comedy of errors finished without further goals.

Both defences had sometimes looked like they were auditioning for *Chuckle Brothers – The Movie*, but the chortles would have been less fulsome from the travelling fans than those from the Londoners.

Sandwiched between the defeats in the capital, a happier, and altogether saner Sunday match in the first week of February saw Town collect a satisfying 3-0 home win over Oxford. This time Maclaren was on target in the right net from the penalty spot, although to score an own goal from there really would have stretched the realms of credibility.

Alan McLoughlin registered his first goal for the Robins just before half-time, and Colin Calderwood completed the scoring in the last minute.

So far, and despite sometimes appearing ready to press their own self-destruct button, the biggest margin of defeat Swindon had suffered was 4-0 at Sunderland back in October. The middle of February brought the reverse fixture as Sunderland visited the County Ground, and the opportunity was presented to avenge the indignity.

Swindon did their best to reverse the embarrassment with a 4-1 victory. Duncan Shearer scored a brace, Steve White scored his eighth of the season and McLoughlin grabbed his second in two matches, all within the space of the first hour. It was an impressive return from Shearer who had missed six matches through a hamstring injury, while midfielder Fitzroy Simpson made his full debut.

The win was the first of seven games without defeat, a run which included an away draw at Leeds, a win at Ipswich and another three points at Bournemouth. Coupled with home victories against Leicester and Hull, Town scored 12 times and let in five over the seven games. None of the goals conceded resulted in the loss of any points.

The victory over Leicester was particularly welcome, considering the way that two of the three points had slipped through the fingers at Filbert Street back in October. Tom Jones, on as a substitute for the injured Ross Maclaren at half-time, netted the important 80th-minute penalty when he took over spot-kick duties.

'It was fortunate for me that Ross went off, although it was bad luck for him,' said Jones afterwards. 'He is the normal penalty taker and would have taken it, but it gave me the chance for my first home goal.'

The Foxes' Mike Newell had powered home three minutes before the break, with Shearer capitalising on a White knock-on after Jones had placed a corner on White's head on the hour to equalise. Jones finished the turnaround, and Town had grabbed their first win of what would turn out to be four in a row.

Steve White was on the mark twice at Portman Road four days later as Swindon made it two on the trot at Ipswich. He modestly described his 90th-minute winner, 'I knew which general direction the goal was in and just tried to get the ball towards the far post. In the end it went in, but I didn't actually see it.'

It was Swindon's first win in Suffolk for 38 years and was no more than they deserved, having dominated the chances for most of the match, but still falling behind to the home side with 60 minutes gone. Ron Fearon fumbled a corner 18 minutes from time and White poached to equalise, setting himself up to complete his double and claim the win.

A 1-0 home win over fellow promotion-chasers Hull produced County Ground talk of a challenge for a place in the First Division, and when a Steve Foley brace and a Tom Jones single earned victory at Bournemouth, Swindon had lifted themselves up to the very edge of the play-off zone.

It was a great run, and perfectly timed. By mid-March, they had reached seventh place in the table with around a quarter of the season still to run, needing one last extra push to finish the campaign in a play-off place.

A goalless home draw with West Bromwich Albion was followed by another four goals conceded, this time at Plymouth Argyle. The result seemed disappointingly out of keeping with preceding performances, but it would have little consequence as Town drew breath for the big finish.

If the comedy routines of the previous game at Chelsea had deserved to be on April Fool's Day, an altogether more sensible 1-1 home draw with Blackburn Rovers took place on 1 April, although the opportunity was there for some fun and games with the potential divine intervention of an official team of Messrs Vickers, Bishop and Priest.

Sadly, few miracles were in evidence for the 90 minutes, but Lou Macari would have banned the water turning into wine in the changing room anyway. Steve Foley continued his impressive goalscoring run from midfield, compensating for a strangely misfiring front two of Shearer and White, who hadn't registered a goal between them in four matches.

The season had entered the penultimate month of the regular competition and there were ten matches to go, equally split between home and away fixtures.

The one loss suffered during this sequence was perhaps unsurprisingly, and certainly without shame, at Maine Road in a 2-1 loss to the team destined to finish second behind Chelsea and gain automatic promotion.

It was the second time that Town had fallen by that scoreline to Mel Machin's Manchester City, but with a bit more luck the outcome this time could have been different.

Duncan Shearer consolidated his return to goalscoring form after his winner against Bradford City the previous Tuesday, with a 35th-minute opener following great work by Jon Gittens and Tom Jones. But a controversial penalty, given by referee John Key seven minutes later when Wayne Biggins appeared to have dived, presented Andy Hinchcliffe the opportunity to equalise.

Steve White, continually falling foul of City's well-marshalled offside trap, tried to set up Shearer when he perhaps should have gone for goal himself, and an unmarked David Oldfield scored what turned out to be the winner for City shortly after.

And that concluded the defeats for Swindon for the rest of the regular campaign. It was 8 April, there were eight games to go and none of them would be lost.

White was back on the scoresheet for the first time in eight matches, and his 13th-minute strike claimed a point against Watford on 15 April.

All footballing matters however were thrown into sharp relief with the news that disaster was claiming multiple lives at Hillsborough at the FA Cup semi-final between Liverpool and Nottingham Forest that same afternoon. No words expended here could possibly confer sufficient perspective on the events of that day.

On Tuesday night three days later a Ross Maclaren double grabbed all three points at Birmingham. Not to be outdone, Steve Foley notched his own brace at Brighton for another maximum haul the following Saturday, and it was midweek again when Town faced a side who they had already played three times that season – and had lost the lot.

Crystal Palace visited the County Ground on 25 April and this time Swindon emerged victorious and it was Steve White who scored the 36th-minute goal which was enough to separate the two sides.

Ross Maclaren fired a long ball into the Palace penalty area and the visiting team hesitated, perhaps anticipating that Colin Calderwood was in an offside position. Referee Paul Vanes didn't think so though, and White controlled the loose ball then crashed it past Perry Suckling to give Town the lead.

Maclaren was to see his penalty saved by the visiting goalkeeper and ten minutes from time Palace's Gary O'Reilly struck the crossbar, but Town had won three games on the trot and the Eagles went back to London with their tail feathers between their legs.

It was the first time that Swindon had beaten Palace in 25 years, and it would soon seem a good time to strike form against Steve Coppell's side.

The win left Swindon in sixth place in the Second Division table, occupying the last of the play-off spots with two home and two away games to play. Nerves were beginning to fray as a third promotion in four seasons looked a possibility.

With the score 1-1 at half-time at Walsall on the last Saturday of April, Duncan Shearer had steadied the travelling fans' worries with a sixth-minute opener. Then the Saddlers' Stuart Rimmer equalised five minutes later.

Midway through the first period Shearer had his second of the match chalked off as Chalkie White was adjudged to be standing in an offside position, and the second half was just a minute old when former Town man Howard Pritchard found himself unmarked to give Walsall the lead.

Calderwood made the scores level again soon afterwards, and both sides had opportunities to add to their tallies, the best of which saw Mark Goodwin strike Fraser Digby's post in the closing stages. Final score 2-2.

Phil King claimed the match's only goal at home to Shrewsbury Town on the first day of May despite an unconvincing display by Macari's men, and the last home game scheduled for the season came when Stoke visited Wiltshire and suffered their second defeat to Town, this time 3-0.

Duncan Shearer, back to his poaching best, scored the first on the hour and added his second two minutes from the final whistle, by which time Tom Jones had eased any tensions with a goal in the 86th minute.

By the time Town visited Oldham Athletic for the last match on 13 May, they had been holding tight to the final play-off place for nearly a month. A 2-2 draw completed the job. Alan McLoughlin and Steve White had both scored in the first half, and the point was all that was necessary to conclude the season with a two-point gap between Town and seventh-placed Barnsley, who just missed out on the end-of-season activities.

Town's 76-point total was five shy of third-placed Crystal Palace, who had missed out on an automatic promotion place by just one point, and it was those two who would face each other in the two-legged play-off semi-final.

Also claiming an interest were Watford and Blackburn, and English football's top tier awaited whoever of the four would prove victorious.

Coming sixth was an improvement of six spots on the final position gained the season before. Lou Macari had now seen his team improve their league finish for five consecutive seasons, and while this rise represented the smallest increase of all five, it was enough to ensure Town's best league finish since 1970.

The play-offs were just three seasons old, yet Lou Macari had now led Swindon to compete in them twice, and with just 20 teams now in the top tier it meant that Swindon could justifiably claim to be the 26th-best team in the country.

There were eight days until Town were to face Crystal Palace in the first leg of the semi-final, and he chose to prepare his team in familiar style: the Robins were off to an army training camp.

Approaching the big day of Sunday, 21 May, goalscoring midfielder Steve Foley passed a fitness test to put himself in contention to face Palace, and the press carried remarks from Macari, and ex-Manchester United team-mate Steve Coppell, manager of the Eagles.

Palace had been denied a play-off place the previous year with defeat to Blackburn in the final game of the season and they would have been keen to put that right.

Asked whether he and Coppell were friends, Macari joked, 'You could say that, but come 3pm on Sunday, I'll hate his guts. Without a doubt it would be nice to have a lead to take into the second leg, but whatever happens on Sunday the tie will still not be won or lost.'

Stratton Bank was handed over to the visiting supporters, allowing 16,656 to witness the tense spectacle, and before the game captain Colin Calderwood voiced his own comments, 'We have done the hard work all season to get this far, now we are going to give it a really good go. It's now just like a cup competition with a very big prize at the end of it. A place in the First Division next season.'

The first half produced chances for both sides but remained goalless. Ten minutes in, Foley started justifying his selection with a determined run and pass to Shearer, but the marksman blasted his volley over the bar. Twenty minutes later the same man was unable to get a header on target and placed the ball just wide of Perry Suckling's post.

Then, eight minutes after the break, came the vital opening goal.

Foley again proved the wisdom of his inclusion when he fed the overlapping David Hockaday who drove a ball into the danger area. With Steve White waiting in anticipation, Palace defender Jeff Hopkins, who had arrived from Fulham in the summer for a tribunal-set £240,000, slid in to prevent the ball reaching White, and only succeeded in placing it past his own goalkeeper.

Much of the big crowd were very happy with life, while a smaller proportion held their heads in their hands.

White had the chance to double Town's lead eight minutes later when he raced on to a through ball from Ross Maclaren and homed in on the visitors' goal. Placing his shot wide of the approaching Suckling, the ball struck the underside of the crossbar, bounced on the line and stayed out.

Where do you find a Russian linesman when you want one?

Then with ten minutes remaining things nearly took another turn for the worse for Coppell's men. Defender Rudi Hedman blocked another cross into the box, and memories of Hopkins's recent mistake must have invaded his mind.

The ball struck the crossbar and rebounded to Steve White who completed the relatively simple chance to net Town's second goal. Except that a linesman had a raised flag, adjudging White to have been in an offside position.

Minutes later the game came to a conclusion, leaving Swindon with a narrow one-goal lead to take to Selhurst Park. Town's central defence of Tim Parkin and Colin Calderwood had denied Palace's dangerous strike force of Mark Bright and Ian Wright much of a sniff of a chance.

Macari was unimpressed with the referee's decision to disallow White's second effort, stating, perhaps with a little exaggeration, 'It must be the worst decision ever made in the history of the game.'

With the second leg set for Wednesday, 24 May, thoughts turned to the last time Town had played a play-off match at Selhurst Park. Steve White's two goals had earned Town promotion against Gillingham two years earlier. Could a repeat be on the cards?

'It couldn't happen again, could it?' White mused. 'I'd settle for just the one goal because if we score, I can't see them beating us.' Town set off for Bisham Abbey two days before the second game, using the centre as a base to concentrate their attentions, just as they had against Gillingham 24 months earlier.

Unsurprisingly, with everyone determined to play their role to become part of Swindon Town history, no one wanted to rule themselves out through injury. Steve Foley was again given a late checking over, and again was declared fit to play.

Ex-Swindon manager Bert Head, still living locally at Minety and also a former Palace boss, declared the first 30 minutes of the game to be crucial.

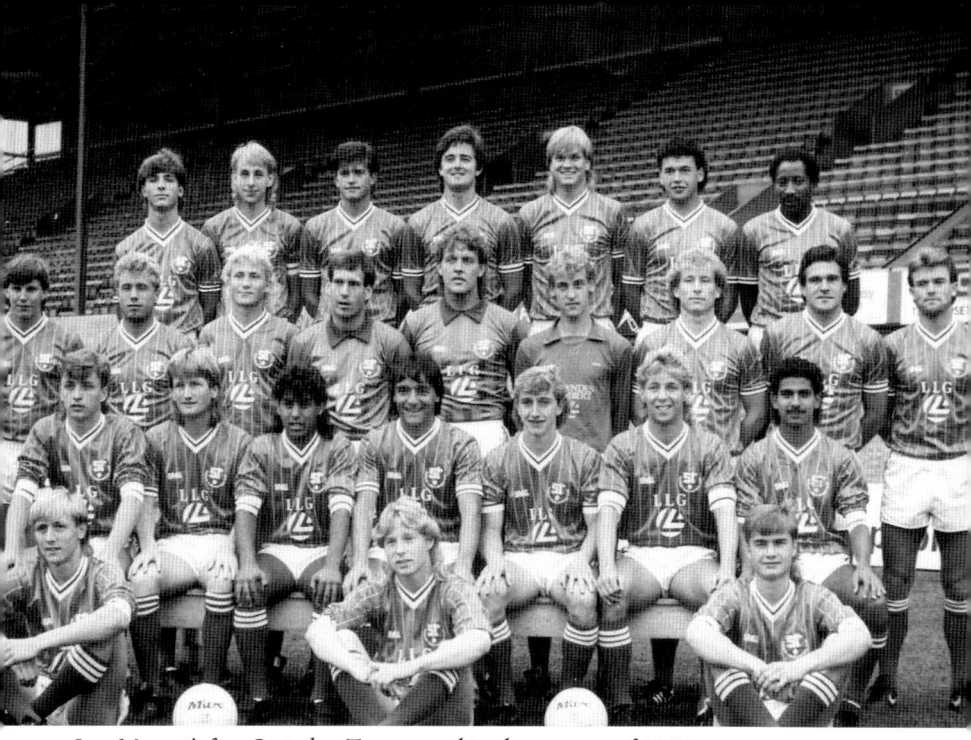

Lou Macari's first Swindon Town squad in the summer of 1984.

There are some glum faces as Swindon Town players see what is expected of them from their new manager.

Decked out in his new club's colours.

Dictating play. Lou Macari the Swindon Town player.

Training gets serious.

Training gets fun.

Bryan Wade wheels away after scoring at Newport County in September 1986.

The fruits of all the efforts. Five Manager of the Month awards.

Celebrations begin with the Fourth Division trophy, May 1986.

Steve Foley scores against Watford in the League Cup in November 1987.

Peter Coyne scores a 119th-minute penalty against Bournemouth in the Associate Members' Cup in January 1987.

Lou and Rocky inspect the County Ground pitch in February 1987.

Dave Bamber jumps for joy after Jim Quinn draws Town level at Wigan in the Division Three play-off semi-final of May 1987. Promotion was to follow.

Chris Kamara nets against Reading in September 1987.

Bobby Barnes slides in to score against Manchester City, November 1987.

Derby County's Peter Shilton beaten by David Hockaday's 'wonder goal' in December 1987. Wonder if he meant it?

Chalkie White slots home against Chelsea in January 1988.

Dave Bamber heads home at Norwich City in the FA Cup in January 1988.

Duncan Shearer nets with his head against Chelsea in October 1988.

Proving that the Midsomer Norton-born man held the Robins in higher regard in his heart, he said, 'It would have been easier on the nerves if Town had managed another goal on Sunday. For the first half hour tonight, they must defend their lead with their lives. If they do that, I think they will pull it off.'

Head's assessment proved spot on.

Nine minutes in, Mark Bright, shackled so well by Parkin and Calderwood the previous Sunday, drew the scores level.

Fraser Digby had punched a free kick away uncertainly, and the keeper then failed to hold the resultant shot from Dave Madden from the edge of the penalty area. With the ball dangerously loose, Bright pounced to punish some unusual defensive sloppiness.

But before that had happened, Duncan Shearer had been unable to capitalise on a great through ball from Tom Jones just two minutes after the start. The Scotsman had shot powerfully 18 yards out, but had not been able to beat keeper Suckling.

Had each of the events had different outcomes, the momentum of the match could have been so different.

But instead Ian Wright, the other much-lauded striker who had been rendered almost anonymous three days earlier, volleyed home seven minutes from the break after collecting a header from partner Bright.

Despite looking suspiciously like offside the goal stood, and it was Palace who were through to the play-off final when victory over Blackburn would eventually lead them to the holy land of First Division football.

When the Town team boarded the coach for the trip back to Wiltshire, Lou Macari was notable for his absence. As time dragged on, puzzled players and officials waited anxiously until the decision was made to leave for home without the manager. The night had ended in disappointment, and the season had also ultimately failed to deliver the much hoped-for promotion.

At the very beginning of the season, Macari had bemoaned the attitude he was encountering in his dealing with players, 'It's getting increasingly difficult to find the kind of players we are looking for, because attitudes are stinking.'

The pressures of the job seemed to be getting to the Scot. Was he becoming disillusioned with the game?

'I was disappointed with comments made by some of the players when they left last summer, suggesting we had not made reasonable offers for them to stay. It's a slight on the people within the club. The chairman offered to sponsor one of them to the tune of an extra £250 a week out of his own pocket. A sponsor also offered £150 a week to keep another. Why did they give the impression we'd only offered them about a tenner to stay?'

To paraphrase Bob Dylan, 'The football times, they were a-changing.'

Before the first ball of the season had been kicked, Swindon had lost the services of Jim Quinn and Dave Bamber, scorers of almost 50 of the 73 goals that had been scored in 1987/88.

Their departures allowed Steve White to step up to the plate, as he partnered new arrival Duncan Shearer.

While by the end of 1988/89 the two had collectively managed only 30; goalscoring contributions from their colleagues, most notably Steve Foley, helped to make up some of the difference.

Town managed five fewer goals than they had with Quinn and Bamber up front, but a tightening of the defence meant that they conceded seven fewer as well. That left the goal difference at the end of 46 league games an extra two to the good.

All those were similar statistics between the two seasons, but the telling factor was that Swindon benefitted from the distribution of goals on a match-by-match basis by gaining an extra 17 points, finishing six places higher than the previous campaign, and earning a play-off place.

For the fifth season on the trot, Macari's team had improved on their previous league finish.

A review of the attendance figures at the end of his last season as manager also makes for interesting reading.

Over the 46 Second Division games that Town played in 1988/89, 14 were in front of a gate of more than 10,000. With so many high-profile clubs in the Second Division, it would be tempting to assume that the highest attendances would be at the homes of the biggest opponents.

And so they were. There were over 22,000 in the ground at Manchester City and Leeds on the days that the home team welcomed Swindon. There were almost 18,000 at Stamford Bridge when Town travelled to face Chelsea, and more than 13,500 at Sunderland.

But the next highest league attendance that Swindon entertained that season wasn't at an away ground at all.

It was at the County Ground when they faced West Bromwich Albion and 12,240 turned up. Sceptics will immediately wonder just how much of that gate was swelled by travelling Albion fans, but in comparison, the corresponding match at The Hawthorns was watched by just 7,500.

Of those 14 games with attendances in five figures, half of them were at the County Ground, home of little Swindon Town. When recently relegated Watford and Portsmouth arrived in Wiltshire, each match was watched by more supporters than watched the corresponding fixtures at Vicarage Road and Fratton Park. The same was true in the case of Ipswich and Portman Road.

And at the end of January, Swindon had faced West Ham in the FA Cup at the County Ground. An astonishing 18,627 were in attendance.

In five seasons, the Robins were finally being reconstructed as a club that was suitable for 'the fastest-growing town in Europe' as Swindon was so often described at the time, and attendances were proving able to support that.

At last, the football club of Swindon Town was matching the often pretentious representations of the town of Swindon, and the time seemed right for both enterprises to make plans for the consummation of a bright future.

But on 3 July 1989, Lou Macari accepted West Ham's offer to become their manager.

After five seasons, 285 matches and a rise of 59 league places, the Scot's revolution was over.

8

1989/90: from 26th to 24th

Consequences

ON 19 July 1989, Argentinian international Osvaldo Ardiles formally took the reins at the County Ground as the replacement for Lou Macari, who had departed for West Ham United. Just as Macari had five years earlier, Ardiles undertook the role of player-manager, with the expectation that he could ease himself into the hot seat while still influencing things on the pitch.

Ardiles inherited a team that had just finished agonisingly close to reaching the First Division and hopes, perhaps expectations, were high that the achievement could be repeated and possibly even bettered. But there would be different and greater challenges ahead for Ardiles than had been experienced in the five years of Macari's reign.

Ossie began the squad restructuring that any new manager expects to undertake, but seemed in general ready to allow his new charges to demonstrate their abilities before he made too many decisions. After appearing on the substitutes' bench for the first two matches of the season, the new boss hung up his boots for the last time, and Swindon Town again had a manager rather than a player-manager.

Initially the season started slowly, but by mid-November Town had hoisted themselves into sixth place in the Second Division table after a 2-0 away win at Middlesbrough. But then things started to take a dramatic turn, in a direction that would have devastating results.

On 13 November, the FA announced that they had begun an investigation into allegations that Swindon chairman Brian Hillier had placed a bet on his team to lose the FA Cup tie at Newcastle United the season before.

Publicly, things then went quiet for a couple of months. Wheels at FA headquarters rarely turn quickly, and it couldn't have been easy for players or manager to keep their concentration on on-pitch matters. Commendably things carried on as normal, and come New Year's Day another 2-0 away win, this time at Watford, saw Town commence 1990 in fifth place in the table.

Then on 5 January the FA made their next move, charging Hillier and Lou Macari with their alleged involvement in the unauthorised bet. It was announced that a special FA commission would be set up to hear the case, and people all around Swindon and the surrounding areas were left to sweat on the outcome.

And sweat they did until 12 February, when the FA made their next announcement. Hillier, who had admitted the betting indiscretion, was fined and issued with a six-month ban from any involvement with running a football club. Macari also received a fine, and despite the ructions within the media, even the FA described the action as 'a foolhardy misdemeanour'.

Hardly the most damning indictment to bring against the club.

Six days later, West Ham visited the County Ground for a Second Division fixture, and it was noticed that Macari was not in attendance. The following day it was announced that he had resigned as manager at the Upton Park club.

Lou explained later, 'I shouldn't have offered my resignation to West Ham. They were not looking to disassociate themselves. The club secretary advised me not to, saying it [his fine] was not a resigning matter, but I felt at the time it was becoming a bit of an embarrassment for the club. The newspapers built the story up to be bigger than Watergate. Leaving West Ham is the biggest regret of my managerial career.'

Both men appealed the FA's decision, and on 3 April Macari's fine was upheld, but in what seemed like a fit of pique, the FA increased Hillier's ban from six months to three years.

While all this was going on, Ossie Ardiles was doing an incredible job of keeping his team focused and a 3-0 away win at Plymouth Argyle on 10 March took Town up to second in the table.

Later, when May broke, all hell was let loose.

On the first day of the month, Hillier, Macari, the club accountant, and Swindon skipper Colin Calderwood were all arrested and taken to Bristol Central police station, where they were questioned by the Inland Revenue regarding alleged tax fraud conspiracy.

Calderwood was quickly released without charge and the following day the Football League, who were now making their own investigations into the club, announced they would hold back from any further actions until the Inland Revenue's case was concluded.

But on 3 May, when the three men still detained appeared in front of Swindon Magistrates' Court accused of tax offences, it was the turn of the Football League management committee to throw their own spanner in the works by announcing they would carry out their own investigation into the financial dealings of the club.

Just how any football club can be expected to perform under these circumstances is difficult to fathom, but on 5 May Town travelled to Stoke City, where they claimed a 1-1 draw in the last match of the Second Division season.

Town had finished six points behind third-placed Newcastle United, but were one of three clubs on 74 points, each of whom filled one of the remaining three play-off spots. Swindon's superior goal difference left them top of the group of three in fourth place, and a play-off semi-final with Blackburn Rovers was confirmed.

Despite all the incredible distractions, Ardiles's side had managed to keep their concentration, and had even improved on Macari's sixth-placed finish the previous season.

For the third time in four seasons, and now with a different manager at the helm, Swindon were to compete in the play-offs, with a place in the top flight of English football the prize for the second successive year. And this time the final would take place at Wembley.

Sunday, 13 May 1990 saw Town and Blackburn face off at Ewood Park in the first leg of the semi-final. The game was 30 minutes old when Steve White hit his 26th goal of the campaign, finishing some great approach play from right-back David Kerslake with a drive from the edge of the penalty box which left Rovers goalkeeper Terry Gennoe helpless.

Half-time had come and gone when Steve Foley added to his own goal tally in the 55th minute with a terrific volley which again had Gennoe rubbing his eyes in disbelief. A goal-bound thunderbolt from Duncan Shearer was gratefully kicked away by Gennoe, and further opportunities fell to both White and Shearer as Town threatened to run away with the game.

When Ross Maclaren lost possession in midfield on 72 minutes, allowing Andy Kennedy to race at Fraser Digby to pull a goal back, the home supporters would have been hoping for a resurgence from their side, but Swindon were not to be denied. A 2-1 lead to take back to the County Ground for the second leg just three days later would do very nicely.

Ossie Ardiles said afterwards, 'It's not over yet and we must not be complacent, but I was tremendously pleased with our style of football.' White, meanwhile, said, 'We are in the driving seat now and we are determined we will make no slip-ups.'

True to his word, neither Town nor White were to do any slipping at all.

Chances fell to Shearer and Jon Gittens inside the first ten minutes of the second leg, but the crucial breakthrough came 11 minutes from the half-time whistle, and it was courtesy of some sloppy defensive work from the Lancashire team, coupled with the expected predatory instinct of Shearer.

Gennoe rolled a ball out to defender David Mail, whose return pass lacked decisiveness. Shearer nipped in to dispossess the pair and placed a curling effort beyond the goalkeeper to increase Town's aggregate lead.

And within three minutes Shearer had this time turned architect. Swinging an inviting ball towards the near post from the left-hand side, Mail was again caught out, this time by White who just beat the defender to the ball to steer it home.

Now 4-1 down, Rovers did their fair share of attacking in the second half as they looked to reclaim some impetus. Howard Gayle grabbed a goal back when his 25-yard drive was deflected past Digby off Maclaren with a little over 20 minutes remaining, but when the final whistle blew, Swindon had claimed a play-off final spot, and a first trip to Wembley for 21 years.

Sunderland, with what must have been a hugely satisfying win over arch-rivals Newcastle in the other semi-final, awaited at Wembley on 28 May.

Long queues formed outside the County Ground for tickets for the big day, and the Football League remained silent about their intentions regarding the financial investigations into the Robins.

Skipper Colin Calderwood explained, 'This is going to be the biggest match of my life.' Goalkeeper Fraser Digby concurred and added, 'Obviously I'm going to be nervous, not because it is Wembley, but more because of what the match means to everyone at the club.'

Boss Ardiles said, 'I'm happier winning 5-4 than 1-0, even if it's not very good for the heart.' Answering questions regarding the potential of the Football League rendering the outcome irrelevant, he added, 'It's not in our hands. The only thing that is, is playing the game.'

New chairman Gary Herbert praised the supporters, saying they were 'the best behaved in the Football League. I just hope they carry on supporting the team next season, hopefully in Division One.'

The game itself turned out to be a hugely one-sided affair, but with only one defining moment 26 minutes in.

David Kerslake won a ball in midfield in what seemed a fairly innocuous part of the pitch. Collecting the opportunity, midfielder Alan McLoughlin advanced a few yards and let loose a shot that could well have been goal-bound but was of sufficient distance that it may not have troubled Sunderland goalkeeper Tony Norman unduly.

But as it travelled it cannoned off defender Gary Bennett, looped over the wrong-footed Norman and found the Sunderland net to give Swindon the lead.

The goal, while perhaps slightly fortunate in its execution, was no more than Town deserved at the time, and would prove to be far less than they deserved by the final whistle. Once a brief bright start made by the Wearsiders had been weathered, the match was all one way in favour of Swindon.

Steve White fired over, then the same striker had a shot well saved by Norman. Then White was at it again when his effort rolled against a post with Shearer not able to capitalise on the rebound.

Tom Jones had a shot blocked by Norman's knees, then the always-industrious Steve Foley headed just over. White, Jones and McLoughlin all had chances to add to the score, but half-time arrived with Town still just one goal to the good.

The second period then continued in much the same vein as the first.

Shearer steered a shot just wide, White was denied by a double save from Norman with Foley unable to finish the move, and then finally Norman used his fingertips to prevent Shearer from adding to the margin of victory.

Back in Swindon, ready to greet the returning and surprisingly thirsty supporters a couple of hours later, a chalkboard outside a Swindon Old Town pub was to exclaim 'Swindon Town 1, Sunderland absolutely bloody nothing'. It was an accurate reflection of the afternoon's events.

The following day the newspapers all carried similar sentiments. 'Now let us stay up begs Ardiles'; 'Don't boot us out'; 'Don't break our hearts say the fans'.

The Football League, having gained the kudos and income from their new, flagship, end-of-season,

Wembley-based play-off final, pontificated. PFA chief executive Gordon Taylor was reported in newspapers to have said, 'It would be an unfair penalty on the supporters of Swindon Town and the players if, despite the efforts of the manager Ossie Ardiles and his players to achieve promotion, this was all to be thrown in their face if points were deducted or they were relegated to Division Three. I have made this point of view well known to the Football League.'

On the morning of 7 June, goalscoring hero Alan McLoughlin was reported to have said, 'The players have worked hard for promotion all season, and all this business has nothing to do with that. Having let us play in the play-offs it would be a kick in the teeth if they did anything to us now. The repercussions for the club could be horrendous.'

But by the end of the day the Football League, after an eight-hour deliberation, announced that Swindon, rather than being promoted to the First Division, would be relegated to the Third Division as a result of 36 breaches of the body's rules, 35 involving irregular payments to players.

There was much soul-searching to be done in Swindon, including the observation that if the Football League had made its announcement a week earlier, the organisation would have been denied the vast sum of money spent by supporters in their fruitless trip to Wembley.

And the question was raised, had their ticket money, parted with under the expectation that the outcome of the game would determine the composition of the following season's First Division, been taken under false pretences?

On 13 June Swindon announced that they were to apply to the High Court for an injunction to set aside the decision to relegate the club, but on the same day, as if to emphasise their authority, the Football League announced that Sunderland would be promoted to the First Division in the Robins' place.

The following day Gordon Taylor was back in the papers, disclosing his view that the Football League's reaction to Swindon's case was over-reactionary and suggesting that most other clubs were in breach of the same allegations, 'The PFA are appalled at the severity of the penalty, particularly as it hits supporters most. The Football League delayed their inquiry, allowed Swindon Town to take place in the play-offs, and have snatched it back from them, and to add insult to injury, have relegated them.'

In scenes reminiscent of those seen when Lou Macari had been sacked in 1985, demonstrations around the streets of Swindon took place, petitions were signed, and Ossie Ardiles flew back from holiday in Argentina to add his effort to the perceived injustice.

By the middle of June, Swindon announced their reluctance to appeal to the Football Association over the Football League's decision and would instead consider pinning their hopes on the High Court finding in the club's favour.

There were real fears that, just as had been seen with the increased sanction applied to Brian Hillier after he had appealed against his own penalty, the football authorities would lay down an even harsher punishment than had already been imposed. So, when on 2 July the FA met to review the punishment, fingers were crossed across Wiltshire.

By the evening, the decision was announced that Swindon were no longer subject to relegation to the Third Division and would remain in the Second Division to start 1990/91.

There was still a feeling of injustice among many supporters who felt the club and fans had been robbed of the promotion to the top division that had undoubtedly been earned. But there was also a feeling of weary relief that the matter had at last been concluded and matters could once again focus on pitch-based activities.

Ossie Ardiles tried to rally his troops and fans and to instil some optimism, 'I expected to be managing Swindon Town in Division Three and now I will be managing them in Division Two again. We are confident of going up again, as we were confident last time.'

All the off-pitch activities that had taken place since the start of 1990 had commenced from Brian Hillier's decision to place a bet on the outcome of an FA Cup match at Newcastle United.

That his actions were unwise could not be contested. That they contravened football's rules was also undeniable, but whether they had been designed to do anything other than protect Swindon's finances should the club suffer the expected loss at Newcastle was doubtful.

At worst, the bet was a naive attempt to offset the potential loss of revenue caused by exit from the FA Cup. A misjudged form of insurance. There was never any suggestion that the outcome of the fourth-round tie had been adversely influenced. Was it fair to punish the club for naive management?

In July 1992, Lou Macari was cleared at Winchester Court of any involvement in tax conspiracy.

Once the newspapers had Swindon in their sights it was open season. With much of the football world in tacit agreement that such activities that were beginning to surface were nothing unusual within football, the authorities seemed to have recognised the opportunity to make a statement to all by making an example of the Robins.

At the height of the revelations, one of the national papers ran a headline of 'The Club that Died of Shame'. It was a caption that was as hurtful as it was inaccurate.

Swindon Town were not dead, but the club had suffered severe injury.

Time had moved on, the club needed to regenerate, and it was time to prove there was life in the old dog yet.

9

Lou's Views

SO FAR, this book has been a retrospect of a five-year period of the history of Swindon Town, told from the perspective of a long-term supporter, but midway through the writing I was delighted to receive a call from Lou Macari.

I had first considered telling this story over a decade previously, and at that time I had managed to get a message to Lou asking for his input. He was very helpful in offering me a contact number, but to my shame I didn't follow it up until over ten years later when, more out of hope than expectation, I found the number and sheepishly sent a text to it.

To say I was pleased to receive a call back would be a huge understatement. Particularly as, after waiting a decade, I'd had the very bad sense to send my message less than an hour before Scotland kicked off Euro 2024 against hosts Germany.

Lou was most generous in offering his assistance and this is how he himself remembers the events that occurred between 1984 and 1990 and offers an insight into the man himself. 'I was on tour with Manchester United in Hong Kong when I was made aware that there was a job opportunity at Swindon. To me at the time, after 11 years at Manchester United, I wouldn't have known anything about the club apart from Don Rogers, John Trollope and the team that had done so well in beating Arsenal at Wembley to win the League Cup in 1969.

'When I came back from the tour the job was still available. I showed my interest, and an interview was arranged, and I travelled down to Swindon to have my first viewing of the Magic Roundabout. Having got lost a couple of times I worked out how to get off it to the County Ground and I sat down to a meeting with the board.'

I asked Lou about the statement attributed to Maurice Earle, which said, 'We didn't interview him, he interviewed us.' Was that a fair reflection of how he remembered it?

'All I'd ever been in life was a footballer and this was like a business meeting. I'd never been involved with business. I asked a few questions and came away wondering whether it was the right job for me or not. I certainly didn't present myself as someone who, having spent so long at Manchester United and Celtic, had unreasonable expectations or demands. I listened to what was said and asked a few questions.

'The questions I didn't ask were those that would be paramount today ... what's the pay and when's pay day! I had a good idea of what they would be at a Fourth Division club and there was no point in asking whether it would be £20 more or less than I expected. That was pretty irrelevant. I didn't expect similar money to what I was on at Old Trafford.

'Obviously things hadn't gone right under Ken Beamish otherwise they wouldn't be looking for a new manager. I don't remember it being a disaster at Swindon at the time, but plainly a 17th-placed finish wouldn't have been considered great. The year after I joined, promotion and relegation were introduced between the Football League and non-league.

'I waited a few days and got a message asking whether I was still interested and I accepted what was on offer. I do remember it being pointed out that I had no managerial experience and I remember pointing out back that that was obvious from the start. My history was well known. I'd never been a manager, but Swindon had previously appointed managers with experience and that didn't appear to have worked out.

'I got the job and told the family we were moving to Swindon.

'Having never been a manager I didn't really know the best way to set about things and keep everybody happy. When you have no experience, everything is a bit of a shock. I quickly realised that everyone would be different and that some would continue to question my appointment regarding my lack of managerial experience.

'The financial state of the club was obvious to me after the board meeting. Apart from Lowndes Lambert throwing in a few quid the bank balance was zero. That didn't bother me. It was just part of the job. I didn't expect anyone to be shelling out hundreds of thousands of pounds at Swindon.

'After I started, I got to know the staff, which was as few as the club could possibly exist on. That was not being detrimental to Swindon. No club wanted to spend more than thought necessary in salaries.'

I asked Lou whether there were any specific influences from his previous manager at Celtic, Jock Stein, that would go on to dictate his managerial style.

'In my opinion, Jock Stein was a genius, getting Celtic to win the European Cup. That couldn't happen at Celtic today. Without a doubt he influenced my style. Jock's style was quite simple. No one was bombarded with systems, formations or tactics. Individual players did their own thing, Jock didn't do tactics. Get the players fit, get them committed, dedication … all the things you want. There was only one coach … although we didn't call them that at the time. You didn't get coached. You got trained.

'I didn't know any of the personnel as I set about preparing for the new season and we didn't get off to a great start. I upped the training at the training ground in Shrivenham Road. I knew what Jock Stein had demanded and I followed that example. Things improved as time went on.

'I inherited the wage structure and bonus system, and I realised that once players' mortgages and bills were paid there was very little left for them. When attracting players to Swindon, the property prices they encountered caused them problems. With Swindon being considered a booming town, it was an added problem in attracting players to the area.

'I re-introduced John Trollope to first-team activities from the reserve team setup. He was very fit which challenged everyone to meet his levels. I was also fit and tried to lead by example. It became a talking point running up through Old Town, the Downs, Barbary Castle. At Celtic we used to run to the training ground, and we did the same at Swindon. Of course, by doing so you are becoming part of the community, saying "hello" to people as you ran, and it was a good start to set a good impression to supporters to have that contact.

'Even reaching eighth that first season was an achievement that got recognised. The players got a feel-good factor and there was a better feel about the club than there had been in the past.

'Of course they were footballers. They were athletes. They should be fit. That was their mission.

'For the first couple of seasons there was no finance to splash in the transfer market. Among my first signings were striker Colin Gordon, a big lad who was good in the air, and Peter Coyne, good on the ground and who gained us a few penalties. They were both all-round improvements on what we had. We improved others only by increasing their fitness levels. There were a couple of players who didn't appear popular with supporters and improving their fitness improved the performance and their popularity.

'We brought in Colin Calderwood. I was certainly pleased with the price and what we got, apart from a good footballer, was a very decent guy.'

When I asked Lou whether he would name Calderwood among his best recruitments, he was loyally defensive about all his acquisitions and loath to pick out individuals for specific praise. 'Everyone thought training was a bit too hard,' was his assessment of all his playing staff.

Next, I asked Lou whether he had heard Brian Hillier's comment, that perhaps he lacked the strength of character to deal with the problem he had encountered with his second-in-command, Harry Gregg.

'I think Harry Gregg was a bigger problem with the players. I think they couldn't deal with him. It was me who eventually dealt with Harry. I brought him in because of the references to my lack of managerial experience. I'd said I would bring someone in, and afterwards I realised I'd done the wrong thing. I didn't really know Harry well before.

'I often felt undermined. If I told a player to do eight laps of the track, and the player complained, Harry would agree with him. If you are number two to the manager and you publicly disagree with him ... well that's wrong. It certainly wasn't me who wouldn't challenge Harry. I did challenge him, and I made it clear to the board that I wasn't happy with his approach. I left it up to them to deal with it, and their way of dealing with it was to get rid of us both! They were more terrified of him than I was.

'I realised that people had seen an improvement, and I got my job back. We made real progress and became a force to be reckoned with.'

When I asked whether Lou was aware of the strength of feeling from supporters that Swindon were on the cusp of something noteworthy, and objected strongly to his dismissal, he responded, 'No. I wasn't aware of that at all.'

Continuing our reminiscing, Lou went on, 'We started to gain a reputation of how tough we were to beat. We went on great runs in cup competitions and became recognised as a team people didn't want to be drawn against, especially at the County Ground which became a fortress for us. Everything was dropping into place.

'The next problem on the horizon though, with all the triumphs in the cups, was the payment for that. You could only pay players what was in their contracts. If you beat Chelsea instead of, say Carlisle, you couldn't reward players with any extra money. Normally bonuses were £15, and with perhaps 12,000 in the ground and the bonus sheet already filed with the football authorities, there was no way to increase that relative to the extra income the club were earning.

'My idea of football is you reward success, unlike today when all the money comes up front. It became a problem that £15 was the bonus, regardless of whether the County Ground was packed. We were getting results that were beyond belief and the players ended up with an extra £15 in their pocket.

'I attempted to rectify this, and everything discussed was done at board level with all the board there. Everyone agreed to give them an extra £30 or £40 each. With new finances desirable there was a move to add new board members who would be able to inject more cash into the club, and not everyone was in agreement with that.'

Referring to chairman Brian Hillier specifically, Lou commented, 'I've been around football a long time and I found Brian Hillier the most fanatical person I ever met. And his fanaticism was totally towards Swindon Town. That is one of those facts that often doesn't get considered. His motive was plainly to maintain momentum and I never met anyone who was more devoted. I don't suffer fools gladly, and my opinion about Brian was that he was fully committed. Brian was in his dream job!

'When we drew Newcastle United in the FA Cup, it was a dream come true. We had to maximise every penny we could get. If we managed to beat them, brilliant. We were into the next round and in for another bumper pay day. Alternatively, a replay at the County Ground would also be great, but if we get knocked out ... what do we do?

'Someone suggested that Lowndes Lambert insured us against getting knocked out. Everyone was at the board meeting and the main talking points were revenue and expenses for the trip. I'd checked army camp availability and nowhere was close enough to Newcastle. All the board agreed to stay in a hotel, with a considerable increase of the usual £10 a head we usually paid for an army camp!'

In our next chat I asked Lou why he had chosen West Ham United as his next destination as a manager after he had decided to leave Swindon.

'Before I spoke to West Ham I went to Chelsea, spoke to Ken Bates and more or less agreed to take the job as their manager. In a phone call after that he told me he had an assistant for me, which we hadn't agreed on. That man was Bobby Campbell. I said, "No, I hadn't agreed with that," so I turned the job down.

'I had nothing against Bobby Campbell. I didn't know anything about him, but I think it's fair to say Ken Bates had a reputation for controlling everything. Back then it was the manager who was supposed to control everything, so if you failed you could have no complaints about who you put in the side. I told him I wasn't going to accept the job and then I got a call from West Ham. I went along to meet them, liked the club and ownership and got the job.'

When asked whether there had been anyone else over the five years he'd been at Swindon who had enquired of his interest in him joining them, his reply was, 'Yes. But I was settled in Swindon and everything was going all right.

'I had no big desire to move out. I had picked up the vibes from the newspapers that I wasn't ambitious to move on. That wasn't true, I just had a loyalty to any club I'd have gone to. I thought unless I gained a reputation as someone who was not going to move on there was no reason to do so. By the time West Ham and Chelsea came along I was getting that reputation, and that would do me damage.

'I thought that after five years at Swindon no one could say I hadn't honoured my contract. I thought the time was possibly right and that I might not get another opportunity.'

Certainly, Lou's success at Swindon was guaranteed to attract attention, and I pointed out that over his spell at the County Ground he had been responsible for a rise from 85th to 26th in the Football League.

'That's what happened? That is an incredible rise for a manager and the players, but until then there had been no reason to disrupt anything.'

Did he think he had achieved everything he could at Swindon?

'We had achieved a lot and I thought that can't continue. Nothing continues for ever. I'd better make the decision to move on in case the phone stops ringing because nobody wants you.'

Does he look back at his time at Swindon with fondness and satisfaction? There was the potential that the events towards the end, might taint all that came before.

'Oh God yes! Everything about Swindon was good. I moved on from my playing career and everything just fell into place. That was very satisfying, and I can't honestly say I planned it at all. I didn't plan anything. I just reacted to what I found, got the players fit, and realised we were moving in the right direction. It worked out for us, and we dealt with any distractions. I didn't think we'd keep winning the way we were, but we did.'

Did that surprise him?

'It did. It doesn't normally happen, and it's not as if we had any significant financial support.'

The lack of funding must have been a culture shock after leaving Manchester United?

'It was nothing unusual. Nobody had any money worth talking about. There was not the sort of ownership we see today. We rescued ourselves, not by following any financial plan. The winning streak just happened, but the opposite also happens. If you get into a losing habit, you never get anywhere near a win.'

I pointed out that at the time of his appointment at Swindon he was the 15th managerial appointment in the club's 105-year history. At the time of our discussion, Town had just appointed their 45th manager, only 40 years later.

'That goes to show how difficult it is these days.'

Given the opportunity to be 40 years younger, would he like to be starting out again now? Was he envious of managers in football today?

'No, not really. There is no challenge there for most of them today.'

I offered my opinion that top footballers today seem to think their playing reputation automatically qualifies them for a leading club's managerial role when they retire from the pitch, regardless of their lack of managerial credentials. Would no one today expect to start at the bottom as he had?

'No. But I didn't expect to start at anywhere other than the bottom. I was someone with no reputation as a manager. Nowadays there are people going in with millions of pounds behind them. It's a completely different world in football today.'

It was at this point in our conversation that I said something that provoked some minor expletives. I used a word that I only usually use in certain circumstances and in certain company.

It had nothing to do with VAR. It wasn't the phrase that even now I can't complete, referring to it only as 'finan … irreg …', and it didn't even have anything to do with a football club from a neighbouring county, that I usually refer to only as the club beginning with 'O'.

I asked Lou how those in charge of so many clubs today can possibly justify the loss of such vast sums of money when their chosen project fails to bring success.

'You've just used the word project,' he said, indicating his dislike for a word that we hear so much in football today, as I hurriedly apologised for such an indiscretion. Neither of us had to explain just how misplaced we felt the use of the 'P' word is, when a new manager holds his first press conference to explain how excited he is to join the 'project'.

We were both in total agreement that taking charge of a club is not a 'project', and I described how I shout at the TV if any new Swindon managerial appointment has the temerity to refer to 'my' football club as a 'project'.

I ventured that football today exists in its own 'bubble' (I apologised for using another cliché in case it caused a similar reaction) where the people within it believe their own over-egged publicity.

'Things back then were so completely different. So far removed from the present-day way of doing things it's scary. When I watch a match and the pundits say a particular player is brilliant, I'm thinking no, no you've got it wrong, you silly journalist. He's not playing brilliantly. He's dropping back into midfield and doing nothing because his legs are going. I've seen interviews when the BBC are telling a player he's the best player in the world, then, when he goes to a cup final is anonymous.'

Lou and I seemed to be in complete accord. Football in 2024 was not what it had been in 1984.

His comments were being made the day after a particularly lacklustre England performance in Euro 2024. Just coincidence? Possibly.

Lou remarked that his old manager, Jock Stein, 'would phone a journalist who ran a story about how good one of his players was, to tell him that so far, he had done nothing. And he was right. Too much publicity when it's not merited goes to a player's head. The money in the game today is ruining it. The likes of Jock Stein and Alex Ferguson saw it coming and decided to get out.'

Then came agreement and a mutual shaking of heads (it was difficult to be sure of that actually, as we were both on the phone) as we bemoaned the number of games that it is considered acceptable for 'top' players to play in these days. 'If they're fit, players can play twice a week, every week,' was Lou's view.

As our regular conversations continued over a matter of weeks, I realised how much I was enjoying them. Lou is a seriously genuine person who is obviously well versed in all that the football world involves and, as someone who is no more than an obsessive supporter of all things Swindon Town, the opportunity to chat to someone who had such a major influence on the club was almost heaven-sent.

Not only that, but so many of our conversations led to me thinking that there was a real mutual belief that football is not what it was.

I had set about writing a book about Swindon Town, during the years that Lou Macari was the club's manager. But with Lou's participation, I had been given the opportunity to not only add in the perspective of the main man of the story, but also give a glimpse of the man himself.

I was interested in the story that Town had spoken to Paul Rideout with a view to re-signing the striker over Christmas in 1987. Had it been a realistic proposition?

'He was coming back from Italy and he'd been a fans' favourite before. It wasn't something that would have happened when I arrived because the club had nothing. We'd made a bit of progress and had jumped up a couple of leagues. Without that, Paul Rideout wouldn't have been interested, no matter how much we had. Everything rides on success and the fact we'd made progress made it a possibility. Getting from the bottom division to the second from top changed things. On the recruitment front there were names that never came out in the press, but our progression gave us different opportunities.

'With the sums of players moving out it made signing Rideout a possibility. We had assets on the bench we could sell to fund incoming players. There were always lots of players in mind and until you meet them you don't know why joining Swindon Town might be attractive to them ... whether they are really interested or using it to engineer a move to a different club. Agents might use it by saying other clubs are after their client.'

That led me to comment that Lou had appeared to spend much of his last season at the County Ground in particular, scouting for players.

'That was part of any manager's job back then. There was no such thing as a recruitment officer, the recruitment officer WAS the manager. It's nonsense now, for a number of reasons. When a new signing comes along today, and doesn't succeed, he's cost a lot of money and everyone automatically assumes it's the manager's fault, but most of the time it's the fault of the recruitment officer. Nobody would be able to convince me to take a player if I didn't want him, and I've got to go and see him.

'If I was a manager today, I'd be at Euro 2024 and covering as many matches as I could to come up with recruitment targets that were realistic possibilities. I'm talking of Georgia, Slovenia, Slovakia. In my time you went hoping to catch players who nobody else knew about.'

Did Lou spread the scouting workload between himself with Chic Bates, John Trollope, Andy Rowland?

'Not really. I liked doing it. I'd get on the train into London and cover two reserve games in a day – one in the afternoon and one in the evening. Midweek games at Highbury or White Hart Lane, then Crystal Palace and Wimbledon. You'd bump into others doing the same and you get to know who was involved.'

That must have been a big workload.

'Yes. But players are the most important part of your team! If you've got players who aren't good enough you are in big trouble. There is nobody else who can get you up the league table, or get you the sack, other than players.'

I suggested that I couldn't imagine too many top managers today putting in the same effort.

'No chance! That's the recruitment officer's job again. It should be the manager.'

But isn't it not just about whether the player is any good, but whether they fit the pattern that the manager wants his side to play?

'Not too much. If you have a flying winger with unbelievable pace, you'd demand he used that. You'd play him to his strengths. If you had a goalscorer, you wouldn't drop him to midfield because you wouldn't get the best of him. You are seeing in these Euros where they play it along the back ... to each other ... my God, back in my time nobody would have turned up to watch that! The modern-day formula of one man up front and keep possession of the ball ... it looks as though that's here to stay.'

I took a chance and ventured that I don't get as much pleasure watching football today, and that it sounded as though Lou didn't either.

'Without a doubt! Today something dramatic might happen once per match, when in the past that would have happened regularly.'

How did Lou feel about the way the rules of the game seemed to have changed?

'I don't know what the rules are any more.'

And as for VAR?

'Oh my God! Do the people running the game today think it didn't occur to people 30 years ago that TV could be used to help decision making? Of course it did, but they realised it would take too long to make a decision. They do it today, and they still can't work out what's right or wrong. It was supposed to clear things up so you could be 100 per cent certain about decisions, but when they are reviewed today, they still can't be sure.'

Again, I felt Lou's and my views on the modern game were in tune. I was self-indulgent enough to imagine two 'mature' gentlemen, who both loved football, bemoaning the state of the sport as they put the wrongs to right.

Having again fuelled each other's discontentment with football today, we returned to the sanctity of the 1980s. I'd noticed what appeared to be an inconsistency regarding Lou's aborted move to Chelsea. Had he been interviewed by Ken Bates to be the club's manager, or as Bobby Campbell's number two?

'I suppose you could say I'd be in charge, but with Campbell overseeing me and reporting back to Bates.'

Would that not have been reminiscent of the time that Harry Gregg felt he could undermine Lou as Swindon manager back in 1985?

'Correct. I didn't even consider it. It hadn't been mentioned in the first meeting, then when it was discussed, it became a complete nonstarter.'

Our talk moved on towards the proliferation of foreign players in England these days, and how different it was in the 80s when all English players seemed to want to go to play in Italy.

'The damage that the Premier League has done, is that all the money is now here. In my 11 years at Manchester United between 1973 and 1984, I only played with one foreign player – Arnold Muhren.'

With the conversation returning to Swindon Town, I asked Lou which of the players he'd been responsible for at the club had he thought most likely to make successful footballing careers.

'I always thought of my Celtic days with Jock Stein, that the players he brought along … myself, Kenny Dalglish, Danny McGrain and three or four others, that all those who applied themselves had long careers. I was always interested to see what would happen to the Swindon players who had similar upbringings as myself, hard work, training, dedication, they had the same longevity and I never thought that was coincidence. I never thought that anyone brought up applying the principles of Jock Stein wouldn't profit from the same effect.

'Once I left Swindon, I kept in touch with some of the players and saw they were having long careers. I never put that down to good fortune. It was because they were fit, and their attitudes were good. Tactics, the things that are rammed down our throat these days, didn't apply. I introduced the good habits and rewards followed on.'

I referred to players such as Colin Calderwood, Duncan Shearer, Jim Quinn, Paul Bodin and Alan McLoughlin, all of whom went on to have lengthy and successful international playing careers.

'The players you've just mentioned there didn't let themselves down. If you speak to the supporters of any of the clubs they played for, I think you'll find they all say they were good value for money.'

With Calderwood's name now back in the conversation I found I had little choice than to comment on my admiration for him, as an ex-Town skipper, player and for what he had later achieved. Was Calderwood a standard-bearer for Lou's footballing principles? His name is always mentioned as a candidate when Swindon's managerial position becomes available.

'So he should be. He was a gem of a person. I had no idea when I signed him from Mansfield Town that he'd play for Scotland. That doesn't come along often, but it did for him. There was nothing wayward about Colin Calderwood. He was refreshingly football minded. You could tell his career would be good and long, and he deserved to achieve the international career he did.

'It was a bit of a surprise over the years that Colin never became Swindon Town manager. Maybe he didn't apply.'

I mentioned the story that suggested that Calderwood had applied, but that Nottingham Forest, his employer at the time, refused to release him, apparently seeking a compensation deal. With Town not willing to play ball, Swindon turned their attention elsewhere, and as soon as a different appointment had been made, Forest released Calderwood.

'Shame. He would have loved to have been back at Swindon. Alan McLoughlin was another one. Great attitude, lovely person ... all the people you have mentioned had all the right assets. Not only polite, charming and willing to work hard, they had everything you'd want in a human being.'

Did Lou know Alan Mac from his playing days at Old Trafford?

'I did, yes. He was a gem of a lad and character-wise he was almost flawless.'

He was so well respected when he returned to Swindon in a coaching capacity.

'And so he should be. I knew what he was like rather than just seeing him from a distance. I got to know him inside out and I could rest assured that he, and others like him were not messing around and were preparing for their next game of football. They were very easy to manage.'

Duncan Shearer?

'I didn't know a great deal about Duncan, other than his goalscoring record. His character was also very good. His partnership with Steve White was very good. Steve improved beyond belief.'

How about Paul Bodin?

'Another lad who did better than we might have expected. Even the most ardent followers of football didn't know much about him when we signed him. He fitted in well and was a great success for us.

'We had very few who disappointed, and another one was Peter Coyne. Another great character. I didn't need to worry about them. They were honest and genuine. We were very fortunate that come matchday we had so many up for selection of good character. Compared to the modern-day players they were a breath of fresh air. They were all just delighted to be at Swindon and playing football.

'Oh, and the big goalkeeper, Kenny Allen. Bloody hell! Every day was a great day for him! Whether it was peeing down with rain or whatever, everything for him was "brilliant"!'

Probably unsurprisingly, Lou admitted to having a limited recollection of Steve Berry, the midfielder who had contributed so significantly to promotion from the Third Division, but who had such a short Swindon career. Berry's input in the 1986/87 play-offs, important at the time, was a fleeting moment in a five-year saga.

I asked Lou whether he had any regrets about his managerial career. Was there anything he might do differently now, with the benefit of experience?

'Not really. Today, so much is preached about "data" ... that's absolute rubbish. It's about the people who go out on to the pitch. It's about trying to get the best out of them, which data doesn't come into. So much is said about the manager changing things around. Today it's about the managers doing this, doing that ... it's about the players. If a player's no good, he's no good. The

Swindon Town story was not based on data. It was not based on planning. It was based around getting the best players you could and getting the best out of them.'

I took a risk and warned I might be about to touch a raw nerve. Did Lou have any truck with the idea of 'data-driven recruitment'?

'It's absolute nonsense. The game has not changed. If you are a player out there now, and you have to think "what should I do now" what does it say about you as a player?'

Is there a lack of adventure in football today I wondered.

'There was adventure, excitement, commitment, desire back then. We didn't sit in the dressing room poring over paperwork, saying this is what we are going to do. Nowadays they are trying to reinvent the "closing down" we used to have. Swindon were a team who closed down. They're calling it "pressing" these days. Whoever thinks they have invented something new, they are so far from the truth. In the 70s and 80s, it was already there. Every club had it. Nobody is coming up with any new inventions. We all had it in the 70s and 80s.'

I proposed that preparing a team by emphasising the strengths of the opposition seems counterproductive. Bill Shankly and Brian Clough famously belittled the opposition before their team took to the pitch.

'Without a doubt. Not just me, but other managers back then didn't spend time talking about the opposition. They sent their own team out to see what they could do. To see if we could match them and better them. It didn't matter what they brought to the party. Once our team got on the pitch at Swindon, I was always confident we'd win. And in those days the decisions were made by the referee and linesmen.'

That seemed to be a reference to the technology used today. I suggested that football now seems to serve the TV-watching audience, not those who have paid their money and gone to the ground to support their team.

'You're spot on there. It's taken all the entertainment out of the game.'

There was then an element of blame placed on the Referees' Association with Lou suggesting that technology in football today was a job-creation scheme for retired refs.

But when I introduced the name David Hockaday the discussion returned to Swindon Town.

'A gentleman. Another who fell into the category of just putting their boots on going out and playing for you.'

When I asked who in the modern game impressed Lou, there was a long pause. Finally, Ipswich Town manager Kieran McKenna, someone with Manchester United connections, was mentioned.

Inevitably, conversation had to return to the events that led to Swindon suffering censure from the football authorities at the turn of the 90s.

'When players earned a bonus, the money came from the programme sales. Without doubt other clubs were doing similar.'

I asked Lou whether he thought Swindon were being punished in the way they were, in order to make an example of them to other clubs who were acting similarly.'

'Without a doubt. The authorities probably didn't want to do anything to us. This had been presented by the newspapers, so they had to be seen to do something. It was exaggerated by the journalists and made to look 20 times worse than it was. Once the Swindon directors had been made subject to scrutiny all denied any knowledge, leaving Brian Hillier to carry the can on his own. Which was perhaps always the plan of some. Brian was hung out to dry.

'The Inland Revenue had to get involved because it ran and ran. In court, no sums of money were ever declared. The Inland Revenue realised they had been suckered into it … for a case that wasn't worth talking about. The sums of money were conveniently forgotten about. No sums were ever mentioned, and when you go to court with the Inland Revenue it's only sums of money they are interested in. It was only because the sums had been exaggerated that forced the Inland Revenue to act.

'Bonuses were supposed to be an incentive for success, and the bonus sheet at Swindon was an embarrassment.'

Discussing events after his departure, Lou said, 'When Ossie [Ardiles] and Glenn Hoddle arrived, there was no way they would accept the wages I was getting. The club had to find new money and the bonus sheet was reorganised accordingly to make everything black and white.'

I mentioned Ossie's statement on his appointment that he intended to change Swindon's playing style.

'There was no style to change. I didn't have a style. I had professional footballers, and my job was to get them fit, focused and fully committed.'

I felt I'd imposed on Lou's time enough so I asked what he was doing these days, and whether he was using his time to indulge in his other interest of horseracing?

'No. I'm at Manchester United most of the time, particularly on a matchday. I've been there 50 years, player for 11 years, and worked there on their TV channel since 2000 to today. I've stayed connected. It's an achievement to be associated with an employer for 50 years as a player and as a pundit.'

After Lou left Swindon he held managerial positions at a series of clubs, one of which was Stoke City, the place where he has chosen to settle.

And it was in Stoke in 2016 that he spotted a news bulletin about the desperate plight of people living rough in the city. Deciding to see for himself, he took to the streets, and was so moved by what he saw that he was determined to try to help.

The subsequent setting up of the Macari Foundation has seen it develop into a venture which provides accommodation and support to dozens of people, who otherwise would be sleeping rough in the doorways and car parks of Stoke.

The aim is to offer the opportunity for those for whom life has dealt a hugely difficult hand, to turn their lives around and achieve their potential.

'We're looking after homeless people. It's a bit of an eye-opener and a comparison to my Swindon days in the "fastest-growing town in Europe". To experience the opposite end of that, working with people who are complicated ... mixed-up a little bit.

'For many people everything rolls on smoothly, but there's nothing smooth about homelessness. There are drugs and addictions in people's lives. In my day in football, I never encountered drugs, performance-related or otherwise. How much life has changed!

'I never had any talk or concern about drugs. I never had to drug test any of the players. Now I'm sure any football manager has a fear of drugs within his football club. Now the grip they can get on homeless people is horrendous. It's destroying people's lives, not having a bed, a roof or food. We're just trying to do our best to help a bit.'

Lou Macari. Someone who had played football at the highest level and who had been responsible for such great memories for so many people at the clubs he had been involved in.

As our regular chats approached their conclusion, Lou was at pains to pay tribute to those who had shared in the success at Swindon in the 1980s, and who supported him in his endeavours to improve the club's lot.

'There are so many people to mention and there is a risk I could forget someone, but everyone contributed to the progress that the club made during my time there.'

Lou was specific to mention someone in particular, who had passed away even during the few short weeks that we had been sharing phone conversations. Someone who was responsible for some of my own fondest memories, both on the pitch, and in what happened after he hung up a pair of prolific goalscoring boots.

'Andy Rowland was so supportive of me during my time at Swindon, and was hugely responsible in helping everyone to achieve the goals we set out to do. As a right-hand man I couldn't have wished for anyone better and his loss will be hugely felt around the County Ground.'

In all our chats I came across one word so many times which seemed to epitomise Lou's view of people, his football recruitment and his judgement of their values in life.

That word was 'character' and it was something which Lou had obviously valued very highly throughout his life. Lou used it to describe someone for whom he had the utmost respect, and it was something that could perhaps only be trumped in Macari-speak by 'professional'.

Lou Macari, having been the ultimate footballing professional, continues to demonstrate the highest level of character, in exactly the way he would have demanded from any of his players at Swindon Town.

My weeks had been punctuated with lengthy, enjoyable conversations with someone who had been responsible for some of my finest memories from over five decades as a Robins supporter. Conversations with a thoroughly decent man, who seemed to think that some of the best days of football were now in the past.

In 2024, many fellow fans might be forgiven for thinking the same.

10

Legacy

THE FIRST season after the departure of Lou Macari was clearly a tumultuous one, and one which was traumatic to anyone who holds Swindon Town dear.

Ossie Ardiles had built on Macari's legacy, and suffered the consequences of the era that preceded his arrival, in equal measure. And while the off-pitch drama was unprecedented, it cannot be denied that Ardiles's squad was several orders of magnitude better than the one which Macari had inherited when he arrived.

When the Football League intervened and prevented Swindon gaining the reward that went with Wembley victory under Ardiles, Glenn Hoddle took over and finished the job, guiding the club to the Premier League three seasons after they had been denied that place.

Ardiles had left Swindon for Newcastle United in March 1991 after a little under two years at the helm. Despite the hopes that a repeat promotion push could be undertaken, the disappointment of authority-induced relegation weighed heavily, and results couldn't match those of the previous season.

With Town in an unfamiliar fight to avoid relegation, there was a real fear that legitimate on-field results could achieve what the Football League had wanted to inflict in the first place – Swindon Town in the Third Division.

Hoddle was appointed player-manager at the beginning of April and Town avoided the drop by two points. An eighth-placed finish steadied the ship the following year, and in 1992/93, a Hoddle-inspired Swindon finally made the top flight, by now called the Premier League, via the play-offs at Wembley.

The final, a dramatic 4-3 victory over Leicester City, was hailed by neutrals as a classic. For supporters it was seen as nothing less than retribution for the events of 1990.

Ardiles and Hoddle deserve all due credit for their achievements, and the County Ground would finally host football of the highest standard.

Much that followed immediately after Macari's departure could be attributed to the work he had done over the previous five seasons. And it wasn't just the club or subsequent managers who reaped the benefit of his foundation. Many of his players went on to achieve success that might not have been forthcoming without the grounding of Macari's professional ethics.

Several went on to play for their country, some performing on the highest international stages.

A year into Macari's tenure at the County Ground, the capture of Colin Calderwood from Mansfield Town for £27,500 proved to be a masterstroke. Calderwood went on to make well over 400 Swindon appearances over an eight-season spell. Ever-present for five of them, more than 160 matches had passed since he joined Swindon before he missed his first game, over two years later.

Colin led Town as skipper in three different divisions, and it took £1.25m to prise him away to Tottenham Hotspur in 1993 when Ossie Ardiles captured the central defender, who had just captained Swindon to that victory against Leicester at Wembley.

All supporters were disappointed to see Calderwood leave, particularly as Swindon had finally attained the stage of which his skills had proved worthy, but as certain as it was that Town's defence would have been so much more secure in the top flight with him, no one begrudged him the chance to shine at a bigger club.

He played 36 times for Scotland, scoring one goal, against San Marino in a Euro 1996 qualifying match in April 1995. He subsequently represented his country in those finals in England, and then in World Cup 1998 in France.

Duncan Shearer was capped seven times for Scotland over 1994 and 1995, all while at Aberdeen after departing Swindon, and scored in a Euro 1996 qualifying game against Finland.

Blackburn Rovers paid £800,000 for his signature in March 1992; Shearer had finished as Swindon's top scorer in each of the four seasons he spent in Wiltshire, the last achieved two months after he departed for Lancashire.

With steel magnate Jack Walker's money being spent freely to the benefit of Rovers, it was often believed that the fee was invested as much to weaken fellow play-off contenders Swindon's bid for a play-off place, than to enhance Blackburn's.

Credence was offered to the conspiracy theory when Shearer was sold to Aberdeen within weeks of his arrival at Ewood Park, after which Rovers had overhauled Swindon's own top-six bid and clinched promotion to the top division.

Mancunian Alan McLoughlin became a pseudo-Irishman and went to the World Cup in 1990, courtesy of his Irish parents.

His Wembley goal against Sunderland in 1990 caught the eye of Republic of Ireland manager Jack Charlton, and McLoughlin was rushed almost directly from Wembley to the airport to catch a plane to Italy for the 1990 World Cup finals. A debut against Malta in a pre-tournament friendly was followed by two substitute appearances in Italy.

It was a seven-figure sum that took McLoughlin away from Wiltshire to the south coast in December 1990 where he joined First Division Southampton. Never the success of a move that would have been hoped, McLoughlin moved on to close rivals Portsmouth and was part of the team which just failed to make the Premier League in 1993, losing in the play-offs.

Four years later his goal against Northern Ireland in a 1994 World Cup qualifying match helped to take his country to the finals in the USA. All told, McLoughlin claimed 42 caps for the Republic of Ireland, scoring twice, the second against Macedonia in April 1997.

McLoughlin rejoined Swindon Town as academy manager in February 2018, duties which he performed in parallel with those of under-18 coach. Tragically, cancer claimed his life in May 2021.

Paul Bodin, known throughout his Town career as 'Zippy', left Swindon for First Division Crystal Palace for £550,000 in March 1991, a move which never fulfilled its potential, and Ossie Ardiles renewed acquaintances when Bodin joined Newcastle on loan in December 1991.

Just ten months after leaving Swindon, Paul was back at the County Ground when new Town boss Glenn Hoddle spent £225,000 in January 1992 to reunite the left-back with the red shirt.

Paul cemented his place in Robins history in 1993 with his match-winning spot-kick against Leicester at Wembley taking Swindon to the Premier League.

He played 23 times for Wales, making his debut in 1990, but heartbreakingly missed the penalty against Romania which would have taken his country to the 1994 World Cup.

Bodin was back at the County Ground yet again in 2001 when he was appointed to the youth team coaching set-up and went on to hold the caretaker managerial reins in 2011 after the sacking of Paul Hart.

Jim Quinn went on to score 12 times for Northern Ireland, making him one of his country's all-time top scorers. He played 46 times for his country over a span of 11 years, making his debut in a friendly against Israel in October 1984.

Quinn scored the goal against Romania which did much to qualify Northern Ireland for the 1986 World Cup finals in Mexico, and he played in the goalless draw against England which completed the job.

He was appointed joint player-manager of Reading in December 1994, and despite leading the Royals to second place in the First Division, automatic promotion was denied as the Premier League underwent another of its periodic restructuring when it was once again reduced in number. Reading lost out in the play-offs. While at Reading, Quinn signed ex-team-mate Paul Bodin from Swindon in July 1996.

Quinn rejoined Swindon as manager in October 1998 and battled against the usual financial difficulties, ultimately losing against the odds. With the club slipping into administration, aged 40 he was forced to come out of playing retirement to make up the numbers on the pitch, adding a further seven appearances to his Swindon total.

When relegation to the third tier came at the end of 1999/2000, and with the club unable to record a win in 19 attempts, Quinn was elbowed in favour of Colin Todd.

Bradford-on-Avon-born Fitzroy Simpson moved on to Manchester City for £500,000 in March 1992. He went on to make 43 appearances for Jamaica between 1997 and 2003, playing in the World Cup finals in 1998 for the Reggae Boyz. He scored twice during his international career.

While Martin Ling didn't appear on the international stage, just like Jim Quinn, he was another ex-Town player who went on to manage the club. His six-week tenure in 2015 was brought to an abrupt halt due to health reasons.

His first spell at Swindon as a player had lasted for just four months, while his third, this time as manager, lasted half as long. In between Martin shone brightly in midfield over five seasons and was one of seven Macari signings who went on to pull on a Swindon shirt in Premier League combat.

Completing the list of Macari's captures who appeared in the Premier League for Swindon in 1993/94 were Steve White, Nicky Summerbee, Ross Maclaren, Paul Bodin, Fraser Digby and Nicky Hammond.

Much was owed to all for contributing to the journey from the Fourth Division to the very top, four years after Macari had left Town for other challenges.

By Macari's own estimate he left behind players who would raise £8m in transfers when they departed from the County Ground.

Headline figures can be notoriously inaccurate, but suggestions that the sales of Calderwood, Shearer, Gordon, Quinn, Bamber, Bodin, King, Summerbee and Simpson alone would have brought in over £5.2m are probably not too wide of the mark, although some of the incoming cash would have been lost in sell-on clauses.

Throughout the entire story of the Macari years there was one particularly consistent member of the playing staff. His name has popped up from time to time in the previous pages but, perhaps somewhat unfairly, David Hockaday's contribution during Town's greatest-ever elevational period has remained substantially glossed over.

He'd been signed by Ken Beamish in August 1983, and by the end of his first month had scored his first Swindon goal. While Beamish has received more than his fair share of brickbats, this piece of transfer business should secure the manager who oversaw Swindon's worst-ever campaign finish a more reasonable hearing than he has so far been granted.

No money changed hands when Hockaday arrived at the County Ground from Blackpool, but the right-winger played in 46 matches in his first season and contributed four goals. Any footballer who can count the melodically named Billingham Synthonia, his first, and hometown, club on his CV deserves to be able to sing his own praises.

Injury limited Hockaday's opportunity to impress new boss Macari for the first three months of 1984/85, but once available he secured his place for most of the last three.

In the promotion season that followed, Hockaday first of all made the wing role his own, but then replaced defender Paul Roberts in defence for the last few months. And a defender Hockaday was from then on.

Able to operate on either side of the back four, Hockaday appeared in 40 of the 46 matches in the next promotion season, and with the arrival of new regular left-back Phil King, he settled permanently in the right-back position in the Second Division, missing just one match in Macari's fourth campaign.

Absent for just a couple more games in 1988/89, Hockaday was selected by Macari 234 times in the 285 matches that the Scot oversaw. In other words, whenever Macari was looking to choose a matchday squad, the majority of which came when only one substitute could be named, he chose Hockaday on 82 per cent of the occasions.

He was named in Macari's first Swindon team on 25 August 1984, and his last on 24 May 1989.

David Hockaday played a huge part in the rise of Swindon through the five seasons under Macari. While others may have grabbed greater glory, his versatility and dependability must have been any manager's dream.

With the arrival of Ossie Ardiles, Hockaday's days were numbered. A run of starts to November 1989 was ended with the arrival of the cultured David Kerslake who dislodged the stalwart from the right side of defence and displaced him to substitute duties.

Soon after the start of the following season Hockaday moved on to Hull City, and Ardiles's own evolution was under way. The reliable, intelligent Hockaday, often referred to as 'Professor' by his team-mates, was off to pastures new.

Hockaday had cost nothing to recruit, raised £50,000 on his departure, and in between pulled on a Swindon shirt more than 300 times over an eight-year stay.

Rarely one to make the headlines, of all the players who served under Lou Macari and helped bring so much success, perhaps it's fair to pinpoint David Hockaday as one of those who most epitomised the standards that Macari set.

11

87th

The Summer of 2024

THE WRITING of this book began in the spring of 2024 and Swindon Town had just completed a season of strife. The club had just finished in 19th place in what was now called League Two, but which was still known to all those old enough to identify it as such as the Fourth Division.

This was two places lower than the disastrous campaign led by Ken Beamish back in 1983/84, just before Lou Macari arrived at the County Ground.

Much of Town's Football League existence has been spent in mediocrity; the Third Division was indisputably the spiritual home of the Robins. It took until 1963 for Swindon to leave it, claiming their first promotion 43 years after first joining the Football League in 1920.

The merging of the Third Division's north and south competitions in 1958 to form the national divisions, the bottom two tiers of the Football League, placed Town in the upper of the two but opened up a whole new potential of failed status. Purely by competing in the newly formed Fourth Division meant that the highest place any team within it could achieve was 69th in the Football League of 92 clubs.

Descending to the Fourth Division in 1982, it was the first time that Swindon had dropped that low in 62 years as a Football League member, and in 1984, under the stewardship of Ken Beamish, the club were officially the 85th-worst club of the 92.

It would have been understandable if expectations were low among Swindon supporters. Fingers had been crossed in hope for too long, and some fans wondered whether a string of Town goalkeepers with modest abilities had played with their digits arranged in a similar configuration.

Gallows humour and irony are useful tools in the face of constant disillusionment.

By the time Swindon started looking for a new manager in the summer of 1984, supporters may have felt justified in believing they had long been addressing their own fears, in their own version of room 101 that George Orwell had already made synonymous with the date. But, in the words of one of Orwell's fellow novelists, Aldous Huxley, a brave new world beckoned.

And in 1984, there had been much that Lou Macari needed to be brave about.

Stein's team, engineered from locally grown, apparently non-exceptional individual talent, was moulded into such a formidable and cohesive unit that they won the European Cup in 1967. Lou used that inspiration to start assembling his team at Swindon, a tenure that was to last four years and 342 days, with a five-day break over the Easter weekend of 1985.

It seems only fair to comment that the no-nonsense attitude of Macari was not everyone's football managerial cup of tea. There were those who had described the style of play of his teams to be too functional. Too basic. Too direct.

During the 1980s it became fashionable to denounce the style of certain teams if they did not satisfy the eye of the pundit, with perhaps Wimbledon the first target of scorn for their apparent lack of panache according to the 'knowledgeable'.

It was a disrespectful assessment that suggested that some clubs, some footballing methods, were somehow less worthy of success than others, and in the age of vilification of 'long-ball football' Macari's style was sometimes not considered sophisticated enough for the purist.

There can be no doubt that during his spell at Swindon he placed high expectations on his players, but that he also considered the limits of their abilities and didn't ask them to perform in a manner in which they were not capable. He cut his sides' playing style cloth, to suit what he had available.

He recognised that, in order to be successful, his team had to play to their individual strengths and collective abilities, and his choice of recruit had to be suited to the challenges of the day.

He demanded no less than total commitment from his players in delivering that.

As a racing enthusiast, Macari would be more than familiar with the phrase 'horses for courses', and his recruitment of players who were able to meet the challenges presented at any given time was plain. He worked tirelessly to find the next bargain to improve that stock, and there were very few accusations that his team was not fit.

His readiness to face a challenge meant that he was not afraid to undertake the hard work and difficult decisions that others might shy away from. And that was just as well, and something that all Swindon supporters of a certain era will be for ever grateful.

Without someone prepared to roll up their sleeves and undertake the hard miles, Town would have never found the person able to lift a club in a desperate, some feared terminal decline to the levels which Macari was to achieve. For the Robins he was the right man, in the right place, at the right time.

Perhaps by the time Macari left, he had taken the club as far as he could.

The foundation on which Macari built the club was capitalised on by future managers to everyone's benefit. Ossie Ardiles and Glenn Hoddle took the legacy they inherited and shaped it to attain even greater heights, but it could be argued that neither would have lifted the club that far in the first place.

Would they have been prepared to toil away at the basement of the Football League to elevate the club to such a level that they would be able to exert their playing style on the field of play? Would they have been loyal enough to continue the work through the course of five seasons? Would they have been able to attract the appropriate quality of players to the Fourth Division to bring about the needed progression?

Just 12 months after Macari departed for other challenges, and now under the managership of Ardiles, Swindon won the right to play in English football's top flight, only to have the prize wrenched from their grasp.

Three seasons later, when Town reached the Premier League in 1993, it was Glenn Hoddle who led them there.

As achievements go, Ardiles and Hoddle deserve huge credit in qualifying a provincial club to dine at the top football table, but both had reaped the benefits of the foundations laid by Macari.

Lou left Swindon in sixth place in the second tier, which made them the 26th-best team in the country. By the time Hoddle raised them to fifth and qualified for the play-offs, two extra teams had been added to the Premier League once more.

Swindon were then actually only the 27th-most successful team in England, and ironically Hoddle had taken them to their greatest-ever achievement but had overseen a drop of one Football League place.

In contrast Macari had overseen a rise of 59 places, and never before had Swindon seen such a prolonged spell of constant progression.

When Ardiles replaced Macari as manager in 1989, his announcement that he was to change Swindon's playing style to one perhaps considered easier on the eye was met with some concerned scepticism among supporters.

Did he not understand the limitations of the players he was now responsible for? Did he not realise that Swindon had only been successful due to the manager's acceptance of the players' limited abilities and their readiness to play to their 'simple' strengths?

The story of Martin Ling's time under Macari makes for interesting recollection.

Ling had joined Swindon at Macari's seeking, but for one reason or another he had not been able to satisfy the needs of his manager. Years later Ling would return to the County Ground, this time at the request of Ossie Ardiles.

A new manager, new expectations, a new level of football, but the same club, and this time Ling's success for his manager, player, club and supporters would be more than fulfilled.

Horses for courses.

There can be little doubt that Lou Macari is a man of integrity. He doesn't suffer fools gladly and he appears to be frustrated about the apparent laissez-faire attitude demonstrated by some present-day footballers toward their profession.

Few players in the 1980s, and even fewer in the third decade of the 21st century, would accept army barracks for training camps.

The passage of time recalls a quote from L.P. Hartley's book, *The Go-Between*, 'The past is another country. They do things differently there.'

Football is not what it used to be.

It is something that is perversely synonymous with Swindon Town, that the highest finishing position the club has ever achieved to date is 22nd in the Premier League. Perverse, because the club's very best position culminated in finishing bottom of the table.

That was in May 1994, and when it came, the slow descent back to whence Swindon had come had begun.

Consecutive relegations took Town back to the Third Division. It was officially called the Second Division by then. But it was the Third Division.

Immediate promotion followed. A championship trophy even. Three mid-table finishes, then bottom of the table and relegation again. Three more consolidation seasons included yet another renaming of the divisions in 2004, which meant that Town were now in what was called League One. But it was still the Third Division.

Relegation came and Swindon were now in League Two. Or the Fourth Division as we knew it was really. It was now 2006 and Swindon Town were back where they had started, pre-Lou Macari.

In truth there have been dawns, false or otherwise, but over the following seasons there has been a common theme running through them all. Town would start to rebuild, perhaps break out of the bottom division, sometimes even with a trophy, flicker briefly then drop back to the bottom.

In two separate campaigns, Swindon were one Wembley play-off final victory from promotion to the Second Division, what the football world now knew to be the Championship. Each time the opportunity was lost, and each time, ultimately the only resulting direction was downward.

THE SUMMER OF 2024

Promotion from League Two to League One in 2020 was followed by immediate relegation 12 months later, and a play-off semi-final defeat to Port Vale in 2022 was one of another four seasons in the very bottom division of the Football League.

Every time Swindon flattered to deceive, there has been another reinforcement of the club's diminished position in the football world. Their natural position in the pecking order of football has been redefined as one of a club which alternates between Leagues One and Two, apparently trying to choose which of the two it feels most comfortable with.

In the 17 seasons between 2006/07 and 2023/24, Swindon have been stranded in the lowest division of the Football League for almost half of them. Unsurprisingly, morale among the gathered throngs at the County Ground has diminished accordingly.

When Lou Macari joined Swindon there were limited funds, players with limited ability and a feeling of despair around the club. He exploited every avenue to turn that around and he did it with huge success. No one who enjoyed that journey would forget what he brought to the County Ground. There is perhaps an understandable belief among the supporters of any club, that their club is bigger than it is. Perhaps there is a delusion of grandeur.

After all, it's to those supporters that their team is the most important.

But perhaps that demonstrates the very gist of this book.

For five short years, plus a few more which were built on those foundations, Macari allowed Town supporters to believe that the status of the club was being redefined. That it could be a bigger club, if it only allowed the recently acquired, more senior status to become the new normal.

It certainly had greater potential than was being fulfilled in 2024, when all that progress appeared to have been wasted.

In 2023/24, what was undoubtedly the worst afternoon of the season came in the first round of the FA Cup.

After an hour Town had been seven goals down at home to non-league Aldershot, before recovering slightly to lose by an incredible 7-4 scoreline. They had been knocked out of the oldest knockout cup competition in the world at the first opportunity for the tenth time in 12 seasons, and this time, overwhelmingly convincingly, at the hands of a non-league club.

For many the match was viewed as the greatest matchday embarrassment Swindon fans had ever had to suffer.

The 2023/24 season finished with Swindon in 19th place in League Two. That equates to 87th in the Football League, two places lower than the infamous 'Beamish Line'.

By the time the writing of this book finished, the 40th anniversary of Lou Macari's arrival at the County Ground had come and gone, and after recently setting a new, lowest-of-the-low standard, the real risk of Swindon falling through the Football League's surface crust and experiencing the underworld of non-league football appears frighteningly possible.

And with two teams now relegated from the Fourth Division to non-league status every season, ebb level is barely above critical. Were Swindon supporters becoming conditioned to accept such low standards?

But then again.

It's now August 2024. Yesterday the postman brought my new season ticket for the imminent season. By my reckoning it's the 48th year I've held one, and the first match of the season is little over a week away.

For a few weeks in the spring, I pretended to procrastinate about renewing. Last season wasn't much fun. But everyone who knew me, knew I would.

If there is ever a time for heart-led optimism to conquer head-led realism, pre-season is it. Hope springs eternal.

I hope.

Lou Macari is no longer involved in day-to-day football. Companies House indicates that Lowndes Lambert, the financier of the club's resurrection in 1984, is no longer an active company.

All Robins supporters can do is hold their breath, cross their fingers and pray for the second coming of a messiah.

Who is going to resurrect Swindon Town this time?

YOUR CARRIAGE AWAITS

PULLMAN DINING - £350 Travel in beautifully restored wood panelled vintage carriages

CLASSIC SAPHOS TRAINS

Your Invitation to board
SAPHOS TRAINS
Classic Steam Experience

THE GOLDEN ARROW
SATURDAY 1 APRIL 2023

*In memory of Bernard de Lattre de Tassigny (1928–1951)
Croix de Guerre and Médaille Militaire*

First published in Great Britain in 2017 by
PEN AND SWORD MILITARY
an imprint of
Pen and Sword Books Ltd
47 Church Street
Barnsley
South Yorkshire S70 2AS

Copyright © Anthony Tucker-Jones, 2017

ISBN 978 1 52670 798 7

The right of Anthony Tucker-Jones to be identified as the author of this work
has been asserted in accordance with the Copyright, Designs and Patents Act 1988.

A CIP record for this book is available from the British Library All rights reserved.
No part of this book may be reproduced or transmitted in any form or by any means, electronic or
mechanical including photocopying, recording or by any information storage and retrieval system,
without permission from the Publisher in writing.

Every reasonable effort has been made to trace copyright holders of material reproduced in this book,
but if any have been inadvertently overlooked the publishers will be pleased to hear from them.
Unless otherwise indicated, all photographs in this publication are via the author.

Typeset by Aura Technology and Software Services, India
Editing and additional sourcing of photographs Gerry van Tonder
Maps, drawings and militaria in the colour section by Colonel Dudley Wall
Printed and bound in Malta by Gutenberg

Pen & Sword Books Ltd incorporates the imprints of Pen & Sword
Archaeology, Atlas, Aviation, Battleground, Discovery, Family History, History, Maritime,
Military, Naval, Politics, Railways, Select, Social History, Transport, True Crime, Claymore Press,
Frontline Books, Leo Cooper, Praetorian Press, Remember When, Seaforth Publishing and Wharncliffe.

For a complete list of Pen and Sword titles please contact
Pen and Sword Books Limited
47 Church Street, Barnsley, South Yorkshire, S70 2AS, England
email: enquiries@pen-and-sword.co.uk
website: www.pen-and-sword.co.uk

CONTENTS

	Prologue – 'Where's Bernard?'	4
	Introduction – Imperial Hubris	5
1.	End of Empire	7
2.	Cold War Realities	14
3.	Operation Masterdom	19
4.	Rise of the Viet Minh	25
5.	Get Leclerc	32
6.	France's Expeditionary Force	38
7.	The Hand of Mao	44
8.	Battle for the Red River	51
9.	Victory on the Day River	58
10.	Air War Over Indochina	63
11.	Operation Lorraine	69
12.	Prelude to Defeat	75
13.	Fortress Dien Bien Phu	84
14.	A Dishonoured Man	91
15.	The Vulture Hovers	98
16.	Isabelle is Taken	103
17.	The Cold War Reckoning	114
	Epilogue – The Returned	121
	Appendix I – French Order of Battle, Dien Bien Phu, 6 December 1953–8 May 1954	123
	Appendix II – Viet Minh Order of Battle, Vietnam People's Army, Dien Bien Phu 13 March–8 May 1954	125
	Bibliography	127
	About the Author	128

PROLOGUE – 'WHERE'S BERNARD?'

Just as the Cold War was starting, a young man by the name of Bernard de Lattre arrived in Indochina in 1949. He was a lieutenant in the French Army and a decorated Second World War hero. Bernard was a graduate of the École Militaire Interarmes and, like many of his generation, had volunteered to fight the new menace to world peace – communism. Such a decision was not universally popular at home and France had banned conscripts from shedding their blood in this distant land. His presence was to spark tragedy for him, his family and his country.

Bernard epitomized France's young officer class. He believed in leadership by example and from the front. At 16, he had been wounded fighting the Germans on 8 September 1944 at Atun, for which he was awarded a medal for gallantry. Five years later, still eager for combat, he had volunteered to go to Tonkin in northern Indochina. There, in the face of a burgeoning Vietnamese guerrilla war, he despaired at the lax and uninspired military leadership around him. He urged his father, a famous general in the French army, to come and help, the troops needed him. Then on 30 May 1951, Bernard found himself sharing a sand-bagged dugout, protected by barbed wire, overlooking Ninh Binh on the Day River. Victory was at hand, or so it seemed.

Capture of Hanoi in the 1870s.

INTRODUCTION – IMPERIAL HUBRIS

The revving engines of the cargo planes lined up on the airfield and taxiways were deafening. Across from them were rows and rows of tough-looking paratroopers in their camouflaged uniforms, waiting for the green light. Their faces were a mixture of apprehension, fear and excitement. For most this was not their first jump, but you just never knew what would happen when you hit a drop zone. There is a universal military saying that the plan never survives contact with the enemy. Once lumbering into the sky, each aircraft was packed with eighteen sweating men and all their combat kit, ready for the jump.

The men of the Viet Minh 148th Regiment were on exercise when they were alerted by the steady drone of engines overhead. Something big was about to happen. Their first thought was that bombs were about to fall, obliterating everything in their path. Even worse, it might be the terrible furnace-like fireballs created by exploding napalm. Instead, thousands of parachutes began to billow in the blue sky. They looked like the annual flower blossoms floating in the Perfume river that flows through the ancient Vietnamese city of Hue. Each flower, though, carried a deadly speck beneath it, an enemy soldier, a French soldier. Soon there was the sporadic sound of gun fire. The outnumbered Viet Minh were forced to withdraw – round one to the French.

This is the story of imperial hubris and a place called Dien Bien Phu. It was a village of no great consequence located in a valley in northwestern Vietnam, not far from the border with Laos. Thanks to the Nam Youm (Nam Rom) River, the broad and very flat flood plain surrounded by jungle-covered hills is very verdant. In this valley, the French convinced themselves they could triumph once and for all over Vietnam's communist nationalists.

This is also the story of France's generals: de Gaulle, Leclerc, de Lattre, Salan, Navarre and Cogny, who were committed to maintaining the ideal of the French Union at any cost. They were involved in a long and brutal war in French colonial Indochina that resulted in such a decisive battle that it led to the international humiliation of France and heralded the end of the French Union. It also sowed the deadly seeds of the subsequent Vietnam War.

French Indochina consisted of five separate kingdoms: Tonkin (northern Vietnam), Annam (central Vietnam), Cochinchina (southern Vietnam), Laos and Cambodia, that had been fused together as part of the vast French empire. It was the Japanese occupation of part of northern Indochina in 1940 that precipitated America's entry into the Second World War the following year. However, the Japanese did not occupy all of Indochina until early 1945, by which time the war was coming to a close. It was the resumption of French colonial rule by force that sparked the First Indochina War, which culminated in France's defeat at Dien Bien Phu in 1954.

This colonial conflict was fought against the backdrop of the Cold War, an almost forgotten postscript to the Second World War. From 1945 until 1991, when the Soviet Union collapsed, ideological and military tensions between East and West regularly threatened to drag the world into another catastrophic global conflict. This was narrowly avoided on numerous occasions, thanks only to the spectre of nuclear war. Instead, the Cold War became a series of widespread proxy conflicts that often had little to do with the initial armed stand-off in Europe.

Japanese troops enter Saigon, 1941.

Europe was in economic and political chaos after 1945 – the far left spearheaded by the communists and socialists thought it was their time to overturn the established order. However, the international community was so alarmed by such a prospect, especially in light of the perceived threat from the victorious Soviet Union, that it moved to contain communism wherever it should appear. For France, the Cold War actually commenced in the summer of 1944 when Charles de Gaulle's Free French moved to head off French communists taking power in France's major cities as the defeated Germans withdrew.

At the end of the Second World War in Eastern Europe, Stalin wanted to give mother Russia even greater strategic depth. Never again would Germany be permitted to launch a surprise attack. The Red Army stayed put in its new-found allies. An iron curtain was drawn across Europe and Germany, divided as the new frontline between East and West. Stalin permitted the charade of elections, but the outcome was the same: an armed Soviet bloc was created, hostile to the capitalist Western powers. When communist leaders Tito and Hoxha took power in Yugoslavia and Albania respectively, Britain intervened to save neighbouring Greece from communism as the country slipped into civil war.

Around the rest of the world, communism and nationalism became a heady mixture, no more so than in French Indochina. The catalyst for the expansion of the Cold War beyond Europe was the triumph of communism in China. The victorious Mao Zedong saw Burma, Korea, Malaya, Tibet and Vietnam as fertile ground for the spread of communist ideology. He gambled that with the support of Stalin, the Western powers, weakened by war, would never oppose his march into Asia. As a result, France found itself involved in a much wider conflict, in a type of warfare it was ill-equipped to fight. What followed was a tragedy of Shakespearean proportions. French imperial pride brought the communist world crashing down around it with far-reaching ramifications for America, China and the Soviet Union.

1. END OF EMPIRE

The Battle of Dien Bien Phu took place because of France's refusal to relinquish her vast empire. It was Vichy France's stance during the Second World War that sowed the seeds for the First Indochina War. The helpless French colonial authorities became pawns in Japan's grand strategy for Southeast Asia. This provided a fertile breeding ground for the spread of communism and nationalism.

France was liberated from Nazi Germany in August 1944 and two months later the Allies recognized Charles de Gaulle's Free French government. When Nazi Germany surrendered in May 1945, de Gaulle was at the height of his power. In Europe, triumphant French armies stretched across Germany into Austria. He was head of the French government, which, although it had not been elected and consisted only of his appointees, was recognized by the rest of the world. He had become head of state by sheer willpower and force of personality, though many found him cold and distant. De Gaulle was the undisputed leader of the French empire, to which only Indochina remained to be restored.

There followed a purge of the pro-Nazi Vichy regime, and in the elections of October 1945, there was a very sharp swing to the left. The new assembly was dominated by France's communists who profited from their impressive wartime resistance record. De Gaulle, although de facto president by virtue of having liberated Paris, thanks to General Leclerc's 2nd Armoured Division, forfeited his position by insisting that France should retain its empire.

Many of France's colonies felt the time was ripe for independence. Colonial troops had shed blood for mother France during the Tunisian campaign, in Italy, metropolitan France

French troops attacking Saigon, 1859.

and Germany. This was especially the case with France's tough Algerian and Moroccan divisions. In light of the post-war situation and strained military resources, the French government needed a large defence budget, but the communist politicians opposed this.

De Gaulle was forced to resign in January 1946. He hoped this would spark a political crisis and the government would be forced to recall him. A rumour spread through Paris that de Gaulle had summoned General Leclerc from Indochina to lead a *coup d'état*. Instead, France survived his departure.

That year the Fourth Republic created the Union Française (French Union) to replace the Empire Française (French Empire). This conceived the idea of a 'Greater France', represented by an Assembly of the Union. Thanks to left-wing opposition to empire, this seemed to suggest a much more liberal policy towards France's colonial possessions. In reality, ultimate power remained with the French parliament and the temptation to retrieve lost glory was far too great even for the Fourth Republic.

During the nineteenth century, the French had carved themselves an empire in Southeast Asia and Africa. The region known collectively as French Indochina from 1893 to 1954 is now comprised of three sovereign states: Vietnam (consisting of the three kingdoms of Tonkin in the north, Amman in the centre and Cochinchina to the south), and Cambodia and Laos. The eastern provinces of Cochinchina were occupied by France in the early 1860s.

Cambodia became a protectorate in 1862 and four years later the rest of Cochinchina was taken over. After a series of military operations, Amman and Tonkin came under French rule. Indochina was completed ten years later when Laos also became a protectorate. The French Indochina Union was created in 1887.

The pre-war French power structure allowed for an Emperor of Annam, whose realm included parts of Tonkin as well as kings in Cambodia and Laos. They all ruled within the heavily French-controlled union. Indochina's component states were ethnically and culturally very different. The Vietnamese, generally similar in appearance to the Chinese, contrast with Cambodia's Khmer people who are much darker, having different features and quite distinct cultural and religious origins. Equally distinct are the mountain peoples of Laos. Notably, the Cambodians and Vietnamese were traditional enemies, which helped ensure French dominance.

French military expeditions also ensured control of Algeria, Morocco and Tunisia. In sub-Saharan Africa, France ruled the vast French West Africa federation, which had existed since 1895, encompassing eight French colonial territories. These were French Guinea, French Sudan, Dahomey (Benin), Ivory Coast, Mauritania, Niger, Senegal and Upper Volta (Burkina Faso). The federation was ruled from Dakar, remaining firmly under the control of Vichy during the Second World War. France's other African colonies included the equally large French Equatorial Africa, which encompassed Cameroon, Central African Republic, Chad, Congo (Brazzaville) and Gabon. This had been established in 1910 and was controlled from Brazzaville.

The French Foreign Legion was in the forefront of carving out this empire. It also acted as the glue that bound it together. Particularly in North Africa and the Levant, the Legion built their blockhouses and forts, becoming the symbol of France's overseas military power. As well as taking a lead in empire building, the Legion was instrumental in crushing insurrection. Its success was to entrench military thinking when it came to the handling of France's colonies.

French governor-general's palace in Saigon, 1875.

After the fall of France in 1940, the prostrate country was divided into two. The southern, unoccupied 'Free Zone' was administered by a government based in Vichy. The armistice of 25 June 1940 permitted Vichy a metropolitan defence force of just 100,000 for maintaining public order. This regime, however, did not resist the German invasion on 11 November 1942. General Jean de Lattre de Tassigny wanted to fight and was imprisoned by Vichy for his defiance.

Following the armistice, the French colonial authorities found themselves in an extraordinary situation. Their first loyalty was to Vichy as the recognized government of unoccupied France, not some unknown general who had proclaimed himself leader of the Free French from the sanctuary of London. Yet Charles de Gaulle had raised a banner for all those who secretly felt that the armistice was humiliating. France should have gone down fighting and stayed in a state of war, even if all of metropolitan France had been occupied. Vichy offered nothing but a shaming compromise and smacked of collaboration with the enemy.

The Germans were lenient with France's colonial empire, especially after Dakar repulsed de Gaulle's Free French Forces in September 1940. This showed that France's colonial troops were loyal to Vichy and therefore compliant. North Africa was firmly in Vichy's hands under the supervision of the German and Italian Armistice Commission. Only French Equatorial Africa rallied to the Free French. In Syria, Lebanon and Madagascar, the Vichy garrisons resisted the Allies in 1941. The following year they resisted them in North Africa.

In his youth, de Gaulle was sceptical of the value of the French empire. While on a military course in 1938, he infuriated another student, who had just returned from Indochina, after launching into a lengthy solution for the Far Eastern problem when he had never

French marines in Indochina, 1888.

even been there. Two years later, Equatorial Africa changed de Gaulle's attitude forever. The recruitment of Brazzaville to his fledgling cause was welcome consolation in light of his failure before Dakar. It gave the Free French an independent base, a radio station and some 16,500 men.

The first thing de Gaulle did was to set up the Council for the Defence of the Empire and hold the Conference of Colonial Governors. In expressing his gratitude for the loyalty of his colonial supporters, he inadvertently overstepped the mark by saying:

End of Empire

> In French Africa, as in all other territories where men live under our flag, there will be no progress unless the inhabitants benefit materially and morally in the countries of their birth, unless they can raise themselves little by little to the level where they are capable of taking part in the management of their own affairs in their homelands.

Whilst de Gaulle pledged to preserve French sovereignty wherever it existed, he also offered a move toward self-government, rather than adhering to the traditional concept of integrating French overseas territories with metropolitan France. The cynical might argue that he was simply being pragmatic in the face of rising nationalism in the old empires and America's dominant anti-colonial influence. No doubt de Gaulle hoped his speech might sway the vast bulk of the French empire still loyal to Vichy. In his memoirs, de Gaulle wrote, 'We were giving France back Independence, the Empire, and the Sword.'

In distant Indochina, the French garrison came under pressure from Japan and Thailand. The French governor-general, General Georges Catroux, found himself in an impossible position. On 19 June 1940, the Japanese insisted that he close the border with China, the British would not help, and Vichy instructed that he should comply with all Tokyo's demands. Catroux disapproved of the armistice with Germany and was sympathetic to the Free French. Henri Lémery, Vichy's minister of the colonies, immediately dismissed Catroux. He did not return to France but instead sought out de Gaulle.

Japan, seeking to stop the flow of arms to China and after threatening to invade Indochina, was permitted to station troops in Hanoi and Haiphong. Anyone showing support for de Gaulle's cause was punished by the Vichy authorities. Many were arrested, and even senior officials and demonstrators were fired on.

De Gaulle could do nothing about the pleas for help from Indochina. It was too far away and he simply did not have the resources. Vichy France was intent on doing nothing that would antagonize the Japanese or their German allies. The colony was on its own. Catroux, whom British Prime Minister Winston Churchill vainly hoped might replace de Gaulle, made it clear that Indochina was totally supportive of the Free French cause. De Gaulle recalled, 'At that time, for me Indochina was like a great disabled ship that I could help only after a long process of gathering the rescue apparatus. Seeing her moving farther away in the mists, I swore to myself that one day I should bring her back.'

Meanwhile, Thailand swiftly sought to capitalize on France's defeat and Indochina's disarray by claiming former territories in Cambodia and Laos. This led to a brief border war in October 1940, which, three months later, saw the Thais conduct a full-scale invasion. Although Japan sided with Thailand over territorial concessions, it continued to court Vichy. In December 1941, Japanese troops passed through Indochina with the acquiescence of Vichy in order to attack first Thailand and then British Burma, Malaya and Singapore.

After the Allied invasion of French North Africa, by 1943 every French overseas possession, with the exception of Indochina, which was under Japanese domination, had declared its allegiance to de Gaulle. This made him the virtual ruler of all Frenchmen outside occupied metropolitan France.

The Japanese tolerated Vichy's continued civil administration of Indochina in return for substantial basing and airfield rights until early March 1945. By this stage, Vichy had collapsed and had been replaced by a hostile de Gaulle. The Japanese seized complete control, by either capturing the small French garrison or by driving it into China.

French troops fleeing over the Chinese border after the Japanese took Indochina in early 1945.

The Emperor of Annam, Bao Dai, was permitted to declare Vietnam's independence. Prince Norodom Sihanouk did likewise in Cambodia, as did Laos. In a stroke, French Indochina vanished. De Gaulle was not happy that the one colonial possession he had pledged to restore had suddenly slipped from his grasp, thanks to Japanese duplicity.

In reality, Bao Dai ruled little more than Hanoi. North of the city, the communist-controlled League for the Independence of Vietnam, or Viet Minh, had created a sizeable liberated area. Their leader, Ho Chi Minh, also had supporters in central and southern Vietnam. They not only resisted the Japanese but also removed those seen to be collaborating with the French colonial administration. Although a communist, Ho was seen as a moderate influence, holding in check the more militant leaders such as Vo Nguyen Giap – soon to be known as General Giap, the master of guerrilla warfare – who advocated violence to achieve their goals.

The Viet Minh gained favour with America, that staunch opponent of colonialism, by intelligence gathering. In return, the Americans supplied them with weapons with which to fight the Japanese. The collapse of Japan's war effort in August 1945 presented Ho Chi Minh and his supporters a golden opportunity to finally free themselves of France.

In Paris, de Gaulle had a major problem on his hands with America. President Roosevelt made no secret of his dislike for the man, who he saw as being undemocratic. He also considered France a citadel of colonialism. Britain, Belgium, the Netherlands and Portugal all

Following the liberation of France Charles de Gaulle was determined to reclaim Indochina.

had overseas empires, but in Roosevelt's eyes, France's was by far the worst. He was only too aware of how France and Spain had treated Moroccan independence aspirations in the 1920s: they had launched a series of bloody military campaigns.

Roosevelt's son, Elliot, who travelled to Casablanca with his father in January 1943, recalled the president was not convinced it would be right to restore the French empire 'at all ever, without first obtaining in the case of each individual colony some sort of pledge, some sort of statement of just exactly what was planned in terms of each colony's administration ... How do they belong to France?'

In the case of Indochina, Roosevelt said the locals considered anything was better than a return to France. He was never keen on France reassuming control of Indochina, writing, 'France has milked Indochina for a hundred years. The people of Indochina deserve better than that.'

The fact that the Philippines had been under American protection since 1902 was an entirely different matter. When Roosevelt died in April 1945, his successor Harry S. Truman was no more sympathetic.

2. COLD WAR REALITIES

France saw the opening stages of the Cold War as early as 1944 when Charles de Gaulle's Free French Forces moved to block French communists from seizing power in Paris, Marseilles and Toulon. He had not wanted them forming a rival government that would challenge his power base. At the end of the war, the Red Army remained in Eastern Europe, occupying Hitler's war gains. As a result, all Eastern Europe ended up with communist governments.

In Greece, following liberation, Britain was forced to act against a communist takeover. Beyond Europe, by 1949 the Chinese Civil War had ended, with Mao's communists in power. This encouraged fledgling communist movements in Indochina, Burma, Malaya and Korea.

Unfortunately, in the post-war period, France proved more unstable than any of the defeated powers. The effect of France's devastating collapse and subjugation in 1940 was long lasting and could not easily be remedied. The war gave rise to a strong left-wing revival, thanks to the resistance, local liberation committees and militant unions.

Vietnamese communist leaders Vo Nguyen Giap (left) and Ho Chi Minh, early 1940s.

Regrettably for France, the right wing was discredited and was unable to govern without being tainted by the past. This was unlike West Germany, or Italy, where there emerged a new and strong Christian Democratic Party.

The weak French Third Republic had been swept away, and in 1946 the Fourth Republic began but without de Gaulle. While America was relieved that he had gone, the last thing it wanted was to see France in the grasp of the communists who were aligning themselves with Stalin. At first, a coalition government between radical, socialist and communist parties was attempted, but this quickly collapsed in disarray in 1947.

After the resignation of de Gaulle, drafting a new constitution proved far from easy. After two referendums, it was finally accepted, but turned out to be very much like that of the Third Republic. It suffered the same defects and was very unpopular. It was voted in by 9.1 million to 7.9 million, but with 7.9 million abstentions. The French despaired at all the infighting, and longed for a strong government that could steer France onto the road to recovery and her rightful place in the world.

The country now experienced a swing back to the right. De Gaulle formed the Rassemblement du Peuple Français (Rally of the French People) to gather the right to the new Popular Front government. The party performed well in the local elections. An energized de Gaulle toured the country, making rousing speeches. On 15 July 1947, he told a crowd of 60,000 at Rennes that the war in Indochina and the rising nationalism throughout the French Empire was the fault of both the communists and a regime too weak to control them.

The subsequent elections of November 1948 confirmed France's swing away from communism. The communists were excluded from the government, which fought off repeated left-wing challenges.

Elsewhere in Europe, the Soviet Union's belligerent blockade of West Berlin during 1948–49 heralded the long Cold War between the Western Allies and the Soviet-influenced states to the east. While America had no desire to help Britain and France recover their empires, it had no intention either of tolerating the spread of communism. From Washington's perspective, there was no democratic peace dividend at the end of the Second World War. In Eastern Europe, communist governments had been voted in thanks to overbearing support from Moscow. In the Balkans, both Albania and Yugoslavia had been taken over by their communist resistance movements, while Greece had only just been saved following a protracted civil war.

By far the most momentous and newsworthy event in Asia was Britain relinquishing control of India in 1947. It signalled to the world that European imperialism was no longer sustainable on such an enormous scale. While the Indian communist party had on occasions been a nuisance, it was never a major player within the independence movement. Together with other political organizations, it had been subject to intense scrutiny by Britain's secretive Indian Political Intelligence organization. Surveillance was also maintained on British communists who supported Indian nationalism.

During the Second World War, although the Indian communist party was implacably opposed to British rule, it wanted to do nothing that would aid the Axis powers. Afterwards, in February 1946, when part of the Indian navy mutinied in Bombay, the regional communist party called a general strike. As a result, violence flared, leaving over 200 dead. Fortunately for the British, Mohandas Gandhi had no interest in communist ideology or its predilection for violence. 'India does not want communism,' he said with heartfelt conviction. Although India was never under threat from communism, just three months after the outbreak of the Korean War in 1950, Mao swallowed Tibet without much fuss. Resistance by the Tibetans was short-lived and the Indian Army did nothing to help.

It was Stalin's Red Army that crushed Japan's forces in Manchuria and Korea at the end of the Second World War, not Mao Zedong's communist People's Liberation Army. When the Chinese Civil War was renewed, Mao continued to promote communism beyond his country's frontiers. There was a communist rising in newly independent Burma in 1948, which continued to be a threat until the fall of their stronghold at Prome two years later.

The presence of Chinese nationalist troops in northern Burma also caused the country problems. Chen Ping in Malaya, the communist leader there, after visiting Mao, employed his revolutionary methods of guerrilla warfare. The violence there also began in 1948, continuing for many years until the British and her Commonwealth allies prevailed against a weakened, predominantly Chinese insurgency.

In the case of Burma, the communists were split into two factions, known as the 'Red Flags' and the 'White Flags' that had differing goals. On Independence Day on 4 January 1948, the former was already in open revolt, while the latter followed suit two months later. Their area of control was steadily expanded from the Irrawaddy Delta all the way to Mandalay. To complicate matters, part of the Burmese army revolted, as did the country's Karen people in the southeast, who lived along Burma's frontiers with China and Thailand. In the face of Mao's growing victories, Chinese nationalists, some 12,000 strong, moved into part of Burma's Shan state on the eastern frontier. They were supplied by America and Nationalist Taiwan, in the hope that one day they would return to fight communist China. During 1950 and 1951, the Burmese launched a series of operations against the communists and Karen, greatly reducing their areas of control.

In Vietnam, Ho Chi Minh (born Nguyen Tat Than, then called Nguyen Ai Hoc) had been a communist agent since 1925. While studying in France, he had become a member of the French Communist Party, before returning to Indochina in 1930 as a representative of the Comintern (Kommunisticheskiĭ Internatsional – Communist International). His army, the Viet Minh, formed in 1941, had received training in guerrilla warfare in Yenan from Mao. By 1949, the French had been forced to recognize Vietnam as a political entity, but refused to accept Ho as ruler. Mao recognized him the following year. De Gaulle felt that it was absurd to negotiate with Ho Chi Minh and that it was vital to hold onto Indochina. France needed to send out a strong message that it would protect its colonies even when they were as far away as Indochina.

Mao's triumph in China in 1949 meant it was inevitable that he would throw even greater resources into supporting communist movements in neighbouring Indochina and Korea. The division of the latter at the end of the Second World War, between the communist North and the supposedly democratic South, was a highly dangerous flashpoint. When North Korea invaded the South, the Americans and British, under the auspices of the United Nations, stepped in and found themselves dragged into a three-year conventional war.

In late 1949, the victorious Mao had visited Stalin in Moscow before they signed the Sino-Soviet Treaty of Friendship, Alliance and Mutual Assistance. Mao returned home, confident that China was now a full member of the international communist brotherhood.

Cold War Realities

Chinese troops captured in Korea.

He was to gain the full cooperation of one of the world's superpowers for the next thirty years. In reality, Stalin distrusted the long-term goals of communist China as it posed a potential threat to the Soviet Far East. All the time that China had been weakened by unrelenting civil war and Japanese aggression, she had not been of any great concern.

As well as tying China to the Soviet Union, Stalin needed the cooperation of the Chinese for the expansion of communism in the region. This would ensure that Mao was preoccupied and would be prevented from meddling in Soviet affairs. Mao had intended to demobilize part of the People's Liberation Army, but he was soon to find he had need of its services again.

In March 1949, Korean communist leader Kim Il Sung had suggested to Stalin in Moscow that Korea should be forcibly reunified. At the time, Stalin was still fully occupied with the Berlin crisis, so the situation was not yet ripe for a war in Korea that could antagonize the Western powers further. Kim renewed his request a year later. This time, Stalin relented, promising military aid for the Korean People's Army. Stalin, though, had insisted that Kim get Mao's approval as they were about to start a major war on China's very doorstep.

Stalin's developing Cold War goals were self-evident: the subordination of Mao's aims to a dominant Soviet foreign policy, the integration of a war in Korea into his East Asia strategy, support for Ho Chi Minh's communists in Indochina, and the infiltration of the communist party in Japan. This policy of deliberately creating flashpoints was designed to force America to stretch her defence commitments at a time when she was demobilizing. This inevitably would force Washington to reduce its support for the 1949 North Atlantic Treaty Organization in Europe. Stalin would deliberately extend the Cold War from the escalating standoff in Europe, to one of global confrontation that included Korea and Indochina.

The British Joint Intelligence Committee, in fact, assessed that the Korean War was not part of the Cold War in Europe, saying:

> We believe North Korean aggression was originally launched not with the primary objective of diverting American attention from Europe, or as a prelude to provocative action against our weak spots on the European or Middle East periphery, but as a limited operation within the gambit of an intensified drive to expel Western influence from the whole of the Far East and South-East Asia.

America played right into Stalin's hands when it announced that the U.S. Pacific defence perimeter ran from the Philippines to Okinawa and then back through Japan, but crucially excluding Korea. In January 1950, the Americans confirmed the exclusion of Korea and Taiwan. This gave Stalin almost a free hand to help Kim Il Sung.

While Soviet troops would not be directly involved in the invasion of South Korea, Stalin promised that Mao would release 14,000 battle-hardened Korean soldiers who had served with the People's Liberation Army. In total, around 100,000 Koreans had fought alongside Mao's forces in China. Stalin also promised advisers and weapons, in particular tanks, which was something the South did not have. The plan was to occupy South Korea in a two-week operation.

Stalin and Mao, however, made a strategic miscalculation, for they took the Americans at their word that they would not defend South Korea. However, with American bases in nearby Japan, it was relatively easy to feed troops into Korea. The two communist leaders would have been better off toppling the weak French hold on Indochina. The French military did not have the resources to fight a war across Vietnam, Laos and Cambodia. Should the Americans have decided to intervene to assist the French, their nearest bases were much further away in the Philippines.

Mao's commitment to the Korean War, including vast numbers of Chinese troops, was a fortunate development for Paris. It meant that Chinese support for the nationalists in Indochina would diminish, plus the international community would be distracted whilst it supported United Nations forces committed to the defence of South Korea. For Ho Chi Minh, it represented a significant setback. Despite the enormous burden of the war in Indochina, the French sent an infantry battalion to South Korea, which landed at Pusan on 29 November 1950. It was to remain for the next three years until redeployed to Indochina.

3. OPERATION MASTERDOM

At the end of the Second World War, and despite everything going on in Paris and across the rest of the country, Charles de Gaulle never forgot about Indochina. Nor did he forget his pledge to reclaim it for France. Thanks to the Potsdam Conference in the summer of 1945, it would be an incredibly difficult task. Nonetheless, he had just the man for the job: Philippe Leclerc de Hauteclocque, who was one of his most trusted Gaullist generals.

To protect his family while serving with the Free French, the Vicomte de Hauteclocque assumed the name Jacques Leclerc. He became a national hero. In November 1945, Leclerc was formally added to his family's name. During the closing months of the Second World War, General Leclerc's 2nd Armoured Division had helped with General de Lattre's destruction of the Colmar pocket, before making a dramatic dash to Hitler's mountain lair at Berchtesgaden. Afterwards, Leclerc led his division as the vanguard of the victory parade in Paris. Not one to be idle, he requested that de Gaulle send him to Morocco.

Instead, de Gaulle informed Leclerc that he proposed to redesignate the wartime French III Corps to become the headquarters for an expeditionary force destined for Indochina. This would be created using the 3rd and 9th colonial infantry divisions. Leclerc would be commander-in-chief of this force, answering to Admiral Thierry d'Argenlieu, the newly appointed High Commissioner for Indochina.

De Gaulle told d'Argenlieu that his incredibly complex mission was to recover Indochina from the British, Chinese, Japanese and the Viet Minh, and to re-establish French sovereignty in the region. D'Argenlieu and Leclerc were to make no concessions to the Vietnamese nationalists. All they were to offer, once firmly in control, was limited internal autonomy to each of the states of Indochina within a French Union. Leclerc would be in charge of all foreign affairs, defence policy and internal politics.

While de Gaulle and his supporters were determined that Indochina should be returned to French authority, Ho Chi Minh aspired to full independence for his country. Ho and his supporters saw the impending post-war vacuum as their best chance to attain this. However, before he could even contend with the French, Ho was to find himself caught between the British and the Nationalist Chinese.

During the Potsdam Conference, at which the French were not represented, it was agreed that Chiang Kai-shek's Nationalist Chinese would accept the Japanese surrender in northern Indochina, while the British would accept it in the south. The 16th Parallel was to form the dividing line. The defeated Japanese had two armies in Indochina and Thailand. British intelligence assessed them to number about 70,000, but this was actually too high. About 28,500 men of the Japanese Thirty-eighth Army were deployed in northern Indochina and Thailand. The Japanese Army of the South in southern Indochina, under Lieutenant General Yuitsu Tsuchihashi, numbered about 30,000, including air force and naval personnel.

De Gaulle knew that Washington, with its anti-colonial polices, was behind this deliberate snub, which immediately served to undermine French colonial authority in the region. In practical terms, though, the French were not in a position to accept the Japanese surrender. They did not have the resources to swiftly send large numbers of troops to

Indochina to disarm the Japanese army. Leclerc's men would not reach Indochina until October/November 1945. In contrast, the British and Chinese were much closer to hand.

Such niceties mattered little to the Japanese, who simply wanted to be repatriated as soon as possible. In the north, perhaps in the name of mischief-making, they were more inclined to hand authority over to Ho Chi Minh, and many of their weapons were passed to his Viet Minh guerrillas. Anything that inconvenienced the Chinese was seen as a good thing. Ho certainly had no love for the Chinese nationalists as they had imprisoned him in 1942 and established the Vietnam Revolutionary League (Dong Minh Hoi) as an anti-communist counter to his party. He was only released after he convinced them he was a nationalist first and a communist second, and that they had a common enemy in the Japanese.

At the end of the war, it was not long before a large Chinese army of 'liberation', numbering some 150,000 under General Lu Han, pillaged its way over the border. It was formed of units whose loyalty to Chiang Kai-shek was suspect, so he was probably glad to have them out of the way and preoccupied. Certainly, Lu Han's ultimate sympathies lay with Mao. He was to defect in 1949. It was not long before these Chinese troops had alienated the Vietnamese, French and Japanese in Tonkin and north Annam.

France's initial attempt to reassert sovereignty lacked power, having the air of a comic opera. In late August 1945, two teams, led by colonels who were to act as the administrators for the north and the south, were parachuted in. To the north, Colonel Messmer was immediately arrested by the Viet Minh and forced to flee to China. Colonel Cédile, sent to the south, was ignored by the Viet Min and was left at liberty to liaise with the local French authorities.

The French navy's first aircraft in Indochina were American-supplied Catalinas in late October 1945.

Operation Masterdom

Ho Chi Minh moved from his stronghold into Hanoi, hoping to pre-empt the Chinese as much as the French. On 2 September 1945, he declared the Democratic Republic of Vietnam. Emperor Bao Dai, after abdicating, became chief counsellor to the new government. The communist-dominated Provisional Executive Committee of South Vietnam, led by Tran Van Giau in Saigon, acknowledged the authority of Ho's northern government. Ho, however, was in a very weak position and had to agree with General Lu to dissolve the Vietnamese Communist Party and hold elections to create a broad coalition government.

In France, after his appointment, Leclerc recruited some of his former officers from the 2nd Armoured Division, including his intelligence chief, Colonel Paul Repiton-Préneuf. He also quickly set about familiarizing himself with the region and its culture. Aware that the dark-skinned Cambodians were the mortal foes of the Vietnamese, he forbade the deployment of his colonial divisions' West African units to Indochina. This instruction was not strictly adhered to, nor did it deter the deployment of Algerian and Moroccan troops. During September 1945, en route to Indochina, Leclerc stopped off in Ceylon to consult Admiral Lord Louis Mountbatten, Supreme Allied Commander South East Asia. He also spent time in India, Malaya, Japan and Singapore where he held briefings.

Mountbatten, facing his own problems, warned Leclerc in no uncertain terms that post-war Asia was now a completely different place to pre-war Asia. Both were fully aware that the major colonial powers had been humiliated in the region, and that this was something from which the nationalists had taken heart. Mountbatten said there could be no going back, to which Leclerc responded pragmatically, 'What you say makes sense but is not French policy.'

He then represented France during the Japanese surrender on board an American battleship in Tokyo Bay, and again at the Japanese surrender in Singapore.

Mountbatten had discussed British plans, known as Operation Masterdom, to deal with southern Indochina. This envisaged the movement by air to Saigon, via Bangkok, of the 80th Infantry Brigade, part of Major General Douglas Gracey's 20th Indian Division, plus elements of two RAF squadrons and an Allied Control Commission. The latter was to assist Allied prisoners of war and oversee the repatriation of the Japanese. They would be followed by the rest of Gracey's division, comprising the 32nd and 100th brigades, which would be shipped by sea. In total, almost 26,000 men and 2,400 vehicles were to be deployed to Saigon to maintain law and order. Once in place, Gracey was to wait until the French were in a position to reassert themselves. His task was simply to take control of the large Japanese garrison, which was to be achieved with the cooperation of Tsuchihashi.

The British began arriving in Saigon on 12 September 1945, with a force consisting of Indian Army as well as British units under General Gracey. The 80th Brigade first flew to Bangkok from Burma, and then on to Saigon. It had been almost four weeks since the Japanese emperor announced his country would accept the terms of the Potsdam declaration, and over a week since the Japanese surrendered to MacArthur. In that time, law and order in Indochina had broken down in many areas, and Viet Minh nationalists had seized power in Saigon. Ironically, the Japanese army, once an occupying force, now found itself acting as policeman.

Colonel Cédile and his supporters quickly persuaded Gracey to rearm the local French colonial infantry regiments, which had been held by the Japanese. Much to Mountbatten's displeasure, on 21 September, Gracey declared martial law throughout Indochina south of the 16th Parallel. Two days later, he agreed to the takeover of the government by Cédile.

British-supplied Spitfires were deployed to Indochina by the French air force.

Although Mountbatten felt that Gracey had overstepped his remit, London supported his actions. This was, after all, a French problem.

Also on 23 September, a mixed force of French Gaullists, former Vichy troops and armed French colonists, stormed the Viet Minh headquarters in the Saigon town hall, where they arrested members of the Provisional Executive Committee. The Tricolore was hoisted, but most of the committee members escaped. The Viet Minh now knew that a smooth political transition of power was not going to happen.

Gracey quietly ejected the Viet Min from the city and handed it over to the French. However, when the French 5th Colonial Infantry Regiment attempted to remove the last of the Viet Minh guards, they resisted, resulting in two French soldiers being killed. This sparked a riot on the night of 24–25 September, during which a mob ran amok, slaughtering French civilians. The following day, the Viet Minh set fire to the central market and attacked Tan Son Nhut airfield. Repelling this assault, the British lost a soldier, but killed half a dozen Viet Minh.

Gracey now had a war on his hands, which was something Mountbatten had hoped to avoid. Nonetheless, their troops were hardened Burma veterans and highly experienced in fighting both jungle and irregular warfare. They were more than capable of facing down the ill-trained and ill-equipped Viet Minh. In early October, Gracey secured a ceasefire. At that point, Leclerc arrived in Saigon. Hostilities resumed on the 10th, when the Viet Minh set about a British engineering party near Tan Son Nhut, killing or wounding most of them. Once Brigadier Woodford's 32nd Brigade landed as welcome reinforcements, they were sent into Saigon's troublesome northern suburbs.

Operation Masterdom

When the Viet Minh attacked Tan Son Nhut again, they were once more repelled by Indian and Japanese soldiers. By mid-October, British forces had killed over 300 Viet Minh, while the rearmed Japanese accounted for another 225. Nevertheless, the Viet Minh stepped up their attacks across Saigon and attempted to lay siege to it. In response, at the end of the month Gracey launched an operation to drive the Viet Minh away from the city. Conducted by 'Gateforce' this included a full battalion of Japanese infantry who had little love for the Vietnamese. The latter killed fifty Viet Minh east of Saigon. When the mission was complete, almost 200 insurgents had been eliminated by the British task force. Ironically, the Japanese did not formally surrender to Lord Mountbatten in Saigon until 30 November 1945.

Trouble was brewing elsewhere in Indochina. The Japanese had imposed a prime minister, Son Ngoe Thanh, on the pro-French Cambodian king. The former had broken all ties with France and sought to oust the monarchy. This made Cambodia highly vulnerable to the Viet Minh's Cambodian communist allies. Leclerc quickly flew to Phnom Penh from where he ordered Thanh to attend the British military representative. When he did, the French arrested him and flew him to France.

Having stabilized the situation in neighbouring Cambodia, Leclerc then turned his attentions to the countryside of Cochinchina and southern Vietnam beyond the confines of Saigon. Once the insurgents' stranglehold on the city had been broken, Leclerc's columns fanned out. The Viet Minh and other nationalist groups were poorly armed. They could not match French firepower, so they set about blowing up roads and bridges. Ambushes and snipers also served to hamper the French patrols.

French forces arrived in Indochina with British weapons, including the Bren gun. (Photo Bundesarchiv)

Leclerc relied on speed and surprise as much as firepower. He moved his men up the roads and waterways, often in the dark, to suddenly materialize in the towns and villages of Cochinchina. Infantry sweeps, backed by artillery and aircraft, then ousted the stubborn resistance. Leclerc also conducted a hearts-and-minds campaign by ordering his men to treat the locals with respect. There was to be no breakdown of military discipline with brutality or looting. Leclerc knew that this had to be enforced because many of his reinforcements were former French resistance fighters who were used to doing things their own way.

To the relief of French colonists and plantation owners, much of the region was successfully reoccupied and a network of military outposts established by the end of November 1945. Units were also sent into Cambodia and southern Laos to reassert French authority. Regaining northern Laos was more difficult because of the presence of the antagonistic Chinese, but a small contingent was deployed against local guerrillas. By this point, High Commissioner d'Argenlieu had arrived to take charge of Leclerc.

Gracey happily handed over Saigon's northern suburbs to General Valluy's 9th Colonial Infantry Division in early December. The British 32nd Brigade was then redeployed to Borneo. The last major engagement involving the British occurred on 3 January 1946, when 900 Viet Minh attacked Bien Hoa. The defenders fought throughout the night without losing a single British or Indian soldier, whereas the attackers suffered 100 dead.

That month, French troops, landing from the sea, entered south Amman to take control. Also at the close of January 1946, the British 80th Brigade relinquished its area of responsibility to the French and the 100th Brigade was withdrawn to Saigon. Gracey handed back southern Vietnam to Leclerc, and by the end of March, Britain had all but ended its seven-month operation. A few troops remained to guard the Allied Control Mission, which was wound up in mid-May. An estimated 2,700 Viet Minh were killed during Operation Masterdom. British fatalities amounted to 40 men. In pacifying Cochinchina, Leclerc lost around 630 dead and 1,000 wounded from a force of 50,000 men.

Although French colonial authority had been successfully restored in the four regions south of the dividing 16th Parallel, the Viet Minh were far from defeated. Leclerc and d'Argenlieu hoped that everyday life could now be resumed, but they underestimated the growing strength of the Viet Minh and Ho Chi Minh's determination to be rid of the French. The initial fighting had just been a taste of things to come.

4. RISE OF THE VIET MINH

It was the year after the defeat of France by Nazi Germany that nationalist leader Ho Chi Minh formed the Viet Nam Doc Lap Dong Minh Hoi, or League for the Independence of Vietnam. This was soon shortened to Viet Minh. His military commander, Vo Nguyen Giap, began seizing territory in Tonkin. Four years later, following the collapse of the Japanese in August 1945, the Viet Minh and the much less communist-dominated United Party of Cochinchina were able to fill the political vacuum.

Both Ho Chi Minh and Vo Nguyen Giap were advocates of Mao Zedong's theory of revolutionary war. Mao, drawing on the fighting in the vastness of China, reasoned that the revolutionary, to buy time to mobilize the political will of the people, should trade space. The struggle for ultimate political supremacy would take place through three stages. These consisted of the 'safe-base-areas' preparation phase, a guerrilla-warfare stage to weaken the enemy, and an open-warfare stage when the guerrillas were ready to fight a conventional war. In the case of Indochina, all three were to take place at the same time.

Foremost, the Viet Minh was a revolutionary movement whose goal was the seizure of political power rather than fighting a conventional conflict. Therefore, although Giap organized his forces on traditional lines with battalions, regiments and divisions, the chain of command was firmly in the hands of the political officers. This very much mirrored the control of the Soviet Red Army during the Second World War and the communist Chinese People's Liberation Army during the Second World War, Chinese Civil War and Korean War.

Vo Nguyen Giap with Viet Minh fighters, 1944.

Direction of the people's revolution rested with Ho and his government in exile operating in the mountains of Viet Bac. From there he sought to control every aspect of the conflict. From 1946–47, Indochina was divided up into fourteen Minh regions under the direction of a committee that answered directly to Ho Chi Minh. As the war escalated, these administrative zones were simplified to the three kingdoms that became Vietnam.

By 1948, there were just six inter-zones encompassing northwest Tonkin, northeast Tonkin (the division between the two rested on the Red or Hong River), the Red River Delta, north Amman, south Amman (the demarcation line was the city of Hue), and Cochinchina. Each had a controlling committee responsible to the leadership in Viet Bac. Their main task was to raise and train guerrilla forces. Ho called for a general mobilization of all males and females from 18 to 45 in November 1949.

The most basic Viet Minh unit was the very simple village militia. Made up of farmers, their task was to act as labourers carrying supplies, preparing defences and intelligence gathering. It has been estimated that, by 1954, the Viet Minh could call on over 350,000 militia. They formed a cadre of recruits who could also serve with the regional troops, effectively home guard, commanded by the inter-zone committees. They were responsible for protecting their local zone as well as conducting attacks on isolated local French garrisons.

By 1954, these regional troops totalled around 75,000 across the six inter-zones. They, like the militia, were ill-equipped and did not wear uniforms. This meant that they looked like the classic peasant guerrilla. Their main contribution to Giap's war effort was that

Léo Figuères of the French Communist Party and Ho Chi Minh meet in Vietnam, May 1950. (Photo Stratigraphy)

Rise of the Viet Minh

The Viet Minh comprised village militia, regional troops and Chu Luc or regulars.

they helped tie down French forces the length and breadth of Vietnam. This effectively forced the French to adopt their strongpoint policy in trying to hold and defend territory.

The third element was the Chu Luc, or Viet Minh regular force – also known as the Vietnamese People's Army. This was a conventional army organized to defeat the weakened French military in the open-battle phase of the revolution. The Chu Luc was formed around Ho Chi Minh's original resistance fighters, and were armed with Japanese, Chinese and captured French weapons. Their uniform consisted of black 'pyjamas' and cork, sun helmets, later popularized by the Viet Cong.

In 1950, the status of these units was formalized when sixty battalions were reorganized into five regular infantry divisions. These consisted off the 304th, 308th, 312th and the 316th in the Viet Bac base region, and the 320th in the South Delta base (Red River Delta). They were organized on conventional lines, each with three infantry regiments (of two or three battalions), supported by anti-aircraft guns and heavy mortars. At the end of the year, a sixth 'heavy' division was created, known as the 351st. This consisted of three regiments, with artillery and anti-aircraft guns, and one of engineers. This effectively was a firepower support division.

By 1954, the Chu Luc was over 125,000 strong, with the new 325th Infantry Division in the process of being formed in An Khe province. Although Giap had no naval or air force units, he did get assistance from the Chinese. In particular, there are reports of Chinese officers serving with the Chu Luc divisions and Chinese anti-aircraft units serving alongside the Chu Luc at Dien Bien Phu.

The Viet Minh were completely reliant on Communist China for logistical backing. Ho Chi Minh naturally looked to Mao for ideological and materiel support. He spoke fluent Chinese, having lived in China for over a decade. By the late 1940s, Mao was training Vietnamese fighters. His initial aim had been to send Chinese troops to assist Ho once he had secured the border with Indochina. Stalin would not agree to this as he had bigger plans involving Korea. When Ho travelled to Moscow in early 1950 to meet with Stalin and Mao, he was told military assistance was China's responsibility.

Mao's immediate contribution to the Viet Minh was to build roads up to the border to ferry in supplies. This ensured that the French lost control of the frontier very quickly. In the summer of 1950, Mao announced that he planned to train 60–70,000 Communist Vietnamese soldiers. They probably formed the cadre of the Chu Luc's regular infantry divisions. Mao though, was soon downgrading his support by the autumn in order to concentrate on the much larger war in Korea. His troops were also sent to occupy hapless Tibet, yet another distraction from events in Indochina.

Ho must have wished Mao lavished the same assistance on Vietnam as he did North Korea. The first regular Chinese troops, designated Chinese People's Volunteers to obfuscate China's official entry into the Korean War, crossed the Yalu River in mid-October 1950. The following month, they numbered 200,000 men. By the new year, they were in the South Korean capital Seoul, when another 250,000 men were committed to the battle.

The Viet Minh, unlike their 1960s successors the Viet Cong and North Vietnamese Army, were initially very reliant on weapons captured from the Japanese and the French. Standard Japanese army small arms included the Nambu pistol, Arisaka Type 99 rifle, Type 100 sub-machine gun, and the Type 96 and 99 light machine gun. The Viet Minh also got their hands on Japanese 81mm and 90mm mortars. They would have particularly prized the Type 92/93 heavy machine guns and the Type 98 20mm cannon, which could be used for air defence. Keeping such weapons in the field though, was dependant on adequate stocks of ammunition. This problem was partly alleviated by the generosity of Stalin's Red Army.

Although Japanese pistols were largely inferior to their Allied counterparts, their infantry rifles and mortars were as good as most Allied designs. In contrast, Japanese grenades were often ineffective due to poor fuses and explosives. The Japanese tended to neglect their weapons, so the poor, damp storage of ammunition and explosives cannot have helped the Viet Minh.

French colonial forces often had to make do with fairly ancient weaponry dating from the First World War or even older. Most of the more modern guns had been issued to the metropolitan French army. Nonetheless, the Viet Minh employed the standard French MAS-36 rifle and the MAT-49 sub-machine gun. During the Second World War, some American arms were supplied to the Viet Minh by the Office of Strategic Services for use against the Japanese. In later years, the French also transferred American weapons to Indochina that had been issued to their army by the U.S. under the Anfa Plan.

Mao supplied weapons, many of them simply passed on from the Soviet Union, including the Soviet Mosin-Nagant rifle, PPSh-41 and PPS-43 sub-machine guns and the SKS carbine. China and North Korea also made their own versions of the PPSh-41, known as the Type 50 and Type 49 respectively. The Chinese copied the SKS and Kalashnikov, but these did not appear until 1956. Chinese supplies would have included quantities of the Mauser-based Zhongzheng, or Chiang Kai-shek rifle, captured from the defeated Chinese nationalists, and the older Hanyang Type 88 rifle.

The long-term arming of the Vet Minh was never going to be a problem. In 1949, Mao was sitting on a vast arsenal of weaponry thanks to the Soviet Union and America. The Red Army, after defeating the Japanese in Manchuria in 1945, handed over vast quantities of captured weapons. The Chinese Communists were gifted 300,000 rifles, 4,800 machine guns, 1,200 artillery pieces, over 360 tanks and 2,300 trucks. Once the Chinese Communists went over to the offensive, they captured ever-increasing quantities of arms from the disintegrating Nationalist armies.

Much of the U.S. military equipment supplied to the Chinese Nationalist leader, Chiang Kai-shek, to help in the war against the Japanese, ended up being diverted. It was deliberately held back by Chiang, ready for the resumption of the civil war against Mao. There was enough equipment provided for 30 divisions, plus over 1,000 tanks. After the surrender of Japan in September 1945, American equipment flooded into Nationalist China. Washington pledged to equip another forty of Chiang's divisions. This support, however, made Chiang complacent and overconfident.

Much of this new weaponry was swiftly lost. Mao's forces captured over 140,000 American rifles during the last four months of 1948. When the nationalist armies systematically collapsed during 1946–49, Mao received a massive windfall of 2,000,000 rifles, 250,000 machine guns, 60,000 pieces of artillery, 940 tanks and armoured cars, and over 130 aircraft. Among all this, were large quantities of American guns that would be used against the French.

However, the bulk of these weapons, and the output from Mao's military factories, would soon be soaked up by the voracious appetite of the Korean War.

Amongst the heavier weapons Mao provided the Viet Minh was the American 105mm howitzer, examples of which were captured in Korea and China.

Dien Bien Phu

Notably, by 1950, thanks to Chinese and Soviet aid, the Viet Minh started to deploy automatic anti-aircraft guns. The first loss to such weapons occurred on 19 January 1950, when a French air force P-63 Kingcobra was shot down over Thai-nguyen. Key among these deliveries was the Soviet M1939 37mm anti-aircraft gun based on the Bofors 40mm. This was issued to the 367th Regiment serving with the 351st Division.

Up to two regiments' worth of 37mm guns were deployed at Dien Bien Phu, which ensured the French air force received a hot reception. There have been reports of an entire Chinese anti-aircraft regiment being committed to the battle, but this has never been substantiated. The Viet Minh also had 12.7mm and 14.5mm heavy machine guns acting in an anti-aircraft role.

Viet Minh logistics were surprisingly sophisticated and highly efficient, despite French efforts to cut their supply lines. Ho Chi Minh introduced conscription in 1942, and eventually all peasants were required to undertake three months' labour every year. This usually meant digging defences or acting as porters in support of operations. To keep a Viet Minh division in the field for a month required around 50,000 porters each carrying 20kg. In some areas, bicycles were supplied, which meant porters could manage 70kg on the outward journey.

By 1952, Chinese aid was pouring over the border into the Viet Bac region by rail and then by road at a rate of 3,000 tonnes a month. This was gathered at Bac Kan, then distributed to units in the field. In 1953, almost 600 Soviet trucks were available for this job. The rapid Viet Minh build-up around Dien Bien Phu was, in part, thanks to these vehicles.

Supplies were first delivered to the Chinese rail heads at Hokow (Hokou) and Nanning. The latter offered the shortest route into northeastern Tonkin, with provisions being trucked from Nanning to the border town of Chan-Nun-Kawan, and from there on to Lang Son and Cao Bang. This attracted the attention of the French air force, so some convoys took a more circuitous route heading northwest on the Nanning–Kunming road before turning south to Cao Bang. On either route, movement usually happened after dark. To the west, a narrow-gauge railway ran from Kunming to Hokow, from where supplies could be trucked to Lao Kai. This though was not up and running until 1953, so it was not as important at the Nanning supply routes.

The guerrillas' armoury included a wide variety of booby-traps intended to main or kill. The Viet Minh, and later the Viet Cong, became masters at improvising deadly and often despicable mines and booby-traps. These were used against convoys and foot patrols. They not only employed standard French and Chinese devices, but also produced homemade ones, using a variety of containers and explosives. Mines could be detonated by direct contact with either the mine or an electrical firing device, or by hand-operated electrical firing, or by trip wire. Mines were normally placed on well-travelled roads, trails, road bridges and footbridges. Aerial bombs, grenades, mines and mortar rounds were also used, often placed in trees.

Much more primitive impaling devices were employed, triggered by trip wire or manual release. Such devices included homemade crossbows, the spiked deadfall, mace, the Malayan gate and the trapeze swing. These were usually designed to strike the victim in the chest, and the only way to avoid them was by immediately falling backwards. The guerrillas also dug primitive but effective pit traps, the most common of which was a concealed punji pit full of stakes. There were also ankle traps, spike boards and sideways-closing traps to catch the unwary. These were often contaminated with human waste or other infectious materials containing bacteria. The fear of mines and booby-traps often greatly slowed down French operations.

Rise of the Viet Minh

Ho Chi Minh standing third from the left with an American liaison team in 1945.

As the three phases of revolutionary warfare were largely interchangeable, this made it very difficult, if not impossible, for the French to seize and hold the initiative. The French tactic of taking and securing ground inevitably meant that they had to then wait and see how the Viet Minh responded. Even when they went over to the offensive, such as at Hoa Binh and Dien Bien Phu, they faced the same problem. This meant the Viet Minh held the initiative for much of the war.

The French made little effort to counter the Vet Minh's political campaign to garner popular support amongst the population. Their generals concluded wrongly that, over time, a combination of mobile operations and static defences would defeat the revolutionaries' guerrilla and conventional warfare tactics. They were to be proved wrong.

In their guerrilla operations, the Viet Minh focused on infiltration and ambush to fight the French. The latter had no answer to infiltration, as the guerrillas looked like the peasants, enabling them, as Mao put it, to move among them 'as a fish swims in the sea'. All the French could do was try and seal off areas, for example, with the outposts on the Cao Bang–Lang Son ridge and the De Lattre Line.

The Viet Minh excelled at ambushes, especially as the French insisted on moving mainly along roads and waterways. Even when the French went over to the offensive, such as in Operation Lorraine, they still stuck to the roads and rivers. All the Viet Minh had to do was stop the lead vehicles of a convoy in a steep wooded valley, before pouring fire down to destroy it.

However, when Giap tried to fully enter the conventional warfare stage in 1951, he did this far too soon, resulting, thanks to French defensive measures, in defeat at Vinh Yen, Mao Khe and Phat Diem. The tactics of sending suicide squads to try and break through also favoured the French defenders, who responded with machine guns, artillery and napalm. It would be another two years before Ho and Giap were confident enough to again fight set-piece battles.

5. GET LECLERC

Thanks to British assistance, General Leclerc, with his limited forces, managed to successfully reclaim southern Indochina for France. In early 1946, he began to plan for an amphibious operation to get his men into the port of Haiphong and then onto Hanoi. He was well aware that the position of the 30,000-strong French community in the north was precarious, as they were caught between volatile and competing parties. Beforehand, much diplomacy was required to ensure his men were not opposed.

Leclerc urged Paris that the time was ripe to promise independence for the nationalists within the French Union. He reasoned, after his military landings at Haiphong, that France would have recovered sovereignty throughout the bulk of Indochina, and only such a step would appease the nationalists. His concern was that if this did not happen, he would be confronted by a protracted guerrilla campaign that he did not have the resources to fight.

Leclerc, as military commander, did not have the best of relations with High Commissioner d'Argenlieu. The latter refused to discuss overall strategy with Leclerc, insisting that his role was purely to reassert military control and not worry about the peace settlement. During the negotiating process in early 1946, Leclerc often found himself side-lined. To make matters worse, after the resignation of his sponsor, de Gaulle, he did not get clear support or direction from Paris. D'Argenlieu, influenced by local colonial administrators and residents, was of the view that a show of force would secure outright military and political victory.

In the north, there remained the thorny issue of the Nationalist Chinese and Viet Minh. Leclerc knew that once the Chinese had agreed to leave, he would have to move swiftly to secure Hanoi. At first it appeared as if the French and Viet Minh could reach a compromise. To appease the Chinese, Ho Chi Minh's government included non-communist nationalists, and in November 1945, he even, publicly at least, dissolved the Indochinese Communist Party.

In the face of the British withdrawal from Saigon on 6 March 1946, Ho Chi Minh signed an agreement with the French administrator, Jean Sainteny. Ho agreed to allow 25,000 French and French-officered Vietnamese troops into the north's urban areas. Sainteny recognized Vietnam as both a 'free state' within the Indochinese Federation, and as part of the French Union, and Paris agreed to withdraw all troops within five years, except for those at a few bases. A referendum was to be held on the unity of Vietnam in Tonkin, Annam and Cochinchina.

Leclerc felt that this was a step in the right direction, and d'Argenlieu, who was in Paris, could not interfere. Both sides, though, knew that this agreement was really just to facilitate the removal of the troublesome Chinese. Leclerc appreciated that, long-term, Ho Chi Minh and the Viet Minh were wholly opposed to French control.

At the start of the year, Leclerc developed a three-point strategy to remove the Chinese, who were not popular with the local French or the Vietnamese. However, the Chinese nationalists had no intention of letting the communists take power in Tonkin and northern Amman. They backed local opposition to Ho Chi Minh, which had obliged him to recognize

General Leclerc, seen here with some of the men of the French 2nd Armoured Division, 1944.

Sainteny's authority. Therefore, it was vital that Paris exert diplomatic pressure on Chiang Kai-shek, as well as Leclerc's own officers on the Chinese command in Hanoi, to facilitate the withdrawal. Secondly, Leclerc wanted to build up his forces sufficiently enough so that they were a factor at the negotiating table, and thirdly, talks should be opened with Ho Chi Minh. By early 1946, the total number of French troops had risen to 65,000.

Chiang agreed to allow his army in Tonkin to be progressively relieved by French units during March 1946. In any case, he needed his troops home to redeploy against Mao's Communist guerrillas, but he used the situation to get the French to relinquish their concession in Shanghai. In Hanoi, General Salan and Sainteny negotiated with General Lu Han to accept this timetable. These talks proved problematic with the Chinese, who appeared not entirely keen to leave their new fiefdom. They would not depart until April 1946 at the earliest, which posed problems for Leclerc, whose forces were to land in Haiphong during the first week of March. This meant that he could not be sure until the very day of his landings whether the Chinese would choose to resist.

Just as he feared, on the evening of 5 March 1946, when his force entered the Haiphong River, local Chinese units opened fire. One landing ship was set ablaze and others were hit. Leclerc had no option but to respond. A thirty-minute firefight ensued, as the two sides needlessly shot at each other. The Chinese, deciding that honour had been served, sent a negotiator with the offer of a ceasefire on condition that the French withdrew downstream. Leclerc refused, and a very tense twenty-four hours followed, until the Chinese finally allowed him to disembark 5,000 troops.

The day after the landings, Giap came to see Leclerc to press his case. As fellow soldiers, both showed the other great respect, with Giap offering admiration for the French resistance and the liberation of Paris. Not long after Leclerc met with Ho Chi Minh, the communist leader was impressed with Leclerc whom he felt he could trust. Ho wanted a joint Franco-Vietnamese commission to supervise the ceasefire and administration of south Annam and Cochinchina. Leclerc refused on the latter, but agreed to scale down French operations while contact was made with remaining rebel units. He also supported Ho's call for early negotiations with Paris, which were backed by the pragmatic Sainteny.

Although the rest of Leclerc's force landed without further hitch, another week was wasted while pressure was brought to bear on Chiang Kai-shek. Eventually, the local Chinese commander agreed to coordinate his withdrawal with the French. The Tricolore was flying once more over Haiphong, but at the cost of thirty-seven dead.

Despite this apparent progress, when Leclerc entered Hanoi on 18 March 1946, only French citizens welcomed him. In some areas in Tonkin, the French were met with outright resistance, but in others, Leclerc and Salan managed to develop a friendly partnership with the local Viet Minh. Leclerc knew that with his limited resources the complete re-conquest of Tonkin was simply impossible.

Keen to avoid French involvement in purely internal Vietnamese affairs, and to foster cooperation, Leclerc was soon at loggerheads with d'Argenlieu. The High Commissioner was not prepared to make any concessions. He felt that Leclerc's meetings with Ho and Giap verged on national betrayal. D'Argenlieu was of the view that Leclerc and Salan were straying well beyond their military remit, ignoring the fact that the generals were on the political as well as military frontline when it came to dealing with the communists.

D'Argenlieu, even while still in Paris, did all he could to delay the negations and sought to divorce Cochinchina from the rest of Vietnam. He used his time in the French capital to strengthen his hand and garner support for his hard-line approach. He wanted Leclerc and Salan dismissed and replaced, but he could not achieve this. When he returned to

The French transport fleet consisted largely of the French-produced version of the Junker Ju 52, the Toucan.

Indochina in late March, he completely ignored both generals, and began issuing orders, bypassing the military chain of command in th process.

Leclerc was thoroughly alarmed that d'Argenlieu's actions would inevitably push Ho further into the arms of the more militant wing of the Viet Minh. In Cochinchina, the High Commissioner's proposals resulted in the Viet Minh opening a new guerrilla campaign that the stretched French forces could not contain. When d'Argenlieu finally met Ho, all he would offer was local negotiations – there was to be no high-level international recognition with talks in Paris. Giap responded by demanding full independence encompassing Cochinchina.

Despite his goal of maintaining French sovereignty, d'Argenlieu, in order to keep the Viet Minh talking, had to acquiesce to holding discussions in Paris. Due to the instability of French domestic politics, these were delayed until the summer, by which time d'Argenlieu had forged ahead with his plans by forming a government for Cochinchina. On 1 June 1946, he proclaimed Cochinchina an autonomous republic, in effect a French puppet state. Ho and Giap saw this as nothing more than a French attempt to foist partition on Vietnam. When Ho arrived in Paris in late June to be greeted by Marius Moutet, the Minister for Overseas Territories, it was inevitable that the talks would go nowhere.

By this stage, a dispirited Leclerc had been recalled to France, assuming that his mission had been completed, but also appreciating that he was under a political cloud because of his liberal approach to Vietnam's nationalists. During the Fontainebleau conference, Ho unexpectedly called on him. Leclerc knew better than to criticize d'Argenlieu publicly, or offer any intervention that would ultimately do more harm than good. He was also not duped by Ho Chi Minh's friendly 'Uncle Ho' persona.

Ho Chi Minh signed an agreement that September, but it did not go far enough for Giap, who resumed violence both against the French and their supporters, and even against the moderate Vietnamese nationalists. Between them, d'Argenlieu and Giap ensured that Indochina would not be spared all-out war.

To block supplies reaching the Viet Minh, and to reassert French political authority in the north, soldiers moved to seize Haiphong's custom houses on 15 October 1946. After street fighting broke out on 23 November, the French navy bombarded the port. This reportedly resulted in the deaths of 6,000 Vietnamese civilians. There could be no turning back now. Full, open conflict commenced on 19 December 1946, with a rising in Haiphong heralding the start of the First Indochina War. It took a week of fighting to clear the Viet Minh from the city.

Leclerc immediately found himself summoned by France's new socialist prime minister, Léon Blum, who wanted him to act as his personal representative in Indochina. There he would assess the situation and offer advice. De Gaulle warned Leclerc that this was a purely political appointment that would cause nothing but trouble, but after his first family Christmas in nine years, Leclerc flew back to Indochina.

He was in an impossible position. He had no authority to act as an intermediary with Ho Chi Minh, nor was he military commander. Likewise, his liberal approach was widely frowned upon by Paris and the colonial authorities. Leclerc knew from French history that France had faced similar situations before, under Napoleon I in Spain and Napoleon III in Mexico. He visited both north and south Vietnam and quickly recommended reinforcing the French garrison, knowing full well that France, in the face of the growing Vietnamese insurgency, would have to negotiate from a position of strength.

The American C-47 Skytrain played a key role in the Battle of Dien Bien Phu.

When he returned to France, he was offered the role of military commander in Indochina, but he declined, not wishing to work with the intransigent d'Argenlieu again. Then Ramadier, Blum's successor, even offered him d'Argenlieu's job.

However, Leclerc's conditions were unpalatable, for he wanted an end to direct French provincial administration and negotiations with the Viet Minh. Also, in return for full independence within the French Union, France would retain only a limited military presence. Leclerc argued that full military re-conquest would require 350,000 troops, or 115,000 to negotiate from a position of strength. Either figure was something the French government would not agree to or fund.

Once more, de Gaulle advised Leclerc against taking the post, pointing out that the removal of d'Argenlieu would cause a loss of French prestige. In addition, Leclerc would find himself a scapegoat for all the woes of Indochina. He agreed with de Gaulle and declined the job. Leclerc remarked, 'Colonial empires all have their period of greatness but are destined to disappear sooner or later. Let us hope that ours will disappear in good circumstances.'

It was not to be. As for Leclerc, he was sent to North Africa instead, where he found the situation not disimilar to Indochina. He was killed in late 1947 in a plane crash in Algeria. In Indochina, if the 6 March agreement had been fully honoured by Paris, the disastrous following seven years could have been avoided and the French military not set upon the road to Dien Bien Phu.

French aircraft at Tourane (Dan Nang).

6. FRANCE'S EXPEDITIONARY FORCE

France had a long history of fighting colonial wars and saw Indochina as just another inconvenient colonial revolt that needed to be supressed in the usual manner. This approach was a mistake, but once the Korean War broke out, it was perhaps understandable.

In Korea, the communists had very much gone straight for the conventional-warfare phase. The result was that the French assumed they could bludgeon the Viet Minh into submission through the use of superior strength and firepower. What they did not take into account was the strength of the Viet Minh's ideology. In addition, they were fighting for their country – the French were not.

The spearhead for France reclaiming her colonies was the Foreign Legion. It had a proud and colourful history. During its formative years, the Legion had fought all around the world, including in Indochina. In 1883–84, legionnaires took part in the storming of the forts at Son Tay and Bac Ninh, both held by Chinese irregulars. When the fighting finally came to an end a decade later, the Legion's battalions formed the Régiment de Marche d'Africa au Tonkin, who helped keep the peace largely undisturbed until 1941.

The French Expeditionary Force deployed the U.S. M24 Chafee light tank to Indochina. Its main weapon was a 75mm gun.

France's Expeditionary Force

This tough force fought with distinction during the Second World War. Afterwards, there was no shortage of foreign volunteers trying to escape or forget their troubled pasts. The Legion was happy to turn a blind eye, even to criminals or those who had committed war crimes. During the Indochina war, the Legion's strength would reach 30,000 men. Their training and administrative base at Sidi-bel-Abbès, sixty miles south of Oran in northwest Algeria, in May 1945 started the creation of a *régiment de marche* to be sent to re-occupy Indochina. Most of the Legion contingent in Indochina, numbering 20,000 men, were deployed in Tonkin during the second half of the war. Inevitably, they were to play a key role in the fighting at Dien Bien Phu.

Although the French sought to regain control of Saigon and southern Vietnam in the summer of 1945, it was not until the following March that the French Expeditionary Force was able to enter northern Vietnam. In the meantime, in October 1945, General Leclerc arrived in Saigon with elements of the French 2nd Armoured Division and the 3rd and 9th colonial infantry divisions. They were reinforced by the 2nd Foreign Legion Infantry Regiment (REI) that landed in February 1946, followed by the 13th Foreign Legion Demi Brigade in March and the 3rd Foreign Legion Infantry Regiment between April and June. A 3,000-strong naval brigade was also deployed to patrol Indochina's numerous waterways.

Over the next few years, French parachute units, who were to become famous in Indochina, began to arrive, including the 1st, 2nd and 5th colonial commando parachute battalions (BCCP) and the 1st Chasseurs Parachute Regiment. By the end of 1948, French paras had made forty combat jumps, three of which involved over 1,000 paratroops. The 1st Foreign Legion Parachute Battalion (BEP) arrived late that year and the 1st Indochinese Parachute Company was formed. By mid-1949, the French Union Forces in Vietnam totalled almost 150,000. Most of the fighting, though, was conducted by some 5,700 French paratroops. The most important arrivals that year were the 3rd and 6th BCCP, the 2nd BEP and the 5th REI.

France's colonial forces were always seen as the poorer cousins of the metropolitan French army. In Indochina, this meant that the local commander-in-chief had no autonomy. He was answerable to his military superiors in Paris and his political masters in Paris and Hanoi. Even when the role of commander-in-chief and High Commissioner were combined in 1950 under General Jean de Lattre de Tassigny, political interference continued unabated.

In France, the politicians played to the gallery, with a war that was very unpopular with the electorate. This often led to extraordinarily foolhardy decisions. For example, in 1950, at the point that the Viet Minh were taking the Cao Bang ridge defences, the government cut the size of the forces in Indochina by 9,000 men. Also, to curry favour with the French public, conscripts could only serve in France, Algeria (considered part of France) and French-occupied Germany.

The result of this was that all French citizens sent to Indochina had to be volunteers. Inevitably, this greatly restricted the French contingent. French volunteers never accounted for more than half the total of the French Expeditionary Force – the average was about 52,000, or slightly over a third. What it meant was that the bulk of the ethnic French units bore the brunt of the fighting. They also made up most of the mobile reserve. As mobile infantry, French soldiers travelled in half-tracks, with the support of American-supplied M4 Sherman and M24 Chaffee tanks, as well as armoured cars. Their normal infantry fire power of carbines, sub-machine guns, 60mm and 81mm mortars and .50in heavy machine guns was boosted by artillery. This included 75mm field guns, as well as 105mm and 155mm howitzers.

The paratroop units, which formed the cutting edge of most operations were largely self-contained, though relied on the air force for transport. Initially, transport aircraft were always in short supply. It was not until the early 1950s that American-supplied C-47 Dakotas (or Skytrains) and C-119 'Flying Boxcars' were available to replace the last of the French-built Junkers Ju-52s called Toucans, a hangover from the Second World War. By 1954, the first American-supplied H-19B helicopters also became available.

The French air force's main role, as well as supplying the ground forces, was to provide direct support, especially for troops in contact. Principal aircraft included American B-26 Marauder bombers and F8F Bearcat fighters, along with Canadian-built Beaver and French Morane 500 Cricket reconnaissance aircraft. The French navy provided coastal fire support and river patrols, along with Privateer maritime bombers and F4U Corsair fighters.

The paucity of French regulars meant deploying colonial troops from other parts of the French Union. Throughout the conflict, Algerian, Moroccan, Tunisian and Senegalese troops served in Indochina. Commanded by French officers, they were organized and equipped the same as French regulars. One exception to this rule was the Algerian units. Due to Algeria being considered part of metropolitan France, they were allowed native officers although Algerian losses were lumped in with the 15,000 North Africans killed in Indochina – indicating they were not truly considered 'French'.

At the close of 1952, there were around 175,000 troops in Indochina, comprising 54,000 French, 30,000 North Africans, 18,000 Africans, 20,000 Legionnaires and 53,000 Indochinese. The French air force deployed 10,000 personnel and the navy 5,000. Local national forces were also quite sizeable. At Dien Bien Phu, nearly half the members of 2nd Battalion, 1st Parachute Light Infantry, were Vietnamese.

The French arrived in Indochina with a very wide variety of weapons because of the post-war French army's reliance on America and Britain for arms. One of the most common was the U.S. M1 carbine. The selective-fire M2 and folding-stock M1A1 were also used by French paras. Rifles included the American M1 Garand, British SMLE, French MAS-36, and its folding-stock derivative, the MAS-36CR39 paratrooper carbine. In the early stages, the French fought with the American M1A1 Thompson and M3 'Grease-gun' sub-machine guns as well as the British Sten. By the 1950s, the French-made MAT-49 had largely replaced these.

The standard squad-level light machine gun was the French FM24/29, which first saw combat in Morocco in 1926. French forces also employed the British Bren light machine gun. Legionnaires deployed to Indochina in 1946 with the Bren Mk III, though this again was eventually replaced with French-made weapons. Support weapons such as heavy machine guns, mortars and recoilless rifles tended to be of American manufacture. Ironically, the Viet Minh were armed by China with American weapons captured in Korea, which were usually newer models than the French had, who were reliant on Second World War surplus.

The French employed Second World War vintage tanks and armoured fighting vehicles. The standard tank of the French Expeditionary Force was the American M5A1 light tank, although it was superseded by the American M24 Chaffee from 1944 onwards under

France's Expeditionary Force

As well as a coaxial .30 calibre machine gun, French Bisons were armed with a .50 calibre heavy machine gun.

the U.S. Military Aid Program. It remained in service throughout the war. The Chaffees were dubbed 'Bisons' by the French troops, while the Viet Minh knew them as 'Oxen'.

The French also employed the ubiquitous American M4 Sherman medium tank, M36B2 tank destroyer and M8 self-propelled howitzers. Motorized infantry was transported in M3 half-tracks. The M8 variant of the latter, mounting a 75mm gun, was also used in Indochina. The tank destroyers were initially deployed in case the Chinese committed armour to the fighting in Tonkin, but instead they ended up acting in a fire-support role.

To support amphibious operations in Indochina's flooded paddy fields vast river deltas and swamps, the expeditionary force operated American M29C Weasel amphibian cargo carriers (known to the French as 'Crabes') and tracked landing vehicles known as the Alligator. Both were likewise veterans of the Second World War. The LVT(A)4, armed with a 75mm howitzer, packed a particular punch. The Crabes, although only armed with a machine gun, were eventually formed into effective amphibious fighting units by the Foreign Legion, who likewise used the LVTs.

At the start of the fighting, the tanks were parcelled out in penny packets to protect vulnerable convoys and static outposts. This made them difficult to maintain, thereby reducing their effectiveness. Only after General de Lattre de Tassigny took charge in 1951 were the armoured units reorganized with their own supporting infantry. This led to the creation of the *sous-groupement blindé*, comprising a squadron of tanks and two mechanized infantry companies, and a *groupement mobile* with up to three battalions of infantry, an artillery battery and up to a squadron of tanks.

France attempted to tap into the huge manpower of Indochina, but the French were wary of training a fifth column and local units were never fully trusted. It did not help that the Vietnamese and Cambodians were traditional enemies. The Vietnamese viewed the Chinese in much the same manner. General de Lattre, in 1951, instructed each French unit in Vietnam to form a locally recruited second battalion. He also opened an officer cadet school, followed by two more for reserve officers.

A small Vietnamese National Army was formed under French command, along with anti-guerrilla units raised particularly among the mountain tribes. By 1952, the Vietnamese National Army numbered 50,000 men, the Laotian army 15,000 and the Cambodian army another 10,000. Although the full potential of these Indochinese forces was never realized, some 27,000 Indochinese died fighting for the French.

French training efforts for local Vietnamese units were concentrated in the north. In late 1948, they established the Vietnamese National Military Academy in the city of Hue. This was designed to train infantry platoon leaders with a nine-month officers' course. It moved to Dalat two years later because of better local weather. The latter was home to the armour school, but this moved to Thu Duc, along with the engineer school. By the end of 1951, there were 800 Vietnamese officers serving.

The French infantry were also armed with the American .30 calibre medium machine gun.

The French also set up the national non-commissioned officers' academy in Quang Yen Province, Tonkin, in 1951. The following year, this was followed by a staff college in Hanoi. This was as a result of the French Expeditionary Force setting up a tactical instruction centre, designed to train mobile group, battalion and company commanders. Notably, intelligence and logistics schools were not established until the late 1950s. This was to prove to be a serious omission on the part of the French.

French forces in Indochina included a postscript from Korea. The French Bataillon de Corée (Korea Battalion), which was raised from volunteers from all branches of the French army, metropolitan, colonial and Foreign Legion to serve in Korea, arrived in Indochina in October 1953. This formed the cadre of the two-battalion-strong Régiment de Corée. This was practically destroyed in the central Highlands, around An Khe and Pleiku, while serving with the Groupe Mobile 100 in June–July 1954.

The French logistical supply chain, stretching all the way back to Algeria and France, proved to be the expeditionary force's Achilles heel. In Paris, the war was not a priority. Many either did not support it or simply saw it as an overblown police operation. Shipping or flying ammunition and weapons to Indochina was lengthy and expensive, and was again unpopular for this reason.

Once in-country, the high command in Hanoi struggled to distribute supplies to the troops. In the immediate Red River Delta area around Hanoi, and indeed in the south, it was not such a problem, but getting supplies to the outlying garrisons and large operations was another matter.

The French were reliant on two methods of supporting their soldiers. The first was land-based, using the roads and rivers. Whilst this was relatively easy to do, both were always very vulnerable to ambush. Viet Minh attacks on supply barges on the Black River trying to reach the garrison at Hao Binh contributed to General Salan's decision to abandon the town. French airlift capabilities were simply not sufficient. Initially, they had to rely on old Ju-52s, but even with the arrival of newer C-47s and C-119s, they could never muster more than 100 transport planes. They were required to run supply flights, move reinforcements and drop paratroops. By the time of Dien Bien Phu, they were stretched to the limit.

7. THE HAND OF MAO

By 1949, French intelligence in Paris was increasingly concerned about how the war against communism in China was going. Despite being equipped with millions of dollars of American weapons, Chiang Kai-shek's nationalists were rapidly losing. The city of Hsuchow (Xuzhou) on the North China Plain was in the news bulletins for all the wrong reasons. Chiang was defeated in Manchuria in 1948, with the loss of 30,000 soldiers and all of their equipment. By the end of the year, his remaining armies were completely cut off at Hsuchow.

Chiang was betrayed by General Liu Fei, his military assistant, who revealed the nationalists' strategy to the enemy. On 10 January 1949, some 320,000 nationalist troops were forced to surrender south of Hsuchow. This meant that the communists could march down the Yangtze River, which runs through the very heart of southern China. Ten days later, with his government in chaos, Chiang resigned as president of the Chinese Republic. In April and May, the communists entered Nanking on the Yangtze, and then Shanghai. Once the nationalists were looking to flee to the island of Formosa (Taiwan), it was only a matter of time before Mao's four-million-strong People's Liberation Army reached the border with Indochina.

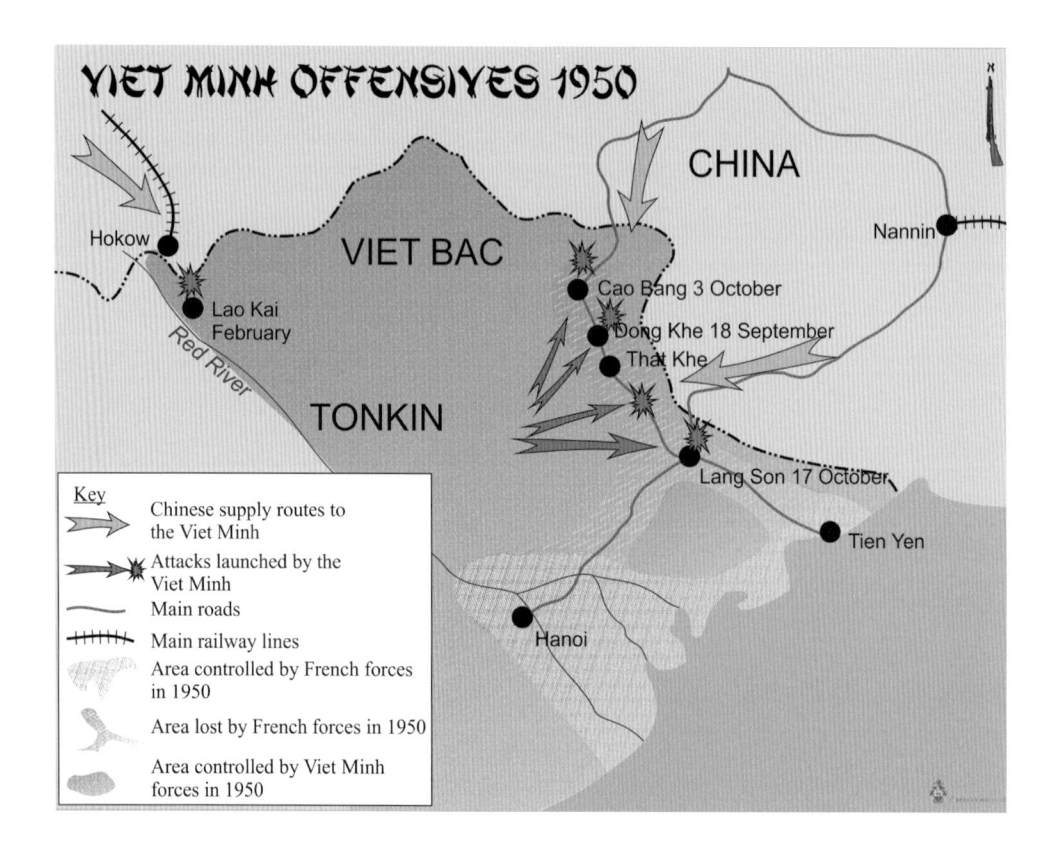

The Hand of Mao

The French military were now taking the situation in Indochina very seriously. France's most senior soldier, General Georges Revers, Chief of the General Staff, flew to Indochina in May 1949 to assess the situation in person. He and his fellow generals knew that Mao's imminent victory would drastically transform the status quo in the region. During his briefings in Saigon and Hanoi, it soon became apparent that once Mao was up against the border backing the Viet Minh, the French military would be unable to hold the frontier.

Revers's report recommended that Lao Kai on the Red River in northern Tonkin, which was particularly isolated, and the Cao Bang-Lang Son ridge on the border northeast of Hanoi, be abandoned, rather than needlessly sacrificing the scattered garrisons. The units could be better used in strengthening the Red River Delta defences. Lao Kai was sometimes referred to as 'the gateway to China'. The delta, General Revers reasoned, would provide a base to conduct pacification operations, followed by a counter-offensive into the Viet Minh's heartland in the Viet Bac.

Revers made an astute strategic assessment that was largely ignored by the politicians. He had accurately predicted Giap's forthcoming campaign. Despite Revers's recommendations, it was felt that the Cao Bang-Lang Son ridge could not be abandoned, because it sat astride Route Coloniale 4. All the time that it was occupied, it prevented Chinese aid from reaching Giap in Viet Bac. This ignored Revers's assessment that the ridge could not be held in the face of a concerted attack.

Although the French had reinserted themselves into Indochina and its major cities, they never really took control of the surrounding countryside. In reality, their authority was confined to the main towns and the roads connecting them and the outlying forts. Even in their Tonkin heartland around Hanoi, guerrilla activity and intelligence gathering by Ho Chi Minh's forces remained unchecked.

The key to the defence of Hanoi and the port of Haiphong was the Red River Delta. Both sides were well aware of this. It shaped their strategic thinking and was to dominate the war until Dien Bien Phu. Giap's immediate task, as predicted, was to secure the very long frontier with China, which ran all the way from the junction with the Laotian border in the northwest, and to the Gulf of Tonkin in the northeast. This would ensure the free flow of Chinese instructors, weapons and ammunition. The campaigning season was limited, so he needed to act before the rains from May to October 1950 severely hampered mobility.

General Wei Guo-qing, leading a Chinese military advisory group some 280 strong, arrived in April 1950. Their role was to guide Ho Chi Minh on the best tactics and strategy to use against the French. It is not entirely clear just how much influence they had, but the size of the group suggests that it was quite considerable. Wei no doubt espoused Mao's doctrine of 'man-over-weapons' to defeat superior French firepower. As manpower was never a problem, the Chinese Communists were advocates of the 'human-wave' tactic, whereby an enemy was simply swamped and overrun. In Indochina, this was to flounder in the face of the French air force's guns, bombs and napalm.

Giap massed fourteen infantry and three artillery battalions with which to attack the French border forts. He struck first at Lao Kai, not far from the Chinese border, in February 1950. The small French garrison found themselves being bombarded by heavy mortars before being overrun. Then, northeast of Hanoi, he attacked the vulnerable Cao Bang-Lang Son ridge. Both these two towns, between which were French posts at

French troops coming ashore on the coast of Annam, July 1950.

Dong Khe and That Khe, sat astride two different roads from China. These in turn were linked by the road that ran south all the way to the French-held port of Tien Yen.

On 25 May 1950, the Viet Minh took the sandbagged outpost at Dong Khe, midway along the ridge, wiping out two companies of North African troops. This was a typical fort, built on a hilltop after the jungle had been cleared from the summit. Giap employed four battalions, supported by small artillery pieces and mortars to overcome the 800-strong garrison. It was the first time that the Viet Minh used the Chinese human-wave tactic. However, his men had to withdraw two days later, when a French parachute battalion arrived on the scene.

In July, General Chen Geng arrived from China at the request of Ho Chi Minh to help with Wei's advisory group. This again indicates that Mao was exerting some considerable influence on the conduct of the war in Indochina. Chen also encouraged Ho and Giap to renew their efforts to take the border forts. At the end of the year, he was to depart for Korea, leaving Wei in charge.

Both sides waited for the summer rains to ease before fighting resumed. By this stage, General Marcel Carpentier, commander-in-chief of the French Expeditionary Force, had about 10,000 troops protecting the scattered forts on the ridge. Giap singled out Dong Khe once again, encircling it with his artillery and mortars. The Viet Minh 174th Regiment built a full-scale replica not far away to facilitate lengthy and detailed training. Nothing was left to chance.

Two companies of legionnaires from the 3rd Foreign Legion Regiment, some 260 men, who were holding Dong Khe were shelled all day on 16 September 1950. They only had two artillery pieces, consisting of a 75mm gun and a 105mm howitzer with which to reply.

Then at dusk, six Viet Minh battalions swarmed forward under covering mortar fire. Desperate hand-to-hand fighting followed. They had killed or wounded 140 of the defenders and driven them out of three of their four sandbagged positions by the following night. The legionnaires put up a heroic defence, but were finally overwhelmed on 18 September. A relief column formed by the Legion's elite 1st Parachute Battalion, who were dropped at nearby That Khe, were ambushed and driven off.

The garrison at Cao Bang at the northern end of the ridge was now cut off from its delta support. General Carpentier finally conceded that Route Coloniale 4 could not be held. On 3 October, it was decided to evacuate Cao Bang. The 1,500 retreating troops and accompanying civilian refugees, however, had first to get past Viet Minh-held Dong Khe to reach That Khe and Lang Son. What followed was a disaster. Despite the French air force flying 844 sorties in support, the French suffered very heavy losses. French pilots were hampered by low cloud and ground mist that helped conceal the Viet Minh's movements.

On 9 October, the withdrawing garrison, plus a 3,500-strong relief force from That Khe, were both separately ambushed and scattered. The two four-battalion-strong French columns were soon surrounded by thirty Viet Minh battalions and overwhelmed. The two columns never managed to meet on the road, and when some of the survivors regrouped, they were attacked for a third time. All order vanished, and the French lost

General Jean de Lattre de Tassigny, third from the right, following the liberation of Marseilles in 1944.

about 4,000 men in the surrounding jungle. A parachute battalion was annihilated while conducting rear-guard actions. Lang Son was abandoned by Carpentier. Likewise, the 2nd and 3rd battalions of the Legion's 3rd Regiment were severely mauled.

By 17 October 1950, all the forts had fallen, resulting in 6,000 French casualties. Giap had secured a strategically important piece of border territory, as well as capturing enough French weapons for an entire division. These included 9,200 rifles, 900 machine guns, 125 mortars and 13 heavy guns, as well as 450 trucks. French morale was crushed, and a wave of alarm passed through the French military and civilian population in Indochina. When the news reached Paris, it was greeted with a mixture of despair and outrage. Heads had to roll. The government's response was to sack both High Commissioner Léon Pignon and General Carpentier.

The French hold on northern Tonkin, Hanoi and the Red River Delta was now precarious. In France, the war was increasingly disliked, with the Cold War in Europe a national preoccupation. The wounded from Indochina were routed home through provincial airports lest they be greeted by hostile demonstrators in Paris. Conscripts could not go

De Lattre, joint Commander-in-Chief and High Commissioner, Indochina.

unless they specifically volunteered, but most were deterred from doing so by a lack of faith in the conflict and by understandably anxious parents. There was an atmosphere of tension, with supplies for Indochina being sabotaged on French trains and in ports. Even getting donated blood out to the troops was problematic. France's communists were opposed to the war, and there were dark mutterings that they were behind the disruption.

The Viet Minh's supply routes from China were now secure, meaning they were now in a position to confront the French with much greater strength than before. Heartened by his victory, Ho Chi Minh boasted that he would be in Hanoi within a matter of weeks. Giap was encouraged to go over to the 'open-battle' phase of their grand strategy. They planned to launch an all-out assault on the delta region, with a view to overwhelming the remaining French strongholds, which would isolate Hanoi and force the French out. What they had not bargained for, however, was the arrival of General Jean de Lattre de Tassigny as joint High Commissioner and commander-in-chief in December 1950.

De Lattre, like de Gaulle, was a war hero and a keeper of the faith. Like de Gaulle, he was autocratic, but he loved his men. He had led the French First Army during the liberation of the Riviera and the long march into southern Germany. This force had included the veteran Algerian and Moroccan divisions. They were the saviours of Strasbourg and Colmar. De Lattre first arrived back on liberated French soil on 16 August 1944 with his 16-year-old son Bernard. De Gaulle had granted the boy special permission to join the army and his father. The diminutive general was photographed with his young son proudly towering over him. During his early career, de Lattre senior had fought at Verdun and during France's wars in Morocco. He was exactly what Indochina's demoralized garrison needed.

In truth, de Lattre was not the first choice for such a difficult mission. Other veteran generals had been approached. Juin, busy in Morocco, had declined, while Koenig said he would only go if the Indochina garrison was bolstered with conscripts. De Lattre was serving as NATO's land forces commander, under General Dwight Eisenhower as Allied Supreme Commander, with Field Marshal Bernard Montgomery as Eisenhower's deputy. It was not an easy relationship, especially as the other two always saw themselves as the dominant military partners.

General de Lattre was very much a French version of Montgomery, and putting them together was never a good idea. It was a titanic clash of egos. Their relationship was so tumultuous it was almost to the point of outright hatred. Their squabbles over the chain of command for the Western European Union were so corrosive that it eventually helped derail France's commitment to NATO. De Lattre was serving as Inspector General of the French armed forces when Montgomery got him appointed commander WEU land forces. Once in post, he would not recognize Montgomery's authority, which led to very public accusations of disloyalty.

Eventually, after a particularly unpleasant confrontation on 10 May 1950, a weeping de Lattre was reconciled with Montgomery. Before his departure for Indochina, de Lattre had tea with Montgomery, who was celebrating his sixty-third birthday. He was touched when the old field marshal cut an extra piece of cake for Bernard de Lattre, who was already serving in Indochina. Whatever their differences, they were brothers-in-arms and they understood each other.

The young Minister for Overseas Territories, François Mitterrand, warned the 62-year-old de Lattre that Indochina would be a poisoned chalice. He cautioned that it could wreck his health and his reputation. Certainly, at that stage in his life, de Lattre did not need this appointment. No doubt he was astute enough to realize that the fighting in Indochina would swing on the pendulum of the escalating Korean War and the meddling of China. Washington had made it clear that it would not tolerate the spread of communism down the Korean peninsula, whatever the cost. Many senior French officers saw Indochina as another front in the same war. The Soviet Union, China, and communism in general wherever they raised their heads, needed to be contained.

Nonetheless, de Lattre had two good reasons for going. Firstly, Lieutenant Bernard de Lattre was there and writing home with very frank assessments of what was happening on the ground. Bernard, like his father, was a soldier through and through. During the Second World War, he had been wounded, earning the Médaille Militaire and the Croix de Guerre. Secondly, every year hundreds of young officers coming out of the Saint Cyr military academy were being killed in Indochina. On 23 October 1950, Bernard had written to his mother: 'Tell Father we need him, without him it will go wrong.' What father could refuse such an appeal from his son? De Lattre felt he could make a difference.

De Lattre did not go alone, for he summoned many of his wartime comrades. He needed men he could trust and rely on. From his 1944–45 staff, he took generals Allard and Salan, and colonels Beaufre and Cogny. They also rallied others, such as General de Linarès, who was already in-country. Great pomp and ceremony was made of de Lattre's arrival in Saigon, where he pointedly ignored his disgraced predecessor, General Carpentier. Once in Hanoi, he reviewed the troops and then addressed his staff. He said it was for the young officers that he had accepted this challenging assignment.

There were no promises on the table. Paris offered no reinforcements, and de Lattre could provide no easy victories. What he could promise them was firm leadership. De Lattre knew from Bernard that among the many shortcomings of the French army in Indochina, there was a lack of firm and purposeful command. This bred poor morale and it was something that had to be addressed immediately – the removal of Carpentier was a start. As well as this, de Lattre knew that his immediate task was to hold the Viet Minh at bay while the Red River Delta defences were strengthened.

Salan was appointed deputy commander for northern Tonkin and de Linarès deputy commander of the delta area. The field command was divided into three divisions and the headquarters reorganized to improve civil/military liaison. While making his preparations, de Lattre lobbied for reinforcements but they would take time to reach him. Everything now hung in the balance.

8. BATTLE FOR THE RED RIVER

In the meantime, Giap was so close to Hanoi that he could not help himself, and decided to cut through the town of Vinh Yen just 65km northwest of the city. Once on the Red River, he could thrust southward. This, Giap and Ho assured themselves, would ensure a swift victory. They gathered a large force of some 22,000 men, comprising the 308th and 312th Viet Minh divisions. In total, there were over twenty-five battalion-size Viet Minh units. Giap, though, made the fatal mistake of making a direct assault on Hanoi without launching any diversionary attacks to dissipate French strength.

Although the French were seriously outnumbered, de Lattre prepared his defences at Vinh Yen very well. He had a thin protective screen of dug-in infantry before the town, inside there was a mobile group, while a second mobile force was deployed to the south, ready to counterattack. The first consisted mainly of North Africans, while the other comprised Senegalese and Muong tribesmen. In total, de Lattre could field only about 7,000 men.

On 13 January 1951, the Viet Minh swiftly pushed the screening French infantry back, moving into the hills between Vinh Yen and the south bank of the Red River. The French outpost at Bao Chuc was overrun without difficulty. The following day, when the first mobile group moved forward to reinforce the infantry at Bao Chuc, it was ambushed. Heavy losses were suffered, but the North Africans fought bravely and the survivors managed to pull back. The Viet Minh's massed human-wave attacks carried them forward towards their objective.

Bison tanks in paddy fields engaging Viet Minh positions.

Despite Viet Minh fighters being within 1,000yd of the airstrip, de Lattre flew into Vinh Yen in a rickety-looking spotter plane to take command on 14 January. His chief of staff was aghast at the great personal risk the French commander-in-chief was taking and radioed his disapproval. De Lattre's response was, 'Well then, come and get me out.'

His presence, though, immediately boosted morale and ensured that the garrison received the resources it needed to repel the enemy. While the second mobile group moved forward, he ordered a massive airlift of reinforcements from as far south as Cochinchina. Allard, the chief transport officer, had to conduct a three-day air-and-road redeployment to bolster the defences. In the air, he could muster just fifteen elderly transports.

An opening east of Vinh Yen could have been exploited by the Viet Minh, but Giap lost his opportunity. Thanks to the vigour brought by de Lattre, and the growing strength of the French air force, the Vinh Yen defences were hurriedly consolidated, while the Viet Minh were held in the hills for twenty-four hours. When Giap opened his attack on 16 January with the 308th Division, his men were cut to pieces as they surged forward in massed human waves. De Lattre recklessly flew over the battlefield in his spotter plane, assessing the situation and directing fire.

He quickly decided to summon almost every combat aircraft available in Indochina and to commit the last of his reserves in an effort to thwart Giap. The following day, a newly formed mobile group, consisting of two Moroccan and one para battalion, joined the fight with considerable air support. The French air force played its part, dropping napalm for the first time on a large scale on 17 January to break up the Viet Minh attacks. The blistering heat incinerated those caught in the open, leaving a trail of charred and smouldering corpses. Those on the periphery, their uniforms ablaze, ran screaming until shot down, or they could roll in the soil to smother the searing flames. It was a hideous sight, but it had the desired effect.

Undeterred, Giap renewed his attack, using the 312th Division. They were stopped in their tracks by French fighter-bombers, again using napalm. Nonetheless, the pointless fighting continued well into the afternoon of the 17th. Two days later, it was all over. The Viet Minh had suffered some 5,000 casualties, comprising 1,600 fatalities, at least 3,000 wounded, and 480 captured. To his dismay, Giap had thrown away his opportunity to end the war. The French lost 43 killed, 160 wounded, and 545 missing or captured.

The Viet Minh had come very close to overrunning Vinh Yen, but that was little solace for such heavy losses. Once the French air force was committed in strength and dropping napalm, Giap should have saved more of his men by calling a halt to the attack and withdrawing. Instead, he very clearly signalled that he was prepared to sacrifice his men to achieve his goals. Giap had every faith in their morale and their commitment to the fight for independence, even to the death.

Vinh Yen provided a much-needed boost for the morale of the men of the French Expeditionary Force, proving to Paris that de Lattre was indeed the man for the job. He concluded that prepared defences, backed by mobile reserves and air power, was the best way to defeat the Viet Minh fighting a conventional war. This conclusion would shape French strategy and lead to Dien Bien Phu four years later.

During the battle at Vinh Yen, de Lattre called on Emperor Bao Dai, requesting more Vietnamese units and, with his candidate, for a new Vietnamese defence minister. Bao was not receptive, but after the French victory, he instructed his prime minister, Tran Van Huu, to dissolve the government and form a new one, including de Lattre's defence

Battle for the Red River

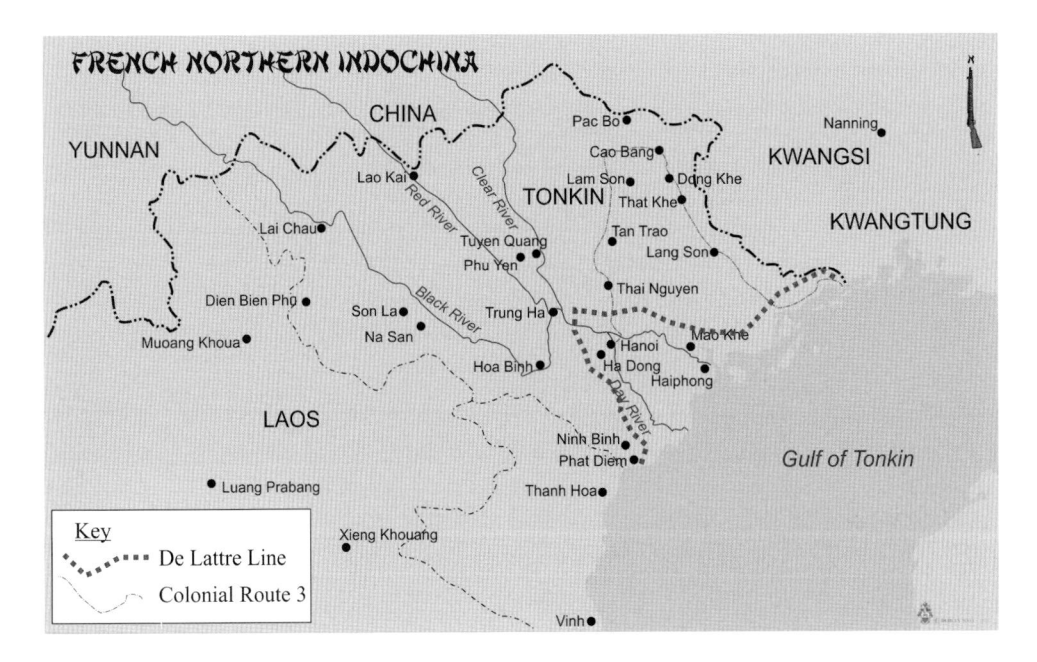

minister candidate, Nguyen Huu Tri. In a message to the Vietnamese, Bao made no mention of the French success, while the enraged de Lattre brazenly held a victory parade in order to salute his men. The Vietnamese government soon broke down, for which de Lattre held the emperor responsible.

De Lattre, now riding high with public and political opinion, understandably renewed his call for reinforcements. He asked Paris to provide twelve infantry battalions, and five artillery units plus support. This was met with opposition and much hand-wringing over how it would be funded. The accountants went to work, seeking to make savings. After much haggling, it was agreed that he could have nine battalions and three artillery units for just eighteen months. De Lattre was probably quietly pleased because, like any good general, he would have asked for more than he expected to receive. Paris also managed to persuade Washington to provide financial aid to pay for French military purchases, especially the equipment for new Vietnamese units. The only drawback was that the money would not be available until the autumn.

Elsewhere, the successes against Viet Minh operations in Amman, Cochinchina, Cambodia and Laos, released French troops for the more fiercely contested delta area. Also, some units were replaced by the newly formed Vietnamese battalions. In Tonkin, de Lattre could muster 68,500 French Union and 18,000 Vietnamese soldiers. In stark contrast, Giap had around 170,000, including 112 battalions, each over 900 strong.

De Lattre decided to fly to Paris to press his case for more men, but twice he had to postpone his departure. The first delay was caused by the Vietnamese government crisis, the second by the fall of the Pleven government in Paris. Unfortunately for de Lattre, Pleven's successor, Queuille, saw the strengthening of the defence of Europe as a key priority in the face of the Red menace over more costly resources for Indochina. The only alternative in Europe was the rearmament of Germany, and no one was ready for that.

53

Morane-Saulniet Cricket spotter plane. General de Lattre landed at Vinh Yen aboard one of these aircraft.

To compound de Lattre's difficulties, the situation in Morocco and Tunisia was a growing cause for concern. It was at this point that his health began to decline due to painful problems with his right hip.

Giap was facing his own issues. The French victory at Vinh Yen had encouraged the creation of the defensive 'De Lattre Line' around the Red River Delta. The French set about constructing some 1,200 concrete blockhouses, running from Ha Long Bay, across to Vinh Yen, and then southeast to Phat Diem. While the rationale for these fortifications was self-evident, they signalled that the French were intent on tying down more of their troops, and that the defences were pointless if the areas behind them could not be pacified. De Lattre hoped that the blockhouses could be manned by local troops, while mixed French-Vietnamese commando units were developed as mobile strike groups to hunt down the Viet Minh. The military authorities were not keen on this combination, having little faith in the loyalty of Vietnamese soldiers.

To pre-empt the De Lattre Line, Giap had little option but to renew his offensive. As his attack to the north of Hanoi had failed, he shifted his efforts to the small town of Mao Khe, just 32km north of Haiphong. While the main attack was towards the port, it appears that the assault was to be supported by an insurgency behind French lines, intended to destabilize the whole of the delta. If Giap got to Haiphong, it would cause de Lattre major supply problems.

Giap was unable to hide his considerable preparations in the massif near Dong Trieu, which involved three divisions. His deception plans failed to work and the French were fully aware of the presence of five Viet Minh brigades (or small divisions), plus a large force of supporting coolie labour. When his assault commenced on the night of 23 March 1951, it had some success against the French outer defences. Three days later, Mao Khe was in danger as the 316th Viet Minh Division massed, ready to overwhelm the defenders. A bombardment by French naval vessels on the Do Bac River, however, caused the force to disperse, delaying the attack. On the 27th, the Viet Minh launched a massed assault on

PostScript

Books by mail since 1987

up to 75% off publishers' prices

Thank you for your order

We hope that you enjoy your books. Our aim is to share new, unusual and almost-forgotten titles with as many fellow readers as possible, at affordable prices. Thanks to our long-standing relationships with hundreds of publishers we are able to pass on discounts of **up to 75% off publishers' prices.**

Refer a Friend and you both receive 20% off your order

Visit your 'My Account' area online to access and share your unique 20% off referral link. As a thank you from us, you will receive 20% off every time a friend makes a first purchase. For full details on our Refer a Friend programme visit www.psbooks.co.uk/refer

www.psbooks.co.uk
Free UK delivery on orders over £25 online*
(*offer only available on orders placed online using standard delivery. This offer can be used in conjunction with other offer codes)

Order line: 01625 897100 (8am-6pm, Mon-Fri)

feefo
Over 8,600 reviews

up to 75% off publishers' prices

Have you tried the Postscript website?

• Browse Postscript's full range of almost 10,000 discounted titles online at www.psbooks.co.uk

• Access exclusive offers, such as 3 for 2 promotions – only available online

• New titles and old favourites which have returned to stock are added regularly, giving online customers access to titles before they appear in a catalogue

• Our 'Recommended for you' function offers suggestions based on the genres, authors and publishers in your previous orders

• Almost Gone pages help ensure you don't miss out on titles that are in limited supply

Free UK delivery on orders over £25 online*

www.psbooks.co.uk
Order line: 01626 897100
(8am-6pm, Mon-Fri)

Postscript Books Ltd., 6 Battle Road, Heathfield, Newton Abbot, Devon TQ12 6RY

Our green packaging

Our commitment to sustainability includes how we produce our catalogues and despatch your books:

• Our catalogue is printed in the UK on paper from sustainably managed forests and is not shrink-wrapped; and many of our in-house Postscript Collections use simple paper bands rather than plastic wrapping

• All orders are despatched in recyclable cardboard boxes, eco-friendly bubblewrap and solvent-free labels, paper and tape

What our customers say

feefo
★★★★★

4.8/5 based on over 8,600 customer ratings

"Easy and quick transaction. Very satisfied buyer."
Firstly, I enjoyed reading their catalogue so that instead of buying one book for a present I bought another for myself. The books arrived very quickly and were well packaged. Ordering them was easy, a really uncomplicated transaction. Thank you.

"Excellent value"
Person on the phone was helpful and friendly. The order arrived within a few days. The books are such good value and my book club members always rate the books highly. Great value and postage is reasonable.

Battle for the Red River

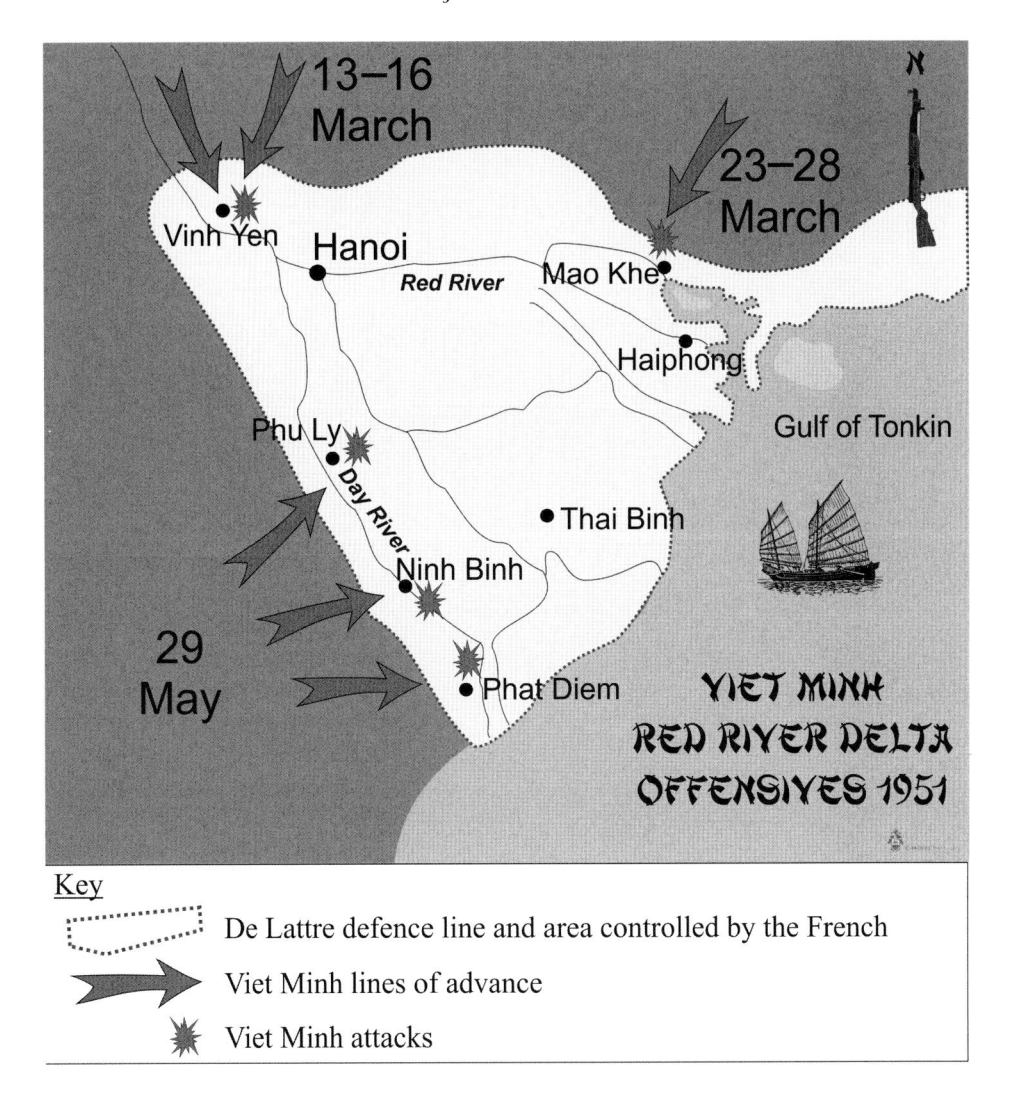

VIET MINH RED RIVER DELTA OFFENSIVES 1951

Key
- De Lattre defence line and area controlled by the French
- Viet Minh lines of advance
- Viet Minh attacks

French defences outside Mao Khe. Although there were some breakthroughs, the town was held.

De Lattre arrived back in Hanoi from Paris, feeling feverish and despondent. Once briefed, he quickly appreciated that Mao Khe, as it was at the exit from the massif, was the key to the battle. Reinforcements were sent up the river, arriving just as the Viet Minh had gained a foothold in the northern edge of the town. The enemy were thrown out and their advance temporarily halted.

Night air reconnaissance, used for the first time, and other intelligence suggested that the Viet Minh had retreated and abandoned any follow-up plans. De Lattre, however, was not convinced, surmising that the Viet Minh were using effective camouflage to hide their movements. He refused to redeploy his forces at Mao Khe, electing instead to place the troops on high alert.

The U.S. first supplied Grumman F8F-1 Bearcat fighter-bombers such as these to the French in Indochina in January 1951. (Photo U.S. Navy)

Just as de Lattre had anticipated, on 28 March 1951, Giap threw his 316th Division into the assault. There was no subtlety in the attack. Human waves launched by twelve 1,000-strong units, were met by artillery, fighter-bombers and warships. Some of the attackers reached the wire, where they were mown down by French small-arms and machine-gun fire. Their bodies lay snagged in the wire like rag dolls, creating a path for those fortunate enough to have survived the deluge of firepower.

Those men who got past the wire, were engaged in vicious hand-to-hand combat. Pistols were fired at close quarter, rifles were used as clubs, bayonets as daggers. The Viet Minh were eventually beaten off with heavy losses. Afterwards, French and Vietnamese troops picked through the scattered, blood-splattered bodies. In five days of fighting, Giap's men suffered 3,000 casualties. It was yet another French victory, thanks to superior firepower and superb defensive tactics.

De Lattre did not wait for Giap to try again. Instead, he moved swiftly to stamp out the insurgency behind his lines in the delta. He ordered his first major sweep with Operation Méduse in mid-April 1951. This, under the local command of de Linarès, and involving three mobile groups, was an unqualified success. His second, Operation Reptile, proved

Vought AU-1 Corsair fighters on the USS *Saipan* being delivered to the Aéronautique Navale at Tourane (Da Nang), 1954. (Photo R.H. Spanioer)

less successful, the French thwarted in part by the Viet Minh guerrillas' ability to blend in with local communities at will.

De Lattre's forces overran training bases and propaganda centres, and disrupted Viet Minh organization. Catching the fighters, however, remained another matter. To stop the guerrillas taking up arms again required a permanent military presence. He knew he had to conduct a hearts-and-minds campaign to sway the population who were caught in the middle.

After Vinh Yen, de Lattre took the Vietnamese prime minister to the scene of the battle, where he reaffirmed that the role of the French army in Vietnam was to secure a lasting independence. Otherwise, he warned, Indochina would fall to communism. He also took great pleasure in presenting Bernard de Lattre with his second Croix de Guerre after his conduct during the latest round of fighting.

De Lattre now felt that he could take time out, so he flew to Singapore to discuss the communist threat to Southeast Asia with the British and the Americans. Whilst the latter were sympathetic to the struggle against communism in Indochina, neither offered troops, even in the event of full intervention by Mao. Both countries had more than enough of their own troubles. De Lattre was about to follow up the conference with a visit to Washington to speed up American material and financial support, when the unbowed Giap struck yet again.

9. VICTORY ON THE DAY RIVER

Following Vinh Yen and Mao Khe, Giap was forced to reassess his flawed strategy. His direct assaults on Hanoi and Haiphong had failed, so he now concentrated his efforts to the south on the Day River. If he could seize this area, it would tie down de Lattre's reserves prior to a renewed effort on the Red River. The French commander in this area, Colonel Gambiez, was half expecting an attack, as this was a fertile part of the delta and the rice crop was approaching harvest. Giap appreciated that, this time, it was vital that the French were distracted from his main operation.

De Lattre and his commanders were therefore kept preoccupied. During April, the French had been kept busy by the Viet Minh 312th Division. This masked the redeployment of the 304th and 308th divisions, who marched to the South Delta Base to join the 320th Division. Giap planned to use them to strike at Phu Ly, Ninh Binh and Phat Diem on the meandering Day River. He proposed to repeat the tactics used for Dong Trieu, with a two-division frontal assault, and a third attacking the flank, while guerrilla operations created mayhem in the rear areas.

The weight of the attack conducted by the 304th and 308th divisions was to fall upon Ninh Binh and Phu Ly. This was designed to tie up French reserves, while, to the south, the 320th Division crossed the river at Phat Diem, linking up with a regiment that had infiltrated French lines a few days before. A move towards the coast near Thai Bin would sever the southern provinces of the delta. This would stop the French moving waterborne reinforcements north, leaving their flank exposed. In principle, it was a very sound plan.

Giap opened his operation on 29 May 1951, with the 304th and 308th divisions crossing the Day River to attack their objectives. In the process, they destroyed a number of French outposts and several gunboats. Late in the afternoon, the 320th Division also crossed the river in sampans at two points, directly opposite Phat Diem and to the southeast. Due to the rains, they soon became bogged down.

De Lattre reacted with characteristic decisiveness. Eight mobile groups and two para units met the Viet Minh. French bombs and shells rained down on the frontal assaults, soon bringing the assailants to a halt. On the water, French river patrols moved to cut the Viet Minh supply lines, sinking any vessels they came upon.

On 30 May, in his moment of triumph, de Lattre's chief of staff brought him some devastating news. Bernard de Lattre, at the age of 23, had just been killed at Ninh Binh. He was told how his son was in his command post on a rocky outcrop with a French lieutenant and two corporals, one French and one Vietnamese, when mortar fire had rained directly down on them. All the occupants were killed or wounded. Out of some eighty marine commandos of the 3rd Naval Assault Division who also fought in defence of Ninh Binh, just nineteen survived.

De Lattre was beside himself with grief. He arranged for a Catholic mass for Bernard in Hanoi Cathedral. Two days later, he flew his son's body home to France, an act that attracted much criticism in the French media. He and his wife held a funeral service at the Invalides. Madame Simone de Lattre requested that the service be expanded to

Phat Diem cathedral. The town on the Day River was the target of a Viet Minh attack in May 1951.

honour the memory of all those killed in Indochina. Their beloved Bernard was buried at Mouilleron. Inevitably, the media attention on the event made the war even more unpopular in France.

When Field Marshal Montgomery heard the sad news, and despite their past differences, he wrote to offer his condolences. Notably though, Monty never recorded what he thought of de Lattre, making no reference to of him in his memoirs. The grieving General de Lattre, with an active combat command, was under enormous pressure. His health was beginning to fail.

Meanwhile, General de Linarès was left to finish the destruction of the Viet Minh assaults across the Day River. By 10 June, Giap had to acknowledge that all was lost. Eight days later, the last of his units disengaged and retired back across the contested river. When the French infantry and tanks re-entered Phy Lu, the river banks were a devastated, smoking wasteland. Giap's forces suffered 11,000 casualties. He was now forced to revert to guerrilla warfare.

Ho and Giap were wrestling with some tough decisions when General Wei announced that Mao's attention was being diverted by the forthcoming Korean War. The Viet Minh had suffered three major defeats in the past five months, losing up to a third of their regular troops, along with much of the equipment furnished by the Chinese. It was clear that conventional attacks on French outposts were no longer paying off.

To the French, these victories seemed to offer hope that the Viet Minh could indeed be defeated. The French succeeded on the Day River because they successfully cut Giap's supply lines and because they had the support of the locals who were unsympathetic to the communists. His greatest error was overextending his forces, leaving himself without reserves. This led to some questioning Giap's competency.

It was Nguyen Binh, in charge of Viet Minh affairs in the south, operating from the swamps near Saigon, who was made the scapegoat. He was blamed for initiating the concept of the Red River Delta operation and for not backing the Viet Minh sufficiently. In disgrace, he was recalled to Viet Bac, but never made it. Nguyen Binh was later wounded in a skirmish with the French and allegedly finished off on the orders of Giap. The latter remained in command and reorganized his command structure. Giap and his officers had little option but to re-evaluate their strategy once again, and scale down their attacks.

Upon de Lattre's return from Paris, his first task was once more to try and supress the countryside insurgency. In reality, he was fighting a losing battle in galvanizing the Vietnamese people and the government against the Viet Minh. Massing six battalions of troops, he conducted a sweep of an area near Hanoi on 18 June 1951. This operation took place in the most appalling weather. At least one major Viet Minh unit was able to slip through the net under cover of the wind and rain.

De Lattre sought to capitalize on local sympathy for his lost son, who was killed serving with a Vietnamese unit, and to ensure that his sacrifice did not go to waste. This gave him the opportunity to appeal to potential young recruits for the local Vietnamese army. To date, attracting peasant soldiers had not been difficult, but recruiting the educated was another matter. De Lattre despaired, because this was exactly the type of young Frenchman who was giving his life for Indochina. In contrast, Vietnamese students remained unmotivated by the war.

He visited a prestigious school where he made an impassioned speech. Before a packed audience, he told the boys that membership of the French Union did not nullify independence. Without France, their country would be dominated by Mao's China and the vengeful communists. He urged them to support Emperor Bao Dai and to fight and save their land, just as the peasant soldiers were doing. The emperor agreed to review a military parade, involving both French and Vietnamese troops. He also agreed to sign a decree officially placing Vietnam on a war footing.

In August, de Lattre took a month's leave, as he was increasingly unwell and privately despondent about his own future. Yet his remarkable drive and energy showed no signs of flagging, and the following month he visited America and Britain. During his American visit, he met President Harry S. Truman. De Lattre's preoccupation during these trips centred on what would happen, and in particular how would China react, once the Korean War came to an end. During his public appearances in America, and these were numerous, he was at pains to clarify that France's war was not colonial, but part of the broader struggle against the insidious spread of communism in Asia. He cautioned that a communist victory in Tonkin would be followed by the loss of Indochina, then Southeast Asia, with the region then posing an eventual threat to India and the Middle East.

While he may have been exaggerating the situation, he knew that France could not dispense with American political support and military aid. The latter was assured but, once again, there were no offers of combat troops. After his visit to London, he spent a few days in Paris attending an army reunion and seeing old comrades. He also gained an unwelcome diagnosis regarding his long-running hip problem that had been causing him such pain. De Lattre went to his wife and told her he had terminal cancer.

Despite this crushing news, de Lattre was as tireless as ever in garnering support for the war in Indochina. On his way back, he stopped in Rome in order to lobby the Vatican to get the Roman Catholic Church in Vietnam, and its one and a half million followers, to put their full support behind opposing the Viet Minh. He landed back in Saigon on 19 October 1951, and was soon en route for Hanoi. He swiftly briefed the local Catholic Church on the Papacy's support for the war against communism in the region. Then with his son's death still heavily on his mind, he summoned Indochina's leading business figures. De Lattre told them that money should be raised so that all of France's troops, be they French, North or Black African, and Vietnamese, could enjoy Christmas.

General de Lattre, with time now running out, turned back to the battlefield with operations at Nghia Lo and Hoa Binh. While he had been away, Giap and his forces had been reasonably quiet as they were still licking their wounds. However, with the end of the rainy season, he wanted to draw the French north so that he could once again infiltrate the delta. The need to do this was urgent, as Giap's men were short of rice and were going hungry.

In early October, Giap struck at Nghia Lo, sited on a ridge between the Red and Black rivers with the 312th Division. General Salan could not abandon this as it would open up a route to Hanoi. Thanks to the French air force and two parachute-unit drops, the town was saved. The French paras then swept an area containing some 360 villages and over 250,000 people. Once more though, the Viet Minh proved elusive and slipped away.

De Lattre wanted to bring the enemy to battle at a location that they would have to defend. He chose their supply centre at the city of Hao Binh, which was to the southwest of Hanoi and outside the De Lattre Line. To the northwest lay a place called Dien Bien Phu. Hao Binh was an important transit point between China and Amman to the south. It was also the main town in the Muong region. These people had a tradition of loyalty to the French. The town lay on the Black River, so it could be a conduit for French waterborne reinforcements and supporting naval firepower. In addition, de Lattre hoped that the taking of Hoa Binh would be the first stage of cutting the Viet Minh in two by occupying their Thanh Hoa province bastion.

The operation was under the direction of Salan and de Linarès. In the opening phase, the town of Cho Ben was attacked and secured to protect a flank. On 14 November, in a show of strength, 2,000 paras were dropped on Hoa Binh. They were followed by fifteen infantry battalions, seven artillery battalions, two armoured groups and two naval assault divisions. Giap, however, refused to give battle. He withdrew, in turn encircling the French. On the 19th, De Lattre said goodbye to the forces at Hoa Binh and handed his command over to Salan.

Officially, General de Lattre flew back to Paris for a meeting with the Grand Council of the French Union. Privately, the real reason was for major surgery on 18 December 1951. This was followed by another operation in the new year, but his condition quickly worsened. His reported last words, on 9 January, were, 'Where is Bernard?' Two days later he was dead.

A grateful France posthumously elevated de Lattre to Marshal of France. Among those who attended his funeral were de Gaulle, Eisenhower and Montgomery. After the service, a turretless armoured car took his coffin to Mouilleron. There he was laid to rest in a grave next to his beloved son, Bernard. De Lattre's legacy was he had shown the world that what had been perceived as a campaign of colonial repression was actually a Vietnamese civil war.

French troops with a captured Viet Minh fighter.

In Tonkin, fighting continued along the Black River during December 1951, with the Viet Minh slowly closing in on Hoa Binh. Salan committed three mobile groups and an airborne group, but the guerrillas withdrew once more, only to return in January 1952. They managed to cut the river, leaving Route 6 as the only way to resupply the garrison. When the Viet Minh tried to cut the road by attacking Xom Pheo, they had to contend with the 2nd Battalion of the Foreign Legion's 13th Demi-Brigade. The tough legionnaires resorted to repulsing them with a bayonet charge. It took a relief force eleven days to fight their way through to Hoa Binh. Reluctantly, Salan took the decision to evacuate rather than risk another encirclement. Under the codename 'Amaranth', this was successfully carried out between 22 and 24 February, under the cover of heavy artillery and air support.

10. AIR WAR OVER INDOCHINA

The air war over Indochina was a decidedly one-sided affair. The Viet Minh did not have the ability to operate an air force, especially one with modern jet fighters. Nor did Mao offer them one. This was just as well for the French, who relied on slower propeller-driven aircraft throughout the conflict. In Korea, Soviet and Chinese-piloted MiG-15 jets operated south of the Yalu, intercepting American B-29 bombers targeting North Korea's defence industries. This led to fierce aerial battles, though the communists ultimately failed to gain control of the air. The North Koreans were supplied the MiG, but they and their allies' jet fighters had little bearing on the ground war as they spent much of their time locked in dogfights.

In contrast, America was soon providing the French with Second World War-vintage naval dive-bombers to support their ground war in Indochina. However, France's greatest failing was its complete lack of a strategic airlift capability and the weakness of its tactical airlift. The French never really generated the ability to support more than one operation at a time, which was to have catastrophic results at Dien Bien Phu.

Once China and the Soviet Union had recognized the Democratic Republic of Vietnam, the Viet Minh began to receive ever-growing quantities of Chinese and Soviet weapons.

A Grumman F6F Hellcat of Squadron 1F landing on the French carrier *Arromanches*, Gulf of Tonkin, 1953.

Subsequently, French reliance on fortified 'hedgehogs' meant aircraft played a key role in the escalating war, providing vital ground support and supplies. The French air force committed around 300 aircraft to Vietnam, while the French navy rotated four carriers with their naval air squadrons in the South China Sea.

Prior to the Second World War, the French Armée de l'Air (air force) and Aéronnautique Naval or Aéronavale (naval air force) had maintained only token units in Indochina. Most of the aircraft there were obsolete, consisting of 1925-vintage biplanes. At the outbreak of the war in 1939, the French had about 100 aircraft, of which just 13 were modern fighters. These accounted for 20 Thai aircraft during the brief border war with Thailand, but they could do nothing to counter the powerful Japanese air force.

The French air force first returned to Saigon on 12 September 1945, when American-built Douglas C-47 Skytrains ferried in 150 French troops to serve alongside the British. Subsequently, C-47 and Toucan (Ju 52 variant) transports were used to drop rudimentary barrel bombs on Viet Minh positions. On their return to Indochina, until 1949, the French feared that America might impose an embargo on spares for U.S.-made combat aircraft and thus greatly limit their deployment options. This concern, however, evaporated once Mao had taken over in China.

Ironically, the Nazi war machine helped equip the French armed forces. The trimotor Toucan was a hangover from the Second World War. While under Nazi occupation, France had been forced to build the German Junkers Ju 52 medium bomber and transport aircraft. These were constructed at the Amiot factory at Colombes. Post-war designated the AAC.1 Toucan, it was kept in production with over 400 built for Air France and the French air force. The drawback with the Toucan, and indeed the Skytrain, was the limited number of men they could carry: eighteen and twenty-eight respectively. This meant that

American-supplied F8F-1 Bearcat fighter-bombers first arrived in Indochina in January 1951. The airfield here is probably Tourane.

Indo China Map

AIRCRAFT USED BY THE FRENCH FORCES

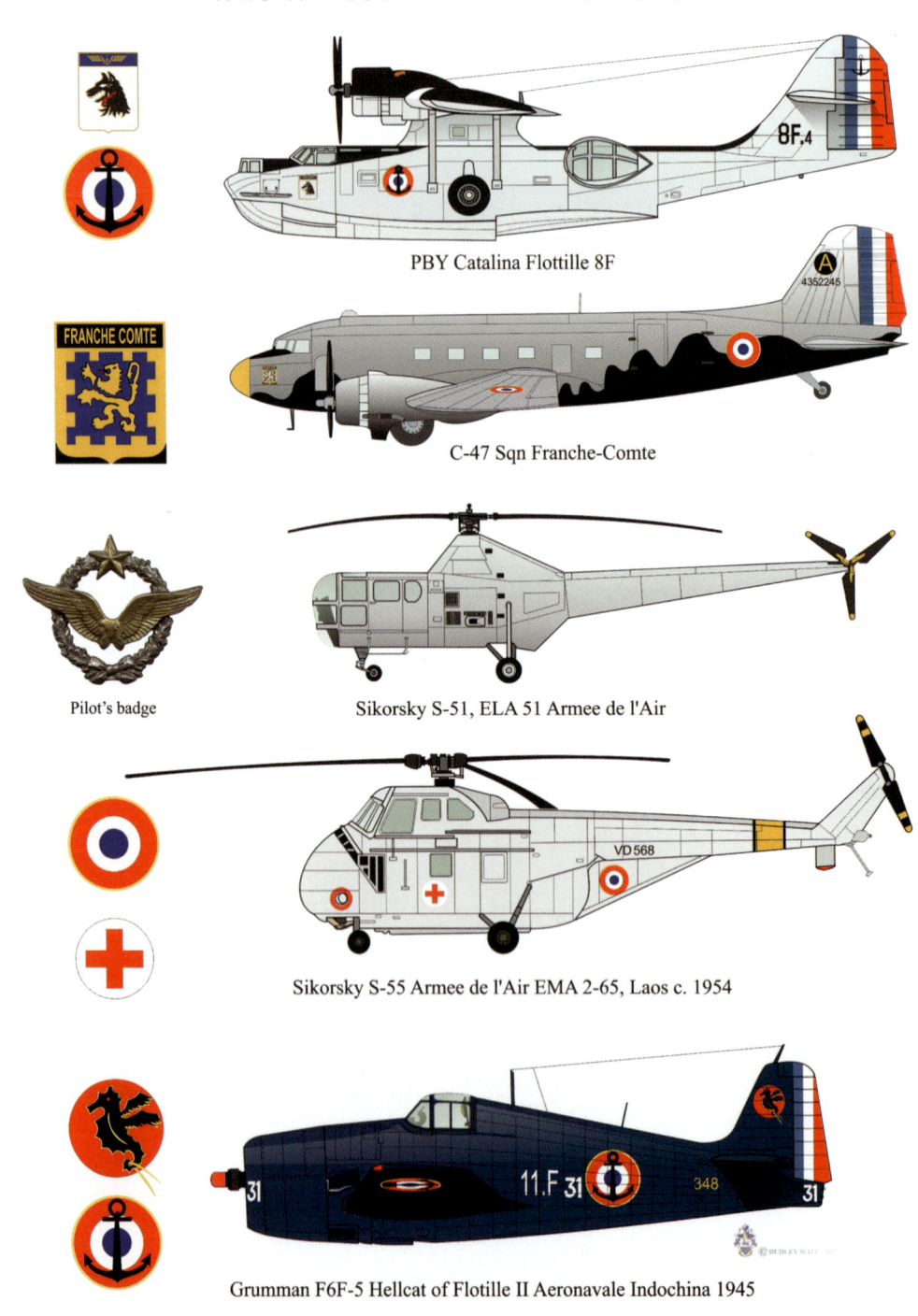

PBY Catalina Flottille 8F

C-47 Sqn Franche-Comte

Pilot's badge

Sikorsky S-51, ELA 51 Armee de l'Air

Sikorsky S-55 Armee de l'Air EMA 2-65, Laos c. 1954

Grumman F6F-5 Hellcat of Flotille II Aeronavale Indochina 1945

Garand

M1 carbine

MAS 36

MAT 49

M1919A4 Browning .30

Chatellerault 7.5mm

Colt 1911 pistol

Bren Gun

WEAPONS AND INSIGNIA OF THE VIET MINH

Mosin Nagant

PPSH

SKS

7.62 x 39mm round

RPD

Viet Minh hat badge

Viet Minh Victory Medal

Ho Chi Minh
People's Revolutionary Youth Union
badge

MEDALS AND INSIGNIA OF THE FRENCH FORCES

Medaille Militaire

Combatant's Cross

Indo China Service Medal

Overseas Service Medal

French Foreign Legion paratrooper badges

French Foreign Legion Second Infantry Regiment pocket badges

Left: Vo Nguyen Giap, 2008. (Photo Ricardo Stuckert)

Below: The 37 mm M1939 (61-K) anti-aircraft gun reputedly used by the Viet Minh at Dien Bien Phu to shoot down three French aircraft. (Photo Binh Giang)

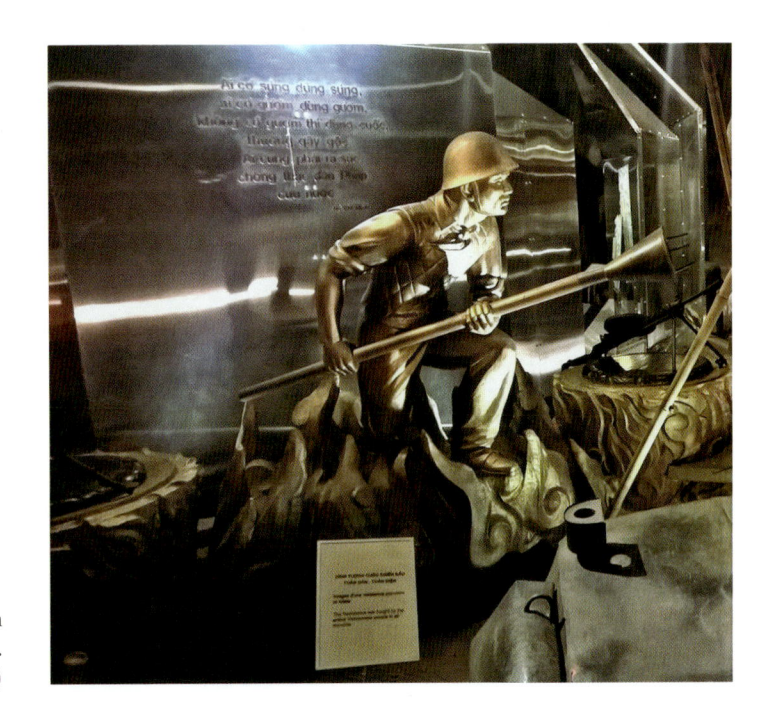

Statue to the Viet Minh who fought the French. (Photo Cookie Nguyen)

Independence statue, Hanoi. (Photo Pilip)

French 105mm captured by the Viet Minh, 1948. (Photo Bui Thuy Dao Nguyen)

parachute and air-landing operations required very large numbers of transport aircraft. In the Second World War, the Axis and Allies conducted such operations, but they always resulted in considerable losses in aircraft.

Similarly, occupied France built the German Fieseler Fi 156 Storch (Stork) reconnaissance aircraft, made famous by Field Marshal Erwin Rommel. It was also kept in postwar production as the Morane-Saulnier Criquet (Cricket). This proved ideal for Indochina because of its short take-off and landing capabilities, plus its low speed, which enabled it to use the roughest of air strips. The Criquet was deployed in Indochina by the French army, Armée de l'Air and Aéronavale for a wide variety of tasks.

The first fighter aircraft sent out were British-supplied Supermarine Spitfires, rather than the Armée de l'Air's American-built Republic P-47Ds. While waiting for them, French pilots conducted hair-raising training flights in a dozen dilapidated and untrustworthy Japanese fighters. The Spitfires though, were not suitable for ground support due to their limited range and small bomb load. Nonetheless, they were flown from Saigon in Cochinchina, Nha Trang and Tourane (Da Nang) in Annam and Hanoi, and Lang Son in Tonkin until 1947. Likewise, the British-supplied, twin-engine de Havilland Mosquito proved ill-suited to the conditions, as the bonded-plywood structure had a habit of falling apart in the tropical heat. Confined to Saigon, they were eventually sent home.

To back up the Armée de l'Air the French navy sought to keep a carrier stationed off the coast of Vietnam, though these deployments really stretched its capabilities, operating so far from home. The escort carrier *Dixmude* (former HMS *Biter*) first arrived in the South China Sea in March 1947, with nine American-supplied Douglas SBD-5 Dauntless dive-bombers – the victors of the Battle of Midway in June 1942. These aircraft made their first carrier sorties on the 16th of that month, with additional raids against targets in Annam and Tonkin.

After problems with her launch catapult, *Dixmude* was forced to return to Toulon for repairs, thereafter making only one more combat deployment the following year. On the return journey, the vessel carried Toucans and Spitfires for the air force. The elderly carrier was then employed as an aircraft-transport vessel. *Dixmude* was photographed in 1950 on the Saigon River with a deck full of F6F-5 Hellcats.

The light carrier *Arromanches* (former HMS *Colossus*) arrived in November 1948, making a total of four combat deployments up to and including 1954. This carrier operated the American Curtiss SB2C-5 Helldiver dive-bomber. While it provided accurate and powerful support for the French ground forces, the Helldiver was vulnerable to ground fire. During these deployments, the aircraft usually operated from forward land bases rather than from the carrier.

The third carrier committed to the war was *La Fayette* (former USS *Langley*), which took over in April 1953, minus its aircraft, ready to take on those from the *Arromanches*. It only stayed on station for five weeks.

The fourth and final carrier, *Bois Belleau* (former USS *Belleau Wood*), only operated from 30 April to 15 September 1954. The navy also deployed amphibious aircraft, such as the PBY Catalina, to patrol Vietnam's coastal waters and the Red River Delta. Additionally, they acted in air-support, transport and medical-evacuation roles. These were replaced by the four-engine PB4Y Privateer, which was the largest aircraft operated by the French.

Dien Bien Phu

Once Mao was in power and the Korean War had broken out, Washington saw France less as an unsavoury colonial power with dubious democratic credentials, and more as a staunch anti-communist ally. The Spitfires were soon followed with American-supplied Bell P-63 Kingcobras, called 'Kings' by their French aircrews. These helped cover the ill-fated withdrawal from Cao Bang in the summer of 1950, but again, could not carry a large enough bombload and could not operate from forward airfields.

What arrived next was much better and just what the French needed. To re-equip French fighter units, the Americans provided the F6F-5 Hellcat and the F8F-1 Bearcat. Both these were designed as carrier strike aircraft, so were capable of relatively short take-off and landing. This meant that they were ideal for forward deployment in Indochina. The Hellcats were delivered by U.S. carrier in November 1950 with the 'Beercats' as the French called them, following in January 1951.

The Hellcat was only intended as an interim solution until all the fighter squadrons could be equipped with the Bearcat – this conversion though, was not completed until early 1953. In contrast, the Bearcat remained in service until the final French withdrawal in April 1956, and fought at Dien Bien Phu. It became the premier fighter-bomber in Indochina, being used almost solely for ground-attack missions. Some 'Beercats' though, were converted to a reconnaissance role by fitting specially modified U.S. drop tanks fitted with two cameras.

In the French armoury was napalm. This jellied-petroleum bomb, developed by the Americans in the early 1940s, and used against the Japanese during the Second World War, was then employed by UN forces in Korea. This terrible weapon, which bursts on contact with the ground into a wide carpet of flame, generates enormous heat and, once stuck to skin, cannot be removed. Used as an anti-personnel weapon, it was devastating. The Bearcat was capable of dropping 100gal. napalm tanks. It was first used by the French on 22 December 1950, against a Viet Minh troop concentration at Tien Yen.

The French air force desperately wanted a twin-engine light bomber, but none was available. It especially needed such an aircraft once the Viet Minh's air defences began to improve. The best available aircraft to fill this role was the American Douglas B-26 Invader, which was known as the A-26 until 1948. While the Bearcat and Hellcat were

A Douglas B-26 Invader light bomber loaned by the U.S. to the French air force in Indochina. (Photo National U.S. Navy Museum)

Air War Over Indochina

An American B-26C invader dropping bombs over Korea in 1951. The French were first supplied this type of bomber three years earlier. (Photo USAF)

surplus to U.S. Navy requirements, the USAF was employing its B-26 as night bombers in Korea. Nonetheless, the first four aircraft were supplied to the French in early November 1950.

The B-26 was the most potent type of air power the French were able to bring to bear during the war, with the ability to carry 2,722kg of bombs, napalm or rockets, and armed with up to fourteen machine guns. Equipping a French bomb group, the B-26s were operated from Tourane. A further two bomb groups were later formed using this aircraft. Despite its growing strength and newfound confidence, the French air force was unable to provide the army with a decisive edge during the inconclusive Black River offensive in the winter of 1951–52. From then until the end of the war, America provided some eighty bombers, fighter-bombers and transport aircraft. Many of these, however, arrived too late to influence the outcome of the war.

Funds were not made available for the acquisition of limited numbers of helicopters from Britain until 1952. America also supplied some rotary-wing aircraft. The French army, air force and navy all deployed helicopters to support their operations. The Groupement des Formations d'Hélicoptères of the French army was created under Commandant Marceau Crespin. In honour of General de Lattre's late son, who was killed in action, the French army's main helipad at Tan Son Nhut air base outside Saigon was named Camp Bernard de Lattre. Army helicopter squadrons were also based at Bien Hoa to the north of Saigon. These were used almost entirely for medical evacuation rather than troop carrying. By the time of Dien Bien Phu, the French had just thirty-two helicopters, most of which were Sikorski S-55s, dubbed the H-19 by the French.

General Salan, relying on the strategy of *les hérissons* fortified 'hedgehog' bases and mobile commando operations, needed the commitment of massive airpower. By this stage, the air force had some 300 aircraft, including four groups of Bearcats and two of Invaders. This strength was to remain unchanged until after Dien Bien Phu, when the third bomb group was added.

After the withdrawal of the antiquated Toucans, there were three transport groups equipped with C-47s, providing logistical support for the ground troops. To supplement this insufficient fleet, the French made use of commercial- and American-supplied Fairchild C-119Cs, which were sent from Japan and Korea. Some aircraft were flown by American mercenaries, operating from Formosa. These civilian pilots could earn up to five times that of their counterparts in the Armée de l'Air. The French armed forces' lack of a strategic airlift meant that to fly troops and equipment from France or the other colonies required the help of Air France. America also stepped in, transporting almost 1,000 military personnel from Paris to Saigon in April–May 1954.

By 1953, the key Armée de l'Air officers were General Charles Lauzin, commander of the French air force in Indochina, General Jean Dechaux, commander Tactical Air Group North (Tonkin), and Colonel Jean-Louis Nicot, commanding the air transport group. Army aviation came under Commandant Crespin, who was responsible for the limited helicopter units.

The French aircraft carrier *La Fayette* in Indochina waters, 1953. (Photo U.S. Navy)

11. OPERATION LORRAINE

For the next seven months following the Black River battles, the French largely remained in their strongholds and the fighting was sporadic. The mobile groups bravely ventured forth to keep the supply lines open, but the area under French control gradually shrank. Their only notable success occurred in central Annam with Operation Sauterelle, conducted on the coast above the Perfume River and Hue. This, and a subsequent operation, accounted for 3,000 Viet Minh killed or captured.

Giap waited for the monsoon to end, as he was planning to take the French positions on the Nghia Lo ridge. This operation was to be a repeat of the Cao Bang-Lang Son disaster of 1950. Giap gathered his 308th, 312th and 316th divisions, with the intention of launching simultaneous attacks on the towns of Nghia Lo, Gia Hoi and Van Yen. In mid-October 1952, Nghia Lo was overrun by human-wave attacks of the Viet Minh 308th Division. The Viet Minh triumphantly photographed a group of eight, apprehensive-looking French officers who were captured during the fighting.

It was clear, with the loss of Nghia Lo, that it would be impossible to hold the other forts in the T'ai Hills. This led to the evacuation of the remaining French outposts and again paratroops were sacrificed to cover the retreat toward the Black River defences.

Under Major Marcel Bigeard, the 6th Colonial Parachute Battalion was dropped to reinforce the post at Tu Le. They were to protect the withdrawal of the 1st T'ai Mountain Battalion, 17th Moroccan Tabor and 3rd Battalion, 1st Moroccan Rifles. The paras were attacked on 20 October 1952, forcing them to conduct a fighting retreat towards the Black River. They ran into an ambush set by the 312th Division. Two days later, the paras, having lost 60 per cent of their strength, reached their destination.

The French defences covering the vulnerable Laotian border were now stretched extremely thin. General Salan knew that the defensive line would not hold in the face of a concerted communist attack. Initially, he had assumed that Giap's attacks were a feint, and that he would turn and strike at the delta once more. Instead, Giap headed southwest. Salan planned to intercept him by moving northwest to block the communists, and force them away from the Black River toward the delta and into open battle. He chose as his area of attack the line of the Clear River northwest of Hanoi.

Dubbed Operation Lorraine, this was to involve the largest French force to date, some 30,000 men. This consisted of four mobile groups, a paratroop group, and supporting units of armour, artillery and engineers. Their task was to seize the Viet Minh supply depots at Phu Doan, Yen Bay and Tuyen Quang, nearly 160km outside the delta defences and deep inside enemy territory. Giap, however, had good intelligence and knew exactly what the French were intending. Nevertheless, he persisted with his push into the T'ai country. As far as he was concerned, his enemies were simply putting their necks in the noose. To delay the French and act as a blocking force, Giap deployed the 36th and 176th regiments.

Lorraine was designed to be executed in four stages. Opening on 29 October 1952, the first would establish a bridgehead towards Pho Tho, 32km to the north, with a task force from Trun Ha on the Red River northwest of Son Tay. In the second, another task force, heading north along Route Coloniale 2 from Viet Tri to the north of Son Tay, would link up at Phu Tho and expand the bridgehead. These two groups would then fight their way further north through Chang Muong towards Phu Doan, where a parachute jump by Airborne Group 1 would meet up with them. Also, forces would push up the Red River to prevent the Viet Minh from escaping westwards. The third stage would involve the destruction of the enemy supply dumps in the Phu Doan area as well as engaging enemy fighters. The fourth, and rather optimistic phase, would be the exploitation of the captured land corridor between the Red and Clear rivers.

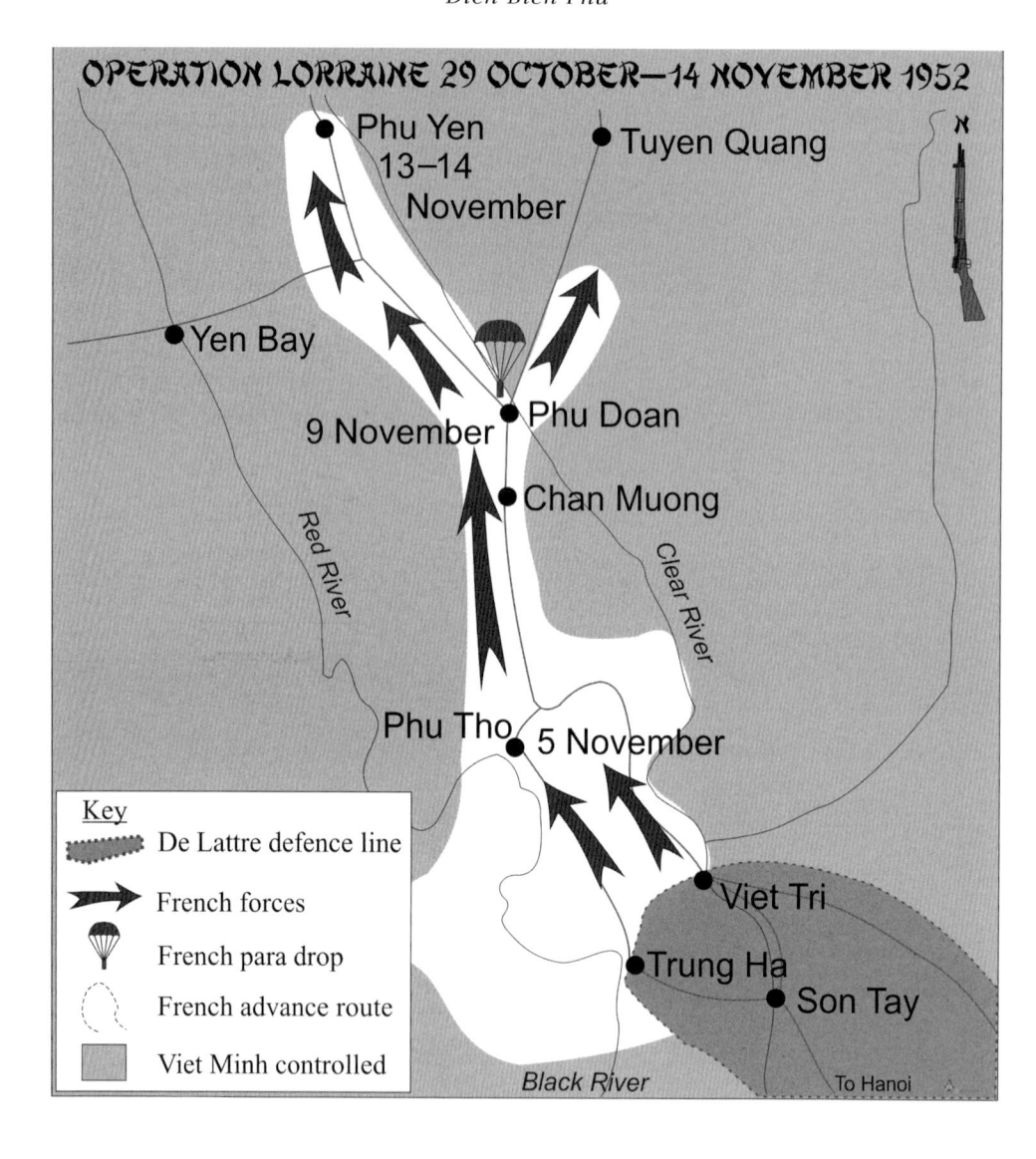

Three Red River bridgeheads were secured by 4 November 1952 and mobile groups 1 and 4 headed towards Route Coloniale 2. Delaying actions by Viet Minh regional troops meant that the link-up did not occur until the following day. However, the lack of opposition from regular Viet Minh divisions encouraged the French to press on.

Operation Lorraine

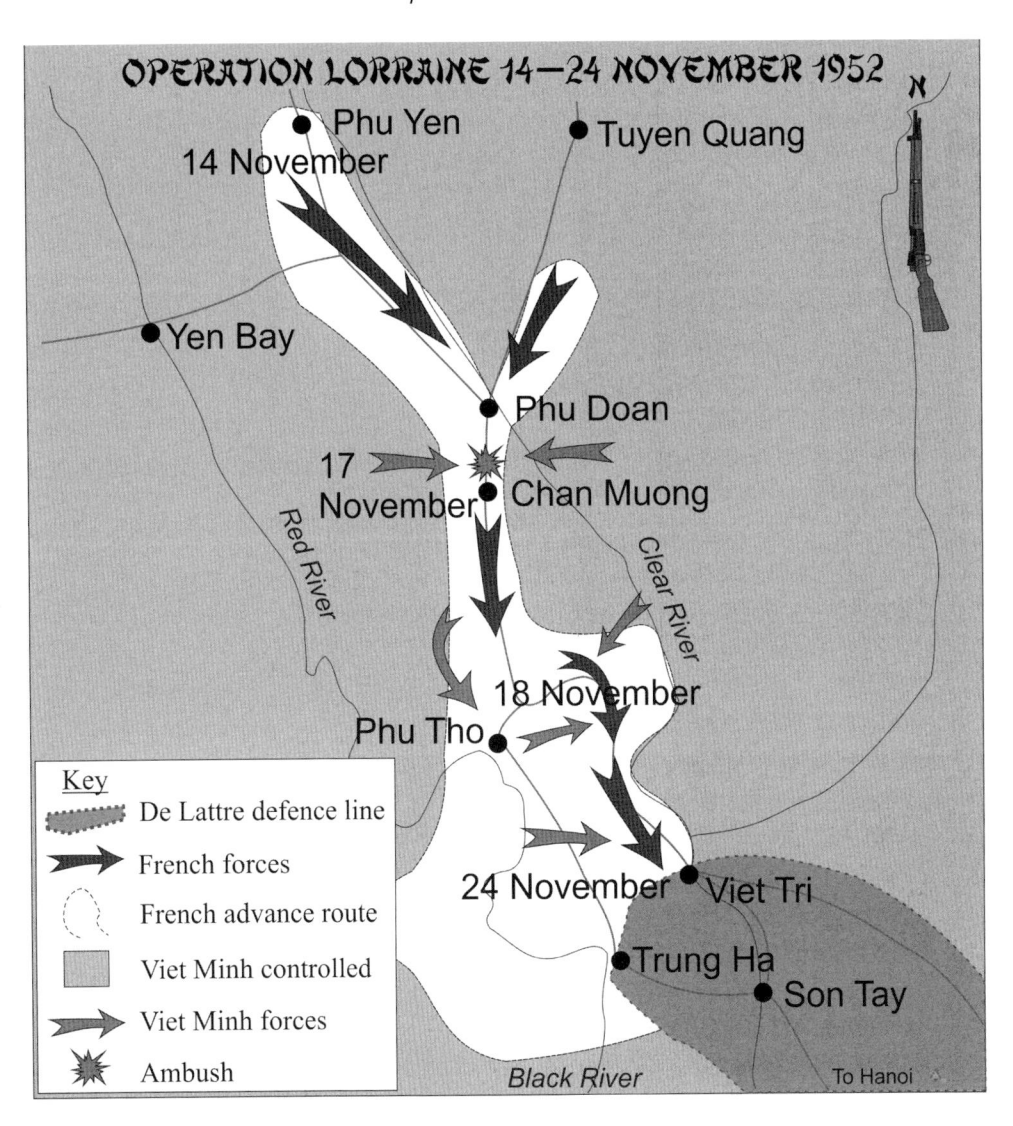

Early on 9 November, the combined task forces, with armoured cars and tanks in the lead, pushed up Route Coloniale 2. In the meantime, the 3rd Dinassaut sailed up the river towards the drop zone. By mid-afternoon, 2,350 paras, belonging to the 1st and 2nd Foreign Legion parachute battalions and the 3rd Colonial Parachute Battalion, had successfully landed in the Phu Doan area where they rendezvoused with the naval force.

Resistance at Phu Doan was light, and with the arrival of the mobile groups, French forces confirmed the village was indeed a major Viet Minh supply depot. They captured a large quantity of supplies, including heavy weaponry such as anti-aircraft guns and mortars. To the embarrassment of French intelligence, they also discovered quantities of Soviet-supplied Molotava trucks. These were being used to move supplies to Viet Minh field units. The French then sent patrols west to Yen Bay on the Red River and to Tuyen Quang to the northeast.

At this stage, Salan should have withdrawn, but instead he opted to conduct stage four of Operation Lorraine, possibly still hoping to force Giap to commit. Salan had successfully captured valuable enemy supplies, but the absence of the Viet Minh's main force meant that his units were now stretched out along a vulnerable and ultimately useless strip of land, well outside the relative safety of the delta defences. The French now moved to extend this corridor by pushing on to Phu Yen, well north of Phu Doan.

Giap, rather than counterattack to retake Phu Doan, was content to wait it out. He instructed the majority of his three regular divisions to remain on the Black River. Just two regiments were sent toward Yen Bay. Giap also moved to pressure Salan to withdraw by authorizing the 304th and 320th divisions, to the north and south of the delta, to conduct guerrilla attacks to distract the French.

By 14 November 1952, Salan's tanks and infantry had reached Phu Yen. It was at this point that Salan, realizing he was dangerously exposed, ordered the withdrawal. Three days later, they had reached Phu Doan without mishap. By now though, two of Giap's regular regiments had reached the midway point between the village and Phu Tho, thereby blocking the French retreat. They were deployed south of the village of Chan Muong in the Chan Muong gorge. This was a steep-sided, jungle-covered defile, through which Route Coloniale 2 passed. It was ideal for an ambush.

Men of the 2nd Battalion, 2nd Foreign Legion Infantry Regiment, the 4th Battalion, 7th Algerian Rifles, and of the Bataillon de Marche Indochinois (a mixed French, Cambodian and Vietnamese unit) drove straight into the trap that was initiated by mortar bombs raining down on them. The French, although suffering heavy casualties in the following enemy infantry assault, quickly rallied and counterattacked. The Viet Minh were expelled from the gorge and the Chan Muong Valley, but the French lost 56 dead, 125 wounded and 133 missing. It was not a good start.

This set the pattern for the next week, as the French struggled to escape south to the safety of the De Lattre Line. The route to Phu Tho was blocked, however, so they turned east and then south toward Viet Tri. The Viet Minh counterattacked again on 18, 20 and 24 November, inflicting yet more casualties.

The French had completely withdrawn all their Operation Lorraine forces back across the Red River by 1 December, having lost 1,200 men. Despite the disruption of Giap's supply lines, Operation Lorraine could be seen as nothing but a complete and costly failure.

This victory, however, made Giap overconfident when he turned his attention back to French strongholds in the Black River valley. Looking at his maps, he decided to attack the isolated French base at Na San. He was partly emboldened by the French failure to adequately supply Operation Lorraine from the air. His diversionary attacks, and the need to sustain the outlying garrisons, had ensured that Lorraine was beyond the French air force's capabilities.

While Operation Lorraine was underway, Colonel Jean Gilles was tasked with building a fire-support base in the Na San valley in Son La Province, to the west of the Black River. This was on Route Provinciale 41, which ran from Hanoi, across the river at Hoa Binh, through the town of Son La, and north to the French stronghold at Lai Chau. It was to be a fully fortified *aéro-terrestre* (air-land) base. The intention was, once again, to draw Giap

Vo Nguyen Giap inspecting Viet Minh during August Revolution celebrations, 1945.

into open battle with a very sizeable entrenched French force, backed by aircraft, artillery and mortars.

In October 1952, the valley, surrounded by hills, hosted a single French outpost and a small airstrip. By the end of November, thanks to the efforts of the French air force, Na San had a garrison of some 15,000 men. Gilles employed the *le hérisson* (hedgehog) tactic. His defences consisted of thirty *point d'appui* (armed positions) that formed an outer and inner ring surrounding the airfield and headquarters, offering mutually supporting fields of fire. Each had good all-round defence, strengthened by trenches, sandbags, barbed wire and mines.

Gilles multi-national forces comprised three battle groups that included Algerian, Moroccan, T'ai and Vietnamese troops, as well as Foreign Legion infantry and paras. They were able to called on dive-bombers from the French navy and bombers from the air force. Artillery included 105mm howitzers and 81mm mortars. This ensured that Na San packed a powerful punch.

Just as Salan had hoped, Giap was provoked into attacking the base using his 308th, 312th and 316th divisions. Giap appreciated that French air power necessitated night attacks, but he knew that if his men could take the airfield then the base would be cut off and helpless. His assault opened at 8.00 pm on 23 November 1952, when a regiment from Colonel Vuong Thua Tu's 308th Division unsuccessfully attempted to take *point d'appui* 8 that formed part of the inner ring. They tried twice, but on each occasion, they were driven back. Then, until the end of the month, Giap conducted night attacks, probing French defences, looking for weak spots.

At 8.00 pm on 30 November, nine Viet Minh battalions attempted to storm positions 22*bis* and 24 in the outer ring, which lay either side of the main French headquarters.

The latter position, on the west bank of the Black River, held on for three hours before surrendering. The 225 men of the 2nd T'ai Battalion holding 22*bis* endured nine hours of attacks before they were overrun. Barely a squad managed to find their way back to the airfield.

The following day, Gilles fought to retake both these lost positions, utilizing the massed fire power available to him, which included a total of six artillery batteries. After an opening barrage, Foreign Legion paratroops secured 22*bis*. It took the 3rd Colonial Airborne Battalion seven hours of tough fighting to retake 24. That night, Giap launched an all-out attack on a number of positions, with 21*bis* and the large defensive-position 26, again in the outer ring, bearing the brunt of the assaults. The Viet Minh's human waves were greeted with flares, bombs, napalm and shells.

The attacks suddenly stopped mid-morning on 2 December. Two days later, Giap, having sustained almost 3,500 casualties, withdrew his battered divisions. Despite suffering about 500 casualties, the French were convinced that their fortified base *aéro-terrestre* and *le hérisson* was a war-winning formula. In the case of Na Son, it was heavily reinforced and kept resupplied entirely by air. As a consequence, it was not overrun and held out, while inflicting heavy losses on the enemy. The net result of this though, was it convinced French planners that they could keep isolated 'air-heads' resupplied from the air – this optimism was to have disastrous results at Dien Bien Phu.

French hearts and minds efforts were never successful.

12. PRELUDE TO DEFEAT

In April 1953, Ho Chi Minh and General Giap sought to stretch the French Expeditionary Force in Tonkin even more, by spreading the conflict into northern Laos. The invasion by the 312th Division had two other goals: the capture of the valuable opium crop and joining forces with the neighbouring communist Pathet Lao guerrillas. Their route of attack ran from Tuam Giao, through Dien Bien Phu, over the border, and down the Nam Ou valley.

General Salan simply did not have any reserves available to reinforce Laos, so the French outposts there were instructed to hold on for as long as they could, while a sustainable defensive system was set up in the region. French resistance was on a line running north–south, centred on Moung Khoua, Luang Prabang, and on the Plaine des Jarres. The town of

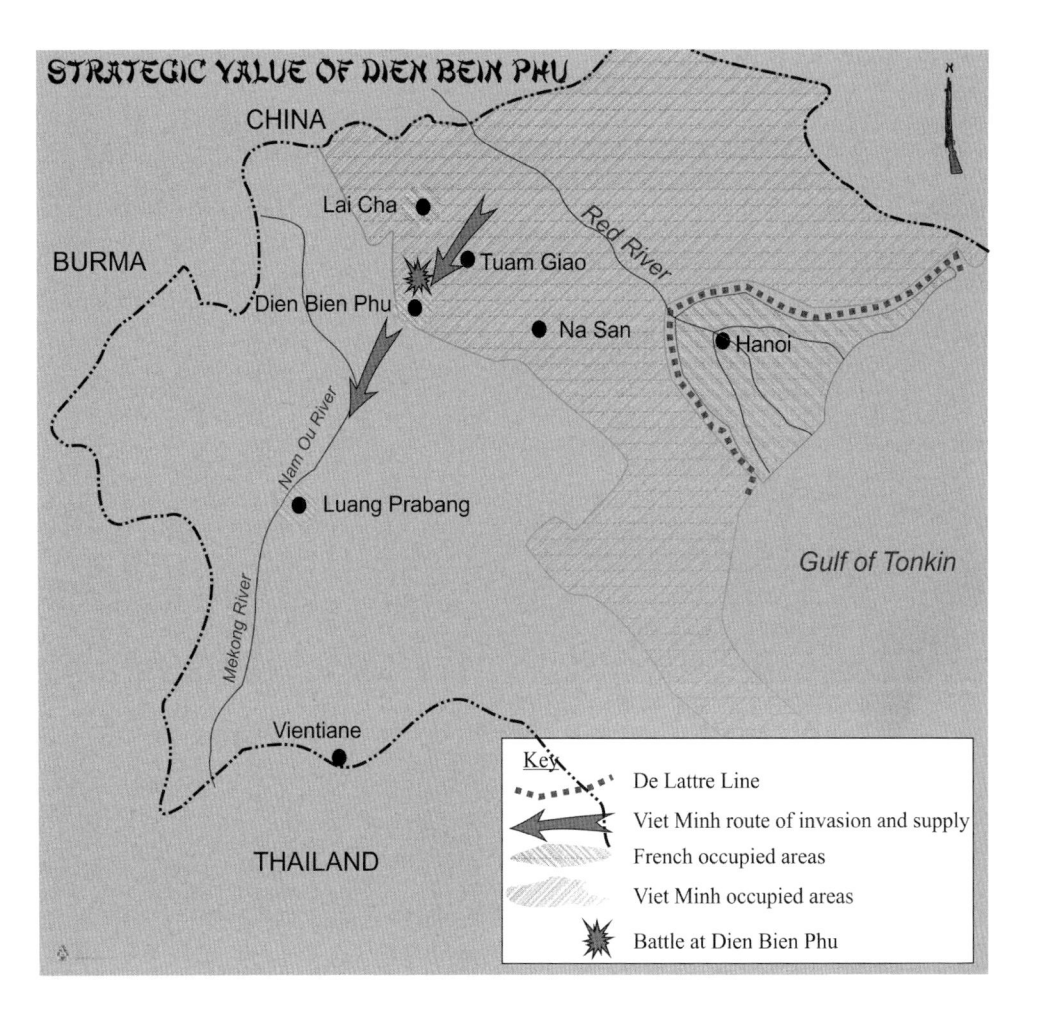

Luang Prabang in central northern Laos was particularly important as its sits on the junction of the Mekong and Nam Ou (not to be confused with Nam Oum) rivers.

Giap's invasion of Laos was a very significant turning point in the war. Previously, the French had been able to largely confine the conflict to Tonkin, with them operating from Hanoi behind the security of the De Lattre Line. Now the *le hérisson* defence would have to be extended around Luang Prabang. It was a step too far.

Although the French Expeditionary Force by this stage in the war numbered 190,000 and the Vietnamese National Army was being formed, Salan had no troops to spare. In northern Vietnam alone he had 80,000 men holding 900 forts who were tied down by fewer than 30,000 Viet Minh, most of whom were peasant militia rather than regulars. This was the situation facing General Henri Navarre when he arrived in May 1953 to replace Salan.

Navarre realized that his immediate problems were much closer to home, so he and his staff set about formulating the so-called Navarre Plan. In southern Vietnam, the troublesome guerrilla war was containable and stable. In the north, the lack of reserves meant that he had nothing with which to counter any Viet Minh attacks in the Red River Delta. His only option was to withdraw some of the outlying garrisons so as to free up troops from static defence. He would eventually be able to muster some 30,000 mobile reserves, but that would take time, so he decided to sit out the 1953–54 campaigning season while developing the Vietnamese National Army. Once the Vietnamese were up to strength they could replace the French and French-led garrison forces in the delta. Washington agreed to support his plans with almost $400 million worth of military assistance. He determined to conduct a number of minor operations to keep Giap occupied before launching a decisive offensive in 1955.

After the departure of de Lattre, René Cogny, who had been on his staff, took a combat command, leading a division in Tonkin and a mobile group in the Red River Delta. Navarre now appointed him ground-forces commander in northern Vietnam. Both men were to subsequently fall out spectacularly over the handling of the battle of Dien Bien Phu.

In the meantime, in Peking, Mao and his advisers decided that they would settle, as they had in Korea, for a half measure in Indochina. By 1953, both sides in Korea, the North backed by China and the South with its United Nations allies, had fought themselves to a bloody standstill, leaving the country divided exactly as it had been before the conflict. The Chinese People's Liberation Army, employing human-wave tactics, had suffered the most appalling casualties. Mao, during the Korean War, had called a halt to large-scale operations in Indochina so that China could focus her resources on Korea. When he took the decision to end the Korean conflict in May 1953, Mao immediately despatched Chinese officers directly from Korea to Indochina.

Mao was looking at the bigger picture: Ho must do enough to drive the French out, but not spark intervention by America. after China's experiences in Korea, Mao was only too aware of the type of firepower the American military could bring to bear. Mao wanted a settlement in Indochina, even if it meant partition, but he did not tell the Viet Minh. He wanted them to escalate the war to a point where it created an irretrievable crisis for the French, but no more.

In July 1953, in northeastern Tonkin, Navarre attacked guerrilla bases in the Lang Son area with Operation Hirondelle, using three parachute battalions. These were then evacuated by sea. He also acted to secure his lines of communication in central Vietnam along the main north–south Route Coloniale 1. Despite a French operation the previous year, convoys on this road were regularly attacked by the Viet Minh's 95th Regiment operating from a fortified region in the sand dunes and salt marshes between Quang Tri to the north and Hue to the south. This had led to the French dubbing the road *la rue sans joie* – the street without joy.

Under General Leblanc, the French gathered some 10,000 men for Operation Camargue, a combined ground, airborne and amphibious operation that was intended to trap the Viet Minh. The 3rd Amphibious Group deployed 160 tracked Crabs and Alligators to get their men ashore and into the dunes. Camargue commenced on 27 July 1953, the landings unopposed. The first resistance was met at Dong Que when the 6th Moroccan Spahis with M24 tanks, the 1st Battalion Moroccan Rifles and the 69th African Artillery Regiment were ambushed. They managed to destroy almost an entire Viet Minh company, but this delay enabled the rest of the 95th Regiment to retreat into the southern portion of the developing pocket.

At 10.45 am, to block the Viet Minh's retreat, elements of the 2nd Battalion, 1st Parachute Light Infantry Regiment, were dropped near Dai Loc, from where they began to push towards the mouth of the Van Trinh Canal to close the pocket. Despite hazardous drop conditions caused by 48kph winds, the 3rd Vietnamese Parachute Battalion dropped near Lang Bao. This helped seal the southern escape routes. However, during the night of 28–29 July, most of the Viet Minh managed to slip the net. The ambitious operation was ended on 4 August, having been a modest success.

General Salan and Prince Sisavang Vatthana visiting the strategic Laotian town of Luang Prabang, May 1953.

During August, as part of Navarre's reduction in exposed garrisons, Na San was evacuated. French air force transport aircraft were assisted by planes from three civilian companies in an effort to complete this mission as quickly as possible. Colonel Gilles conducted the withdrawal without loss, having duped the local Viet Minh. He slowly withdrew his units, collapsing his defences, until just a single battalion was left. A local Viet Minh officer at Na San recalled, 'The enemy was able to escape and save its entire forces because of our poor intelligence.'

Nonetheless, it must have slightly rankled Gilles that having shed so much blood to secure the base, he was now asked to abandon it to the enemy.

That October, Mao got his hands-on France's strategic intentions, when he obtained a copy of the Navarre Plan. China's chief military adviser to Indochina, General Wei Guo-qing, flew from Beijing, handing this to Ho Chi Minh in person. It was this intelligence that convinced Ho to give battle at Dien Bien Phu, although the plan made no mention of the place. It is unclear how this vital intelligence coup occurred, but a copy of the Navarre Plan had been passed to the Americans.

By November 1953, the French position in Indochina had slightly improved, and Navarre began contemplating taking the battle to Giap once more. Disrupting Giap's supply lines seemed the best option, as this would curtail the Viet Minh's war effort. This, however, would require a mission deep into the Viet Bac and, in view of the failure of Operation Lorraine, was not an enticing prospect. Countering Giap's unwelcome activities in Laos seemed to offer a better chance of success, especially if the Na San base *aéro-terrestre* could be repeated to good effect.

Looking at his situation maps, Navarre understood that if his men could dominate the invasion routes into Laos, this would cut off the Viet Minh threatening Luang Prabang. This would either force Giap to fight or withdraw. The best place to block Giap was at Dien Bien Phu, known as Muong Than in T'ai, and the flat valley formed by the Nam Youm river in the T'ai mountains. The region, although dominated by the Viet Minh, was still supportive of the French. Also, the T'ai capital of Lai Chu north of Dien Bien Phu, although cut off, was held by French-officered local units.

Initially, Operation Castor and the seizure of Dien Bien Phu as a base *aéro-terrestre* was intended to distract Giap from Lai Chu and so relieve the T'ai units ready for an evacuation with Operation Pollux. Once French paratroops had linked up with the T'ais they would use Dien Bien Phu as a 'mooring point' from which to attack the Viet Minh's rear areas. This was a terrible gamble because Dien Bien Phu had no ground link with other French garrisons and was 275km by air from Hanoi. Nonetheless, the success at Na San indicated that a garrison could be kept resupplied.

To facilitate Castor, Navarre gathered an initial spearhead of French and Vietnamese paratroops with full combat kit at the Giam-Lam and Bach-Mai airfields just outside Hanoi. These men were under the command of seasoned veterans of the Indochina War, majors Marcel Bigeard, Jean Brechignac and Jean Souquet. On the runways were sixty-seven C-47 Skytrain transport aircraft. Another aircraft carrying Lieutenant General Pierre Bodet, Brigadier General Jean Decheaux and newly promoted Brigadier General Jean Gilles was soon circling over a drizzle and mist shrouded Dien Bien Phu. On their command, three parachute battalions were poised to attack, with the task of seizing three drops zones dotted through the valley.

Prelude to Defeat

Vietnamese National Army on parade, Hanoi, 1951. (Photo Huyme)

Fatefully, on 20 November 1953, Airborne Battle Group 1, consisting of the 1st and 6th colonial parachute battalions and the 2nd Battalion, 1st Chasseurs Parachute Regiment, jumped over the northern and southern drop zones designated 'Natasha' and 'Simone' respectively. Major Bigeard's 6th Colonial Parachute Battalion, landing at 'Natasha', unexpectedly encountered some resistance from Viet Minh regulars who were in the valley undergoing training. Bigeard recalled, 'When we came down on November 20 were told there would be no Vietnamese. But there were two companies exactly where we jumped. Some of my men were killed before they even touched the ground, others were stabbed where they landed.'

His men, recovering tons of equipment, found that many of their radios had not survived the drop and some of their mortars were missing. Bigeard, gathering three of his four companies, and without waiting for support, attacked Dien Bien Phu village. He was met by resistance from Viet Minh regulars of the 148th Regiment, but at 3.00 pm, Souquet's 1st Colonial Parachute Battalion, who had jumped in support, arrived to help. The Viet Minh withdrew in good order and the villagers fled into the mountains. French losses for the day proved to be light, with thirteen dead and forty wounded.

A second force of paratroops jumped into the valley the following day, 21 November, with their commanding officer Lieutenant Colonel Pierre Langlais, who injured a leg, and the overall commander of the operation, Brigadier General Gilles. The Airborne Battle Group 2 comprised the 1st Foreign Legion Parachute, 5th Vietnamese Parachute and the 8th Parachute Assault battalions. A third drop zone, called 'Octavie', was used further south to deliver heavy supplies. The parachute of one of the two bulldozers dropped failed to open fully and it buried itself into the ground.

Dien Bien Phu

By 22 November, after the arrival of a fresh battalion of Vietnamese, there were 4,560 troops at Dien Bien Phu. Langlais, much to his irritation, was airlifted back to Hanoi to get his leg plastered, returning several weeks later.

The paras set about securing the heart-shaped valley, which is 19km long and 13km wide and surrounded by heavily forested hills. They had possession of the village of Dien Bien Phu and a nearby airfield west of the Nam Youm, plus a second one on the east bank to the south of Ban Long Nhai. The first was quickly refurbished, ready for the first C-47 transport aircraft that would form the vital lifeline for the isolated garrison. Defences were also built, while patrols pushed into the hills. At the end of the month, the paras began to pull out to be replaced by infantry. It was now that Giap responded, despatching his 308th and 312th divisions towards the valley.

The first indication that Operation Castor was not destined to go well occurred with the withdrawal from Lai Chau. Although the town had acted as a useful base of operations, it was indefensible, sitting as it did in a valley at the confluence of the Black and Nam Na rivers. It only had a small, exposed dirt airstrip that was prone to flooding. The only other way in and out was by means of a narrow jungle track.

When Lieutenant Colonel Trancart, the French commander at Lai Chau, was told of the planned evacuation in mid-November, he immediately despatched the 700-strong 1st T'ai Partisan Mobile Group to Dien Bien Phu. After a week-long march and a series of communist ambushes, they finally reached their destination. The mobile group's departure

French troops in a damaged village near the Plaine des Jarres, May 1953.

clearly signalled that General Cogny viewed the defence of Lai Chau as untenable, particularly now that Giap's 316th Division was bearing down on the town.

Operation Pollux commenced on 7 December, when generals Cogny and Gilles landed in Lai Chau to personally break the bad news to Deo Van Long, president of the T'ai Federation. French aircraft transported the 301st Vietnamese Infantry Battalion, a paratroop company, elements of the 2nd Moroccan Battalion, 7th Company, 2nd T'ai Battalion and 327 Senegalese of the headquarters staff from the town in over 180 flights. Deo Van Long and his entourage were flown to Hanoi and exile.

To local communist spies, it was all too obvious what was going on. Trancart departed on 10 December after overseeing the destruction of 300 tons of ammunition and 40 vehicles that could not be salvaged. Some 400 mules and pack horses were abandoned. When Giap's 316th Division moved into Lai Chau two days, later they found the French Tricolore still defiantly flying.

Tragically, some 2,100 T'ai irregular light infantry and 36 Europeans were left behind, with the impossible task of fighting their way to Dien Bien Phu. They should have gone earlier with the 1st T'ai Partisan Mobile Group. Instead, many of the remaining T'ai, faced with the prospect of leaving their homes, deserted. The rest, divided into four groups and armed with only rifles, sub-machine guns and a few mortars, were constantly harassed and ambushed by communist and pro-communist forces. They were kept resupplied by air drop.

Seven companies under Lieutenant Guillermit became trapped at Pa Ham Pass and were overrun on 10 December, with just 150 men under Sergeant Arsicaud escaping to Muong Tong, 15km south of Lai Chu. There, 600 irregulars gathered before heading south, hoping to catch Lieutenant Ulpat's column, which included women and children. On 18 December, Dien Bien Phu informed Arsicaud that Ulpat's men, who were just a day's march ahead of him, had been wiped out. His force them came under attack that night and vanished.

Sergeant Blanc, with three other companies as well as elements of the Partisan Mobile Group and dependents from the Vietnamese battalion, were trapped at Muong Pon, 70km from Lai Chu. He tried to get the women and children to a relief column formed by the 2nd Airborne Group that was fighting its way northwards towards him, but failed. His force disappeared while under attack during the night of 12–13 December. The relief column arrived in Muong Pon to find it deserted. Of the twenty T'ai

Colonel de Castries, the French garrison commander, Dien Bien Phu.

companies that had marched out of Lai Chu, the remains of barely half a dozen reached Dien Bien Phu, with just 175 men.

The 2nd Airborne Group also had to fight its way back. In an ominous taste of things to come, reconnaissance aircraft and fighter-bombers supporting it reported being hit by anti-aircraft fire.

The 2nd Airborne Group under Langlais conducted another reconnaissance raid on 23 December, with the aim of linking up with Laotian light infantry and Moroccan Tabors from Laos. The rendezvous point was the Laotian town of Sop Nao, which was in a very mountainous area, thick with jungle and ideal for ambush. Although the link-up was effected two days later, the task force was harried by a mobile enemy and had to return by a far worse route. This again showed that offensive operations conducted from Dien Bien Phu were almost impossible, due to the presence of the enemy and the extremely unforgiving terrain.

Upon gaining intelligence on Giap's movements, Navarre and Cogny began to reconsider their plans. It seemed that Dien Bien Phu might act as bait from where the French could crush the Viet Minh, or at least act as a diversion in anticipation of an attack on the Red River Delta. Also, the almost complete destruction of the T'ai units meant that the original plan to use it as a rallying point was now completely redundant. Dien Bien Phu went from a forward operating base to a fortified camp, defended by a series of armed positions in the same manner as Na San. By the end of the year, there were almost 5,000 French troops at Dien Bien Phu. The scene was set for the decisive battle of the First Indochina War.

Beginning in May 1953, America lent the French six Fairchild C-119 Flying Boxcars.

Prelude to Defeat

All grossly underestimated Giap's capabilities: in Saigon, General Navarre, Lieutenant General Pierre Bodet, his deputy commander-in-chief, General Lauzin, commander of the French air force in Indochina, and Colonel Jean-Louis Nicot, commanding the Indochina air transport group, and in Hanoi, General Cogny and General Jean Dechaux, commander Tactical Air Group North Crucially, they failed to take fully into account the growing power of Giap's artillery and anti-aircraft units, nor did they appreciate his considerable logistical support. They could not conceive that Giap would commit five divisions to Dien Bien Phu. Nor could they conceive that the Viet Minh could capture the surrounding hills and lug their heavy artillery up onto them. If that happened, the French would not be fighting a mobile battle from a fortified base, but instead they would be facing a siege.

General Navarre's hands were now tied, as he noted:

When I occupied Dien Bien Phu I expected to have to deal with two divisions, then eventually two and a half, three ... It was not until 20 December that I learned we would actually be dealing with four divisions. At that point it was too late to evacuate Dien Bien Phu ... If I had withdrawn I would have lost all our men and supplies.

Communist anti-aircraft guns included old Second World War German MG34s.

13. FORTRESS DIEN BIEN PHU

Unbeknown to the French and the Vietnamese, the whole war had led up to this very point in time at Dien Bien Phu. What followed was not a particularly large battle, but it was to prove decisive. Construction of the central base and headquarters area commenced in late November 1953, but work on the perimeter defences did not start until mid-December.

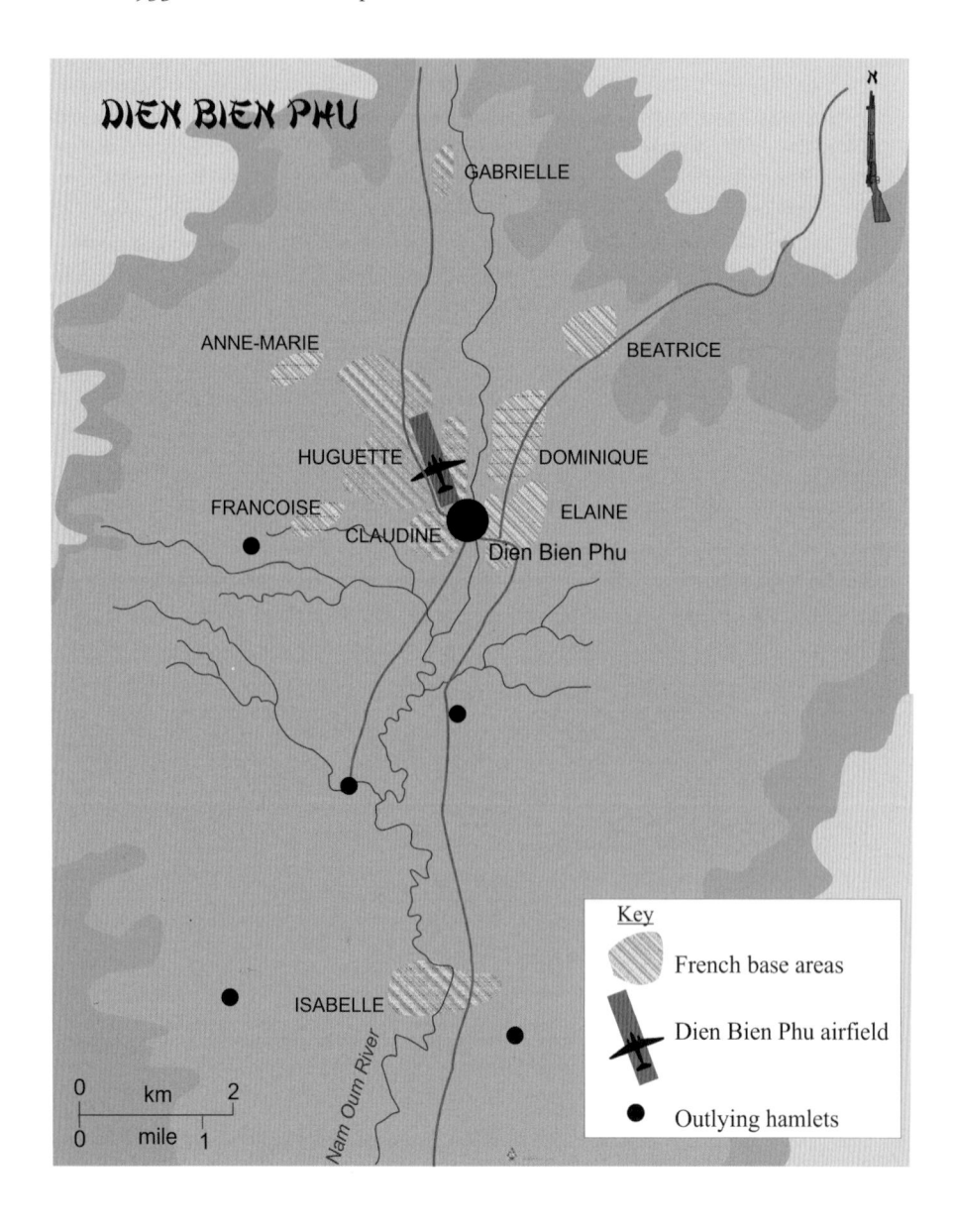

The initial success of Castor, in terms of securing the base, soon meant that Dien Bien Phu was welcoming high-ranking military and political tourists. These included generals Navarre, Cogny and Lauzin, and even the French defence minister René Pleven. Navarre and Gilles were photographed together at Dien Bien Phu in December. They and the six officers behind them all looked in an ebullient mood.

Foreign visitors included the British High Commissioner, Malcolm McDonald, and the British military attaché, General Spears. Among the Americans, was the U.S. army commander in the Pacific, General John 'Iron Mike' O'Daniels. He was a veteran of the First and Second World Wars and had served in Korea as a corps commander. O'Daniels was photographed during his visit and he did not look impressed. Pleven, on the other hand, came away with the right impression.

By the new year Dien Bien Phu, had been fortified with eight defensive bastions, forming an outer and inner ring. To the north of the main airfield, running in an arc through the edge of the surrounding hills, were the defensive positions 'Francoise', 'Anne-Marie', 'Gabrielle' and 'Beatrice'. Gabrielle to the far north was the farthest from the main base. In the centre of the village was the command HQ, with the inner ring comprising 'Huguette' to the northwest of the main airfield, 'Dominque' to the east, 'Claudine' just to the south, and 'Elaine' to the southeast. The most isolated outpost was 'Isabelle', built below the smaller airstrip and some 6.5km from the main base area.

Anne-Marie, Gabrielle, Beatrice and Elaine were built on the lower hills on the fringe of the valley. The rest were largely on the flat valley floor. During a visit, General Navarre had expressed concern that Beatrice, built on a high hill, was isolated, and that if it was captured, it would enable the enemy to overlook the entire base area. He was reassured that if ever this should happen they would be blasted off by the artillery.

Despite any reservations he may have had, General Navarre, having made his decision to fight, poured men and equipment into the valley to ensure that it was the rock upon which the Viet Minh tide would be broken. During December 1953 and January 1954, infantry, armour and artillery units streamed into Dien Bien Phu by air. The garrison at this stage numbered around 10,800 men, backed by two groups of artillery with 75mm, 105mm and 155mm guns, 10 M24 Chaffee light tanks, and 9 Bearcat fighter bombers, stationed on the main airfield.

Viet Minh spies watched with interest as the French set about building their defences across the valley floor. The constant drone of transport aircraft indicated that a major French build-up was underway. From the end of November 1953 through January 1954, an average of 165 tons was delivered every day. It was evident from all the activity to the north around the airfield that this was the focus of the French fortifications, and was therefore where the weight of the Viet Minh assault would take place. Just before battle commenced, Giap had detected 'forty-nine strong-posts, group into three main sectors [around the airfield] capable of supporting each other'.

Many of the French paras, including the 2nd Battalion, 1st Parachute Light Infantry Regiment, 1st Colonial Parachute Battalion and the 5th Vietnamese Parachute Battalion, were withdrawn to act as a mobile reserve. Only the legionnaires of the 1st Para Battalion and the 8th Para Shock Battalion remained. The others were replaced with more heavily armed infantry units and four battalions from the Foreign Legion that included the 1st and 3rd battalions from the 2nd and 3rd Foreign Legion infantry regiments respectively, and the 1st and 3rd battalions of the 13th Foreign Legion Demi-Brigade.

Vietnamese troops digging trenches near Dien Bien Phu's main airfield.

The French showed great ingenuity in getting some of their heavier equipment to the base. When base commander Colonel de Castries requested a squadron of tanks, this posed a particular problem as they were simply too heavy to air drop. The U.S.-built Chaffee tanks had to be dismantled and flown into Dien Bien Phu. Each 18-ton tank was broken down into 180 parts that took six C-47 sorties and two by British Bristol 170 freighters, requisitioned from a commercial Indochinese airline, to deliver. The latter were the only aircraft capable of taking the tanks' hulls. Foreign Legion mechanics reassembled the Chaffees beside the main runway, completing one every two days. Similarly, each 155mm howitzer needed two C-47s and one Bristol 170, plus another seventeen C-47s for the gun crews and ammunition.

The garrison was also bolstered by six battalions of colonial troops, consisting of the 2nd battalion, 1st Algerian Rifle Regiment, the 3rd Battalion, 3rd Algerian Rifle Regiment, the 5th Battalion, 7th Algerian Rifle Regiment, the 1st Battalion, 4th Moroccan Rifle Regiment, plus the 2nd and 3rd T'ai battalions.

Artillery units included the 2nd and 3rd artillery groups, the 4th and 10th colonial artillery regiments, and the 1st Foreign Legion Airborne Heavy Mortar Company. The tanks served with the 1st Light Horse Regiment.

The French air force and navy were called on to support Dien Bien Phu. They operated from four main airfields dotted around Hanoi: Bach Mai to the north, Gia Lam to the east, and Don Son and Cat Bi to the south. Notably, the Flying Boxcar transports of Armée de l'Air flew from Cat Bi. The F4U-7 and AU-1 Corsairs of the Navy's Flottille 14F flew out of Bach Mai. The air force was able to provide two fighter squadrons, two bomber squadrons and four squadrons of transports. Naval aviation comprised two dive-bomber squadrons and a bomber squadron.

A squadron of French Bearcats was deployed to Dien Bien Phu to provide air-to-ground support.

Despite this impressive order of battle, it was nowhere near the strength committed to Operation Loraine. Unlike previous French fire bases, the widely dispersed defences at Dien Bien Phu were far from perfect. It was likened to an idyllic death trap. The picturesque valley was simply too large for a tight all-round defence and too small to manoeuvre in. Notably, the surrounding hills that rise up to 2,500ft easily dominated the principal 1,200yd airfield. The engineers calculated that they required 36,000 tons of equipment – total deliveries for the entire battle only amounted to 22,500 tons. This would have required 12,000 C-47 Skytrain flights from Hanoi. All they received was a third of this tonnage and three-quarters of the deliveries were barbed wire. Here lay part of the cause for the French defeat, because the fortifications were not capable of withstanding an artillery barrage.

To protect the base, Colonel des Castries had just twenty-four American 105mm howitzers, four short-barrelled 155mm howitzers, and thirty-two 120mm heavy mortars. The one-armed Colonel Charles Piroth, commanding these units, considered them more than capable of breaking up enemy attacks. They would provide effective counter-battery fire when the time came. Piroth also thought that the air force operating from the airfield and the delta would pounce on any enemy guns once they started firing. He was completely contemptuous of Giap's gunners, claiming, 'No Viet Minh gun will fire three rounds without being destroyed.'

French troops supported by a Bison light tank.

This was a fatal miscalculation. His batteries were poorly protected. The guns were placed in large circular pits that were very vulnerable to indirect shell and mortar fire.

Piroth, who had lost his left arm in Italy in 1943, was an experienced gunner. Despite his outward confidence, however, he knew his resources were inadequate, pointing out to Colonel de Winter, his superior in Hanoi, that he had fewer artillery pieces than that normally supporting an infantry division. The location of Isabelle particularly hamstrung Piroth's artillery. By the end of January, two batteries had been deployed there, but these were too far away to offer any support to the northern strongpoints. In addition, Piroth's guns relied on observation posts in the hills and six light observation planes. Once the shooting started, these would be lost very quickly. The result was that his gunners would be reliant on spotter planes making a three-hour trip from Muong Sai in Laos.

Concealed in the dense jungles around Dien Bien Phu, Giap and his Chief of Staff, General Hoang Van Thai, began gathering their 304th, 308th, 312th, 316th and 351st divisions, amounting to over 50,000 men. As the latter unit was organized as a heavy division, it had a bigger provision of artillery and mortars, with at least thirty American 105mm (captured in Korea) and eighteen, largely Japanese, 75mm guns, fifty 120mm heavy mortars, and sixty 75mm recoilless guns. Of equal importance, it had an anti-aircraft regiment armed with thirty-six 37mm anti-aircraft guns.

In total, including the artillery battalions serving with the other divisions, Giap had about 145 field howitzers. By early March, he had available some 15,000 105mm and 5,000 75mm shells. Two thirds of the 105mm ammunition was already in the Dien Bien Phu area. However, the Japanese 75mm Type 94 mountain gun was obsolete and much of its ammunition was a decade old.

Once again, the hand of Mao, in the form of General Wei and his advisers, was evident. The Chinese Communists had ample experience with the American M2 A1 105mm howitzer, which had been captured in quantity during the Chinese Civil War and the Korean War. This weapon could drop four high-explosive rounds a minute onto a target up to a range of over 11,000m. According to Giap, the 351st Division received around fifty 105s from the Chinese, most of which had been taken in Korea, and that thirty-six were deployed at Dien Bien Phu. Most of these weapons had presumably been captured from the South Korean rather than the U.S. army.

Equally important was the training his gunners of the 45th Artillery Regiment received on these weapons in southern China. Once they were outside the French base, they ensured their 105s were well dug in and concealed from the air. Dummy guns were also deployed to draw French fire. Artillery observers, with uninterrupted views of the airfield and French defences, took up position to accurately direct the gun fire.

The Viet Minh hacked five routes through the jungle toward the

General Giap.

French base. As well as tens of thousands of porters on foot and using bicycles to shift supplies, Giap's men had 600 Russian-built 2.5-ton lorries, which travelled by night with their lights off to avoid attracting attention. Nonetheless, the weather and French air force together conspired to ensure that this build-up did not run smoothly. The torrential rains turned the valleys into marshes and many fords were impassable. French pilots attacked the Lung Lo and Phadin passes, resulting in sections of the roads sliding into the ravines below.

The French were not ignorant of the Viet Minh build-up, as their air force had detected the movement of men and equipment. By early December, it was estimated that Giap would have about 49,000 men under his command. Aerial intelligence also showed that Giap's 105s had been removed from their rear-base areas. A sizeable attack on Dien Bien Phu was now inevitable.

Giap's logistical support comprised tens of thousands of porters.

14. A DISHONOURED MAN

Giap officially let his presence at Dien Bien Phu be known on 31 January 1954 when his artillery opened fire. They spent six long weeks making and adjusting ranging shots across the base. While the French found it increasingly bothersome, Giap slowly collected very important targeting intelligence. Throughout February, French patrols kept detecting Viet Minh regular units, confirming that Giap had taken the bait and was prepared to fight.

By the middle of the month, any plans to stretch the French defences out to encompass the higher surrounding hills had been abandoned. By doing so Colonel de Castries surrendered the initiative and the vital high ground to Giap. De Castries did not have the manpower to create a wider perimeter, but he should have done his utmost to disrupt the Viet Minh preparations. Instead, he settled back to await Giap's first attack.

General Navarre paid his last visit to the base on 4 March 1954, during which he discussed with de Castries bringing in reinforcements. The general was clearly rattled by the strength of the force Giap had brought to bear on the valley.

'I was much less confident than the local commandant,' said Navarre. 'I thought of suddenly bringing in three additional battalions – and since the Viet Minh were very methodical I thought they would then think twice.'

De Castries reassured him that they were not needed and should be kept in reserve. 'That is what I did,' recalled Navarre, 'I was probably wrong.'

During November and December, the valley was verdant and dotted with trees. By early March, it had been turned into a desolate lunar landscape. The trees had been hacked or blasted down and the banks of the Nam Youm River stripped bare. The central headquarters area on the west bank was a mass of bunkers, earthworks, trenches and revetments. Just to the north were

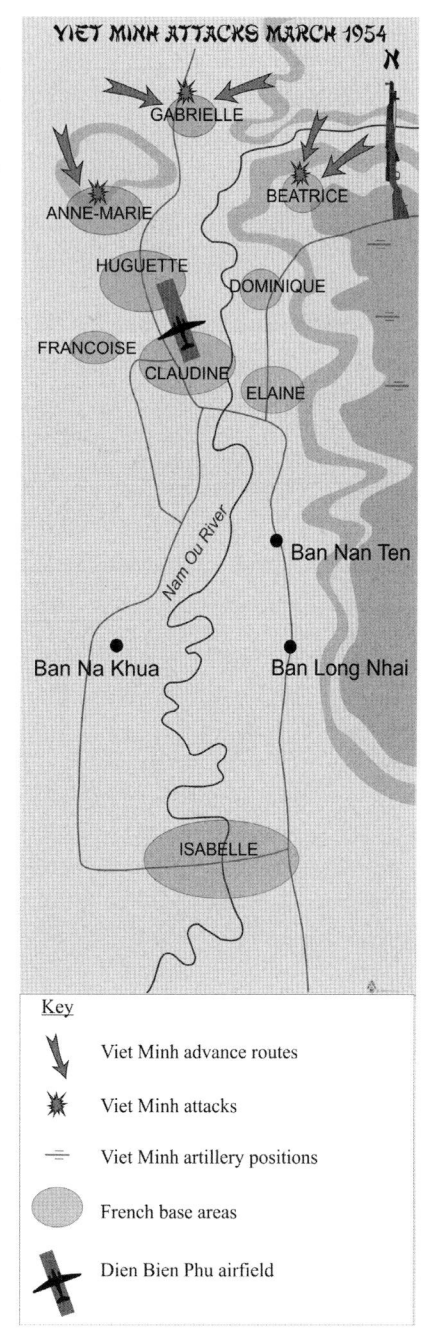

French machine-gunners awaiting attack.

the gun pits for some of the 105s and the 155s. Beyond them were aircraft dispersal pens created by banked earth.

Both sides knew that the fighting would commence to the north. It was the Algerian garrison of Gabrielle that sustained the first probing attacks on 11 March. Giap had a choice to either take Gabrielle or cut it off by capturing Anne-Marie and Beatrice to the southwest and southeast. It was decided to attack all three. However, looking at their maps, Giap and his divisional commanders decided that Beatrice, consisting of four strongpoints that were out on a limb, would be their next main target. The battle of Dien Bien Phu was about to start in earnest.

Colonel de Castries knew roughly where the blow was to fall. The following day, he briefed his commanders to expect an attack on the 13th at 5.00 pm. His suspicions were confirmed when Viet Minh movements were detected in the area of Beatrice and Gabrielle, after two regiments from the 312th Division moved into position less than 100yd from the French defences. The vulnerability of the main airfield and the airstrip near Isabelle were soon illustrated when artillery fire ranged in from 9.00 am on 12 March, destroying two C-47s, while others were riddled with shrapnel on the taxiways or as they tried to come in to land.

Just two Bearcats were serviceable that day, the rest having been damaged by the hail of hot shell fragments. They managed ten sorties between them, buzzing angrily around the valley looking for somewhere to drop their 500lb bombs. The fighter and transport pilots found themselves attracting increasing anti-aircraft fire from machine guns, 20mm cannons and 37mm AA guns concealed beneath the dense hillside foliage. Six Hellcats flying from the carrier *Arromanches* tried to help suppress the flak, but struggled to find their targets and futilely bombed the same locations. Unable to get back to the carrier, one of the aircraft crashed trying to find Cat Bi airfield.

At 5.15 pm on 13 March, Giap's 105s began to drop shells onto Beatrice for the next two hours. It was a shocking taste of things to come. Communication trenches were blasted into oblivion, inadequate gun positions and bunkers collapsed. Deadly flying debris and shock waves killed or wounded anyone caught in the open. French counter-battery fire proved wholly ineffective. Beatrice lost two 105mm guns to enemy artillery fire. The French, in a desperate attempt to protect the three northern outposts, wastefully fired off 25 per cent of their 105mm ammunition in one night. Lieutenant Colonel Jules Gaucher, the post commander, and the men of Major Paul Pégot's 3rd Battalion, 13th Demi-Brigade of the Foreign Legion, braced themselves for the inevitable.

While Beatrice and the airfield were being bombarded, shells also fell on Gabrielle, Dominique and Isabelle. On the airfield, accurate shelling took out the VHF radio beacon, damaged the temporary control tower and blew up two Bearcats. At Dominique, a heavy-mortar platoon, just about to provide counter-preparation fire on the Viet Minh's assembly trenches before Beatrice, was pulverized by a direct hit on one of the weapon pits. Then their ammunition dump containing 5,000 mortar bombs exploded in a brilliant ball of flames. The garrison of Gabrielle was also prevented from providing supporting fire to Beatrice by a series of diversionary attacks.

Crawling forward from their assault trenches, at 6.15 pm, brave Viet Minh sappers blew holes in the remaining barbed wire around Beatrice. Fifteen minutes later, just as their infantry opened the assault, Beatrice's battalion command post received a number

Troops of the 1st Foreign Legion Heavy Mortar company who fought at Dien Bien Phu.

of direct hits. Pégot was killed and Gaucher mortally wounded. Despite losing their senior officers, the legionnaires engaged in desperate hand-to-hand combat as the Viet Minh sought to overwhelm them. By 9.00 pm, just one strongpoint was still holding out. Three hours later it was all over.

The garrison suffered 75 per cent casualties with just over 100 men escaping back to their lines. Giap's artillery stopped firing and a stunned silence fell over the valley. The stench of explosives hung in the air.

Colonel de Castries was shocked that Beatrice had held for just six hours. If Giap could repeat this success, then Dien Bien Phu was unlikely to last much more than a week. In the early hours of 14 March, he reluctantly reported to Cogny in Hanoi that he had lost a battalion and Beatrice. This was at a cost of around 125 dead and some 200 captured, most of whom were wounded. As Giap had intended, Gabrielle was now extremely isolated, and the 88th and 165th regiments from the 308th and 312th divisions moved into position ready to strike.

General Navarre was dismayed by the incoming reports of the strength, accuracy and closeness of the Viet Minh guns:

> All the French and American artillerymen who had visited Dien Bien Phu – and there were many Americans – thought that the Viet Minh would have to stay behind the ridges to fire on the entrenched camp. The surprise was that they managed to bring their artillery much closer than we had thought possible.

Tourane airfield, in 1954, showing 25 Vought F4U-7/AU-1 Corsairs, four Grumman F8F Bearcats and a solitary Douglas C-27 Skytrain.

A Dishonoured Man

On 14 March, French reinforcements arrived in the form of a para drop by the 5th Vietnamese Parachute Battalion, commanded by Captain Botella. De Castries briefly contemplated trying to retake Beatrice, but low cloud and poor weather made close air support impossible. At 6.00 pm, Giap's batteries began shelling Gabrielle, which was held by a battalion of Algerians with eight Foreign Legion 120mm mortars. Although they beat off the first assault, by dawn on the 15th, they were only holding on in one remaining outpost.

Lieutenant Colonel Trancart, who was in charge of the northern sector, was watching the heavy shelling of Gabrielle when a distraught Colonel Piroth came into his dugout.

'I am completely dishonoured,' cried Piroth. 'I have guaranteed de Castries that the enemy artillery couldn't touch us – but now we are going to lose the battle.'

The admission that no one wanted to hear, or acknowledge, was true.

Lieutenant Colonel Langlais organized a counterattack towards Gabrielle, employing two companies of legionnaires and one battalion of Vietnamese paratroopers, supported by six tanks. They fought their way to within 1,000yd of the Algerians, enabling 150 men to escape to safety. De Castries had lost his second outlying strongpoint in just two days. Within the garrison there was a sinking feeling that after all their efforts in building the base's defences, perhaps Dien Bien Phu was untenable.

Unfortunately for them, generals Navarre and Cogny were not Leclerc or de Lattre – both the latter would have quickly taken firm control of the situation and sought a solution to safeguard the garrison. Indeed, neither of them would have ever dreamed of underestimating their enemy and extending French forces in such a manner. The uninspired de Castries seemed to slip into an ever-deepening despondency, while Navarre and Cogny strove to blame each other for the unfolding mess.

Even at this early stage in the battle, everyone at senior level was preparing for a worst-case scenario. The French had the decisive conventional battle they had always hoped for, but they were already losing. They had realized too late that Dien Bien Phu was simply too damn far away. The agony, though, was only just beginning. In Saigon and Hanoi, the only solution was to belatedly send in the paras to beef up the defences. They could come up with no other options.

Langlais, commander of the Airborne Battle Group 2, was furious at how the action was progressing. De Castries was a reflective-looking man, whereas Langlais was wiry, gaunt and tough in appearance. He never seemed to be without a cigarette firmly clamped between his lips. Langlais was described as hatchet-faced, while de Castries was dubbed aloof and highly aristocratic.

Although de Castries lacked neither courage nor panache, he was overwhelmed by unfolding events and did not have the ability to control a battle of this magnitude. To be fair however, he was operating way above his pay grade. He was commanding a division-sized operation that required a general. The French, though, always ran these types of operation employing a colonel, for fear of losing someone more senior. If anyone should have been in command, it was Brigadier General Gilles as the ranking officer.

The angry Langlais took his wrath out on Piroth, whose pledge to silence Giap's guns had come back to haunt him. Despite their best effort, his gunners and the French air force had singularly let down the garrison. Feeling dishonoured and ashamed, on 15 March, while in his quarters, Piroth took a hand grenade and pulled the pin using his teeth. His death was hushed up for fear it would harm already poor morale.

Dien Bien Phu

French wounded being evacuated.

French trenches at Dien Bien Phu.

A Dishonoured Man

Giap's logistical support comprised of tens of thousands of porters.

When Bigeard was informed of Piroth's death he said:

> I had known him as a man of duty and heart who had said that as soon as a Vietnamese cannon was found he would overpower it. But they were invulnerable. We could fire 100 shots on their positions and still be incapable of destroying their cannon. Giap had attacked only when he felt that everything was just right.

The following day, the mood lifted slightly when Major Bigeard and his 6th Colonial Parachute Battalion dropped back into the valley. From 14 March to 6 May, the French parachuted and air-landed 4,300 men to reinforce the base. This boost, however, was short lived, as the 3rd T'ai Battalion holding Anne-Marie knew that they would be next in the firing line and have to abandon their posts. Two companies fled from two of Anne-Marie's four positions. A third of Dien Bien Phu's defensive bastions had now fallen.

In Hanoi, General Cogny was anxious about the situation in the Red River Delta. Intelligence showed that the Viet Minh could muster thirty-nine battalions, of which twenty-four were regulars. Their key units were the reconstituted 320th Division and six regular, independent regiments. Additionally, they had some 50,000 communist militiamen. Cogny had at his disposal around 100 battalions, less than a third of which were mobile, and of them, just sixteen were in the mobile groups. He was also concerned that Navarre was persisting with Operation Atlante in southern Vietnam, which was tying up sizeable forces. The bulk of these, however, were ineffectual Vietnamese troops who were proving that Navarre's 'Vietnamization' process was not working.

15. THE VULTURE HOVERS

By early April 1954, it was clear that something drastic needed to be done to help the trapped garrison at Dien Bien Phu. There were three options on the table. The first and most obvious was to get a relief column through to the base to break the siege, dubbed Operation Condor. Secondly, the garrison could fight its way out with Operation Albatros. Lastly, if Washington would agree to help with Operation Vulture, the Viet Minh could be pounded into withdrawing by American heavy bombers.

What Navarre and de Castries really needed was a combination of all three, which would enable the defenders to withdraw into Laos towards Luang Prabang, as this would be slightly easier to get to than the Red River Delta. The loss of Lai Chau and Na San meant that there was no sanctuary for them in western Tonkin. In truth, though, Giap's strength was such that a successful escape was almost impossible. The only real solution was to kill as many of Giap's men as possible to force him to lift the siege.

Condor had originally been conceived in the event of victory as a linkup between those French forces at Dien Bien Phu and those in northeastern Laos. This would have involved around 5,500 troops. During the first week of April, Navarre sent Colonel de Crèvecoeur, land forces commander in Laos, instructions to revise Condor. Navarre also sent de Crèvecoeur and Colonel Then, his staff officer responsible for operations, a small team to help out.

They had four battalions with just over 3,000 men available, but nearly 1,700 of these were Laotians. Only one unit was European, the 2nd Battalion, 2nd Foreign Legion Infantry Regiment. This force was optimistically designated Mobile Group North. In the light of the Viet Minh's manpower at Dien Bien Phu, these forces were woefully inadequate, even if they were augmented while on the march. There was little de Crèvecoeur and Then could do, but proceed with their mission as they had been given their orders to help.

After some frantic planning, it was proposed that the legionnaires and the 4th Laotian Chasseurs under Lieutenant Colonel Yves Godard would march up the eastern leg of the Nam Ou River bend. A second group, commanded by Major Coquelet, consisting of the 1st Laotian Parachute Battalion and the 5th Laotian Chasseurs, would make their way up the Nam Pak towards Muong Khoua to the west. Then the two columns would merge at Pak Noua and move along the Nam Noua to rendezvous with paras from the 1st and 3rd Vietnamese parachute battalions dropped west of Sop Nao. This force would then proceed through the Massif des Calacaires to reach a point south of Isabelle.

To accomplish this, de Crèvecoeur needed 500 porters and 150 mules to carry supplies and ammunition for Mobile Group North, but these were simply not available. The region had been pillaged following the Viet Minh invasion, and the locals had fled. There was also a shortage of jerry cans to transport water and inflatable rafts to get the force over the innumerable streams and rivers that would bar their way. Navarre's response to this

The Vulture Hovers

was to have mules and 500 prisoner labourers airlifted in, but this put even greater pressure on the already struggling French transport fleet.

On 14 April, Navarre ordered Condor be implemented. Plans were likewise made ready to carry out Albatros. It quickly turned out that he did not have the resources to conduct the airborne phase of Condor and keep Dien Bien Phu resupplied at the same time. To drop the two para battalions would require diverting all the transport aircraft away from Dien Bien Phu for twenty-four hours. Some would also have to be regularly diverted to supply the rescue columns by air during their advance through the jungles of northeastern Laos. This would inevitably severely disrupt vital ammunition resupply flights into Dien Bien Phu.

Behind the scenes, the French government desperately sought help in Washington. The same day Condor was authorized, General Earle E. Partridge, commanding U.S. Far East Air Forces, arrived in Saigon to prepare an American bombing feasibility study. His bomber commander, General Joseph D. Caldera, flew over Dien Bien Phu three times and concluded that a daytime raid would be possible. Both generals, though, were concerned by the French lack of comprehension of the destructive power of a wing of B-29 Superfortress heavy bombers. Nor did the French seem greatly concerned about inevitable 'collateral' damage.

On 15 April, the French Secretary of State for the Air Force, M. Christiaens, publicly announced that France had asked if it could borrow American B-29s that would be operated by French crews. Such a pretence fooled no one, as the French had no experience of operating this type of bomber. At a staff meeting in Hanoi the following day, General Cogny began exploring alternatives to Condor. He wanted another raid on the communist base at Phu Doan and a para drop to cut Viet Minh supply lines at the Meo Pass, but these were rejected as impractical.

USAF B-29 on a bombing mission over Korea. The French had no concept of the damage such a bomber could cause. In mid-April 1954, the French asked to borrow American B-29 bombers to attack Viet Minh positions at Dien Bien Phu.

In Washington, President Eisenhower was presented with plans that envisaged up to 200 American bombers flying from Manila and Okinawa to destroy Giap's positions around Dien Bien Phu. These proposals also considered options for deploying the U.S. Seventh Fleet to provide up to 150 fighters to escort sixty B-29 bombers to Tonkin. Such a commitment would be a significant game changer for the battle.

It was at this stage that the threat of nuclear war once again reared its ugly head. According to Vice-President Richard Nixon, 'In Washington the Joint Chiefs of Staff devised a plan, known as Operation Vulture, for using three small tactical atomic bombs to destroy Viet Minh positions and relieve the garrison.'

In mid-April, French Foreign Minister Georges Bidault claimed that the Americans had offered to make two bombs available for such an operation. Admiral W. Radford, chairman of the U.S. Joint Chiefs of Staff, backed going nuclear in Indochina. America had considered doing so in Korea to stop the Chinese, but decided that this would be a step too far in escalating the conflict, besides which, the decision to authorize the atomic bombing of Hiroshima and Nagasaki continued to haunt American policy-makers.

All this discussion about American bombers and nuclear bombs may have been part of a deliberate ploy to get Mao to pressure Ho Chi Minh and Giap to slacken their grip on Dien Bien Phu. Mao acquiesced to the status quo in Korea, partly due to America's very public threats to use tactical nuclear weapons if a negotiated settlement was not reached. In 1950, President Truman had been ambushed by a reporter into stating that the use of nuclear weapons in Korea was a possibility. He inadvertently added that responsibility would rest with General Douglas MacArthur, whereas such a move actually required presidential authorization. This caused an international furore, particularly in Britain, where politicians were aghast at the idea.

Although Truman sought to sooth ruffled feathers, just two weeks into the Korean War, the U.S. Joint Chiefs of Staff did consider the use of atomic bombs in direct support of ground combat. The deployment of up to twenty bombs was discussed, with MacArthur suggesting one be used to cut off any Chinese intervention. The idea was shelved until the end of the year, when Mao committed his armies in North Korea to drive back the UN forces. The following year, with the development of tactical nuclear weapons, a single B-29 had conducted a simulated atomic-bombing run over North Korea. Sabre rattling or not, it signalled intent.

Two years later, with the U.S. military reinvigorated, President Eisenhower was even less reticent. He had begun looking at potential targets in North Korea, China and Manchuria to demonstrate the power of a tactical nuclear bomb. A warning was passed through the Indian prime minister to Chinese Foreign Minister Chou En Lai that if a resolution was not forthcoming, then America would bomb north of the Yalu River.

Whether Eisenhower was bluffing is unclear, but China and the Soviet Union believed him. In late February 1953, Mao sent his leading atomic expert to Moscow to ask Stalin either for a nuclear guarantee or the means of retaliation if Eisenhower used the bomb against China. Stalin died the following month and Chou En Lai, who acted as a pallbearer at his funeral, returned from Moscow convinced that Eisenhower meant business. The conflict in Korea came to an end.

Eisenhower now faced another terrible decision with Indochina. He had the same dilemma Truman had in not goading China into an all-out war. In 1951, General MacArthur had been sacked for pressing to expand the Korean War into China, despite the fact that Chinese troops were fighting American soldiers in Korea. In the name of maintaining world peace, the conflict had been confined to Korea.

If Eisenhower agreed to help France, then his actions might save the French garrison, but there was no knowing how the Soviet Union or China might react. Using American-crewed bombers to drop conventional or nuclear bombs would signal Washington's entry into the Indochina War. In response, Mao might commit his ground forces, which would simply overwhelm the French if the Americans did not then put boots on the ground in Tonkin.

General Matthew Ridgway, who had commanded U.S. forces in Korea and then served as Supreme Allied Commander Europe for NATO before being appointed U.S. Army Chief of Staff, was implacably opposed to using nuclear weapons. He wrote:

> There is of course the school that argues for the immediate use of nuclear weapons when a stalemate threatens, that talks of "reducing the enemy to the Stone Age" by blowing his homeland to dust. This to me would be the ultimate immorality. It is one thing to do this in retaliation, or as a measure of survival as a nation. It is quite another to initiate such an operation for less basic reasons.

In Saigon, Navarre was nervous that Mao might retaliate by authorizing the Chinese air force to attack the vulnerable French airfields in the Red River Delta. Chinese and indeed Soviet air power, had played a major role in Korea. The French air force did not relish tangling with veteran Chinese or Soviet MiG pilots. This meant that U.S. carrier fighters in the Gulf of Tonkin would have to protect Navarre's airfields as well as striking at Dien Bien Phu. It was hard to see how mission creep could be avoided.

Eisenhower wanted British support with any military intervention in Indochina, but his old ally Churchill would not sanction it. Britain's defence budget was stretched to the limit as it was, and the Korean war had been very unpopular. Churchill was well aware that British intelligence had warned against meddling in Indochina, assessing that, 'Any direct intervention by the armed forces of any external nation would probably lead to Chinese intervention, and there is a danger that it might ultimately lead to a global war.'

In the end, Eisenhower decided against Vulture. The French were on their own.

Everything now hung on Condor and Albatros to retrieve the situation. Intercepted Viet Minh radio messages showed that the 148th Regiment had first reported on the progress of Condor on 20 April. This intelligence also showed that the Viet Minh knew what the French were trying to achieve, and that they anticipated airdrops on Nga Na Song and Sop Nao as they were on the most direct road to Dien Bien Phu.

The following day, Goddard received some bad news: his men captured a small boat on the Nam Ou bearing mortar ammunition. When they interrogated the three-man crew, they discovered that they belonged to a 1,700-strong Viet Minh regiment.

At this point, the vexed issue to transport aircraft became a real problem. On 22 April, Navarre signalled Lieutenant General Pierre Bodet, his deputy commander-in-chief in Hanoi, telling him that the second phase of Condor was on hold until further notice.

By 23 April, the lead elements of Condor force were within 50km of Isabelle, but Giap moved at least four battalions to intercept them. Godard had reached Pak Noua and

Coquelet had reached Muong Khoua. As the airborne element was postponed, Sop Nao was abandoned in favour of Muong Nha as the new drop zone.

Confusion though still reigned over the viability of the para drop and, instead, on 27 April, it was decided to reinforce Godard with two battalions that would somehow be airlifted from central Laos. Two days later, Navarre informed de Crèvecoeur that the airborne phase of Condor could not be conducted for at least another week. Feebly, he washed his hands of the operation by telling de Crèvecoeur it was up to him as to how he wished to proceed. Godard had no choice but go on to the defensive and halt his advance at Muong Khoua.

Colonel de Crèvecoeur's men were left out on a limb in hostile territory. His understandable concern was what would happen to them in the event of Dien Bien Phu falling. By early May, there were ominous reports that some 10,000 Viet Minh from the siege were expected to move into Laos. If that should happen, General Cogny in Hanoi informed him, then Mobile Group North would have to immediately retreat with all haste. He could expect no air support or reinforcements. Effectively, they were being abandoned. De Crèvecoeur and Then must have felt that Condor had been a complete waste of time and that Godard and Coquelet were little more than sacrificial lambs.

U.S. President Eisenhower welcoming president of South Vietnam Ngo Dinh Diem, left, at Washington National Airport, 1957. Eisenhower threatened to deploy tactical nuclear weapons in Korea, but he refused to release heavy bombers or nuclear bombs to support the French in Indochina. (Photo NARA)

16. ISABELLE IS TAKEN

Following the successful capture of Beatrice, Gabrielle and Anne-Marie, General Giap was confident that he could move in for the kill at Dien Bien Phu. The French had completely underestimated his ability to dominate the battlefield, as much as they had overestimated the ability of their fighter-bombers to impede his movements. The French air force only had about 100 strike aircraft, of which three-quarters were committed to the battle, but they could not generate enough sorties to drive the Viet Minh away. Likewise, the French had insufficient transport aircraft.

Now that Giap's artillery completely dominated the main airfield, Cogny could not fly in reinforcements and supplies. The only way to do this was by parachute drop, but the transport aircraft still had to brave enemy anti-aircraft fire on the approach. However, Giap's losses during the frontal assaults had been heavy, and it was decided to revert to good old-fashioned siege warfare before renewing the attack. His men set about completing over seven miles of trenches and approach routes. To the south of the airfield, Viet Minh sappers dug a 50yd tunnel under Elaine and filled it with explosives ready to blast the outpost into oblivion.

It was in the last week of March that what was dubbed rather unkindly the parachute 'Mafia' began to dominate the defence of Dien Bien Phu. The overwhelmed Colonel de Castries informally passed de facto command of the garrison over to Langlais, with the exception of Isabelle, which was under legionnaire Lieutenant Colonel André Lalande. The latter was a highly competent officer who grimly held onto isolated Isabelle, despite constant shelling and attacks. Major Bigeard, who had dropped into the valley with his parachute battalion eight days earlier, was to act alongside Langlais. There could be no hiding de Castries's crippling inertia. Upon his

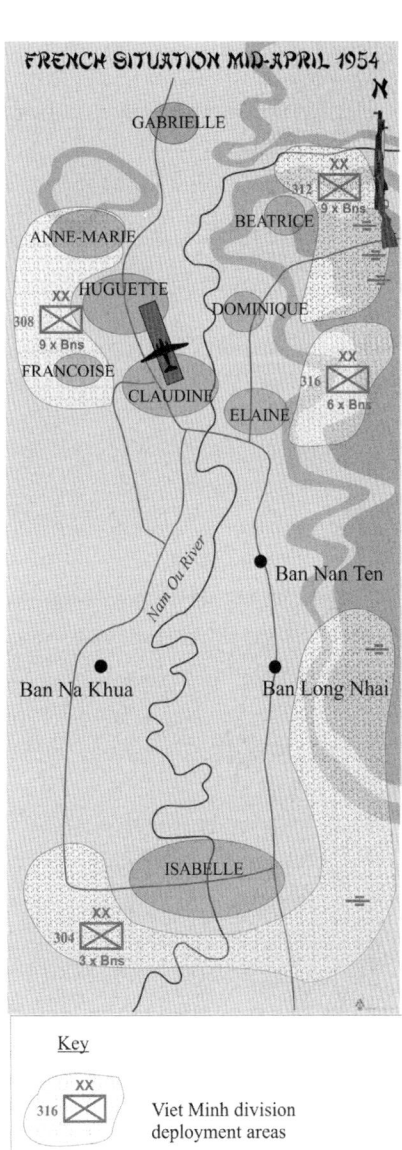

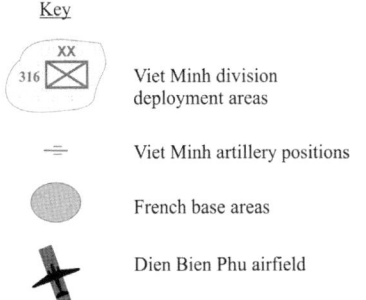

103

arrival, Bigeard recalled he 'found a colonel in command who did not dare come out of the shelter'.

Late on 30 March, after heavy preliminary bombardment, Giap launched his second offensive when the 312th and 316th divisions attacked Domonique and Elaine. Bitter fighting followed, with positions continually changing hands. In a single day, French artillery expended 13,000 rounds of 105mm ammunition while supporting those positions under attack. Over the next few days, the Viet Minh also assaulted Huguette and Isabelle. The pressure on the exhausted garrison was relentless, but they fought back with all their strength.

Napalm, used to such devastating effect at Vinh Yen, proved to be far less effective at Dien Bien Phu because of the density of the surrounding jungle. In a bid to break up Giap's massed attacks, French air force Invader and French navy Catalina bombers dropped 227kg Hail (Lazy Dog) anti-personnel cluster bombs, which contained 11,200 finned missiles. These, technically, were not bombs as they contained no explosive. They were solid, unguided kinetic projectiles that could reach up to 500mph before hitting the ground. While these proved highly effective piercing anything with which they came into contact, unfortunately for the defenders there were not enough of these cluster bombs or aircraft to drop them round the clock.

The French position at Francoise was next to fall. When frightened T'ai troops defending the forward outpost fled, the remaining two Foreign Legion companies holding

American C-46D Commandos were used to fly support missions to Dien Bien Phu. (Photo USAF)

the rest of strongpoint were forced to withdraw to Huguette to the northeast. This loss exposed the heavily shelled airfield even more. Lieutenant Colonel Langlais decided not to take any more chances and ordered all T'ai auxiliaries be disarmed, except for their non-commissioned officers. He was fed up with them being untrustworthy.

Giap's 308th Division was thrown against the defences of Huguette on 2 April. Bigeard responded by scraping together men for a counterattack, using elements of four para battalions. The Viet Minh were driven off, leaving 800 dead in the wire. For a brief moment, morale soared, especially when Bigeard's force went on to recapture one of Elaine's lost strongpoints. French professionalism shone out that day.

In Saigon and Hanoi, all Navarre and Cogny could do to help was to maintain the airstrikes and supply drops, which amounted to ninety tons daily. Frustratingly, up to 30 per cent of this was missing the French perimeter and falling into the hands of the Viet Minh, who were always grateful for extra 105mm ammunition. In terms of reinforcements, they continued to send in the tough paras. Reinforcements from the 2nd Battalion, 1st Parachute Infantry Regiment, under Major Bréchignac, jumped on 3–4 April.

Not all was going well for Giap, however, as French firepower was still exacting an appalling toll on his frontal attacks. By 4 April, he had lost almost 2,000 soldiers. French counterattacks had recaptured Domonique and parts of Elaine. Giap decided to pull his men back to recuperate before discipline collapsed. Nonetheless, his artillery kept firing and his men kept working their trenches ever closer to the remaining French positions.

Langlais, Bigeard and de Castries used the time to reorganize their defences. These were now squeezed into an area a little over 1.5km in diameter, encompassing Claudine, Elaine and parts of Domonique and Huguette, with Isabelle still isolated way to the south. To the west, the Viet Minh's 308th Division, with some nine battalions, was ensconced in the captured positions of Anne-Marie and Francoise, relentlessly firing down on Huguette and Claudine. To the east, the 312th Division, with a similar number of battalions, was positioned around Beatrice overlooking Domonique, while to the southwest, Elaine's garrison was faced by the 316th Division with six battalions. The 1,800 men holding Isabelle were cut off by 7 April, as three battalions from the 304th Division had dug trenches all around them.

Two days later, Major Liesenfelt arrived with his 2nd Foreign Legion Parachute Battalion. Altogether three paratroop battalions had reinforced the garrison since mid-March, which meant that some 16,000 French Union troops were surrounded by an estimated 50,000 Viet Minh. Liesenfelt's men reinforced Bigeard's 6th Colonial Para Battalion during the battle for Elaine on 11–12 April. This fighting also involved the 1st Foreign Legion Parachute Battalion, the 2nd Battalion, 1st Para Light Infantry Regiment, and the 5th Vietnamese Para Battalion.

Despite the French success around Elaine, the situation was getting extremely desperate for the garrison at Dien Bien Phu. By mid-April, food shortages forced them to cut their rations. Critical medical supplies were also running short. Although Operation Condor had been launched from northern Laos, it would take the relief column two weeks to get anywhere near Isabelle. Also, it was hard to imagine how it would prise Giap's vice-like grip from the base. Hopes that the United States Air Force might intervene had been dashed by President Eisenhower. French air force General Lauzin, and his transport commander Colonel Nicot, knew that they could not support both Condor and Dien Bien Phu, but had little choice but to try.

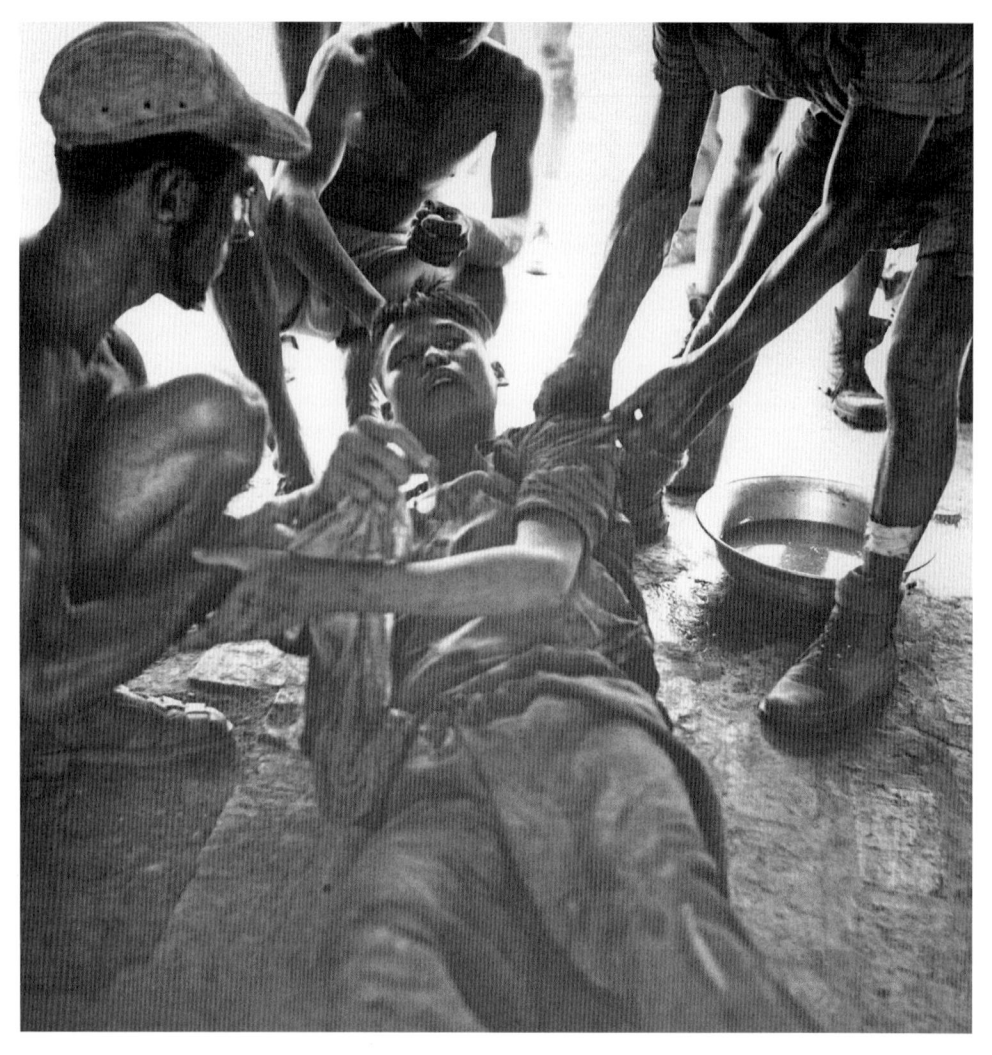

French medics see to a wounded Vietnamese soldier.

Not before time, the French government decided to recognize the efforts of those trapped. The French media was covering the siege and the public were well aware of what was going on. They were captivated by stories of tough legionnaires and paras fending off hordes of communists. Colonel de Castries found himself promoted to brigadier general, while lieutenant colonels Langlais and Lalande were promoted to full colonels, and Major Bigeard to lieutenant colonel. The purpose of these field promotions was not entirely clear.

Meanwhile, Hugeutte to the northwest of the airfield was under constant attack. Supply drops were becoming ever more difficult, which meant a considerable fall in the tonnages being delivered. For the rest of the month, the Viet Minh continued to wear down the battered defences of Huguette. To make matters even worse for the French, on 22 April the monsoon season arrived, with heavy rains flooding their remaining strongpoints. The trenches and dugouts became awash in mud and debris. It was at this point that General Navarre abandoned the second phase of Operation Condor.

Giap and his commanders now realized that the time was right. The garrison, with no hope of rescue, and with the supply situation worsening day by day, were sitting ducks. Langlais, Bigeard, de Castries and all the others knew that they had been left to their fate. Talk of escape was ridiculous – where would they go? Brigadier General de Castries was informed that Condor and Vulture had failed and that Albatros was now the garrison's only hope of salvation. At best, up to 3,000 men in three combat groups might fight their way out. These would consist of Langlais with the paratroops, Lemeunier with the legionaries and Lalande with Isabelle's garrison. They would travel light, carrying only four days of rations and their small arms. Every available piece of artillery and mortars, plus fighter-bombers, would support the breakout. The lightly wounded would also provide covering fire. De Castries would remain with the rear guard and the badly wounded.

Leaving late in the day, the intention was that the three breakout groups, once they had reached the cover of the forest, would head southeast to meet elements of Godard's forces, who would move to Muong Nha. De Castries knew that to stand any chance of success, his men would have to break out in all directions to confuse the enemy, and because the tracks heading south could not handle large numbers of men without causing a dangerous bottleneck.

Cogny was against Albatros and with good reason, for he feared that the retreat would turn into a repeat of Lai Chau. The spectacle of French legionnaires and paratroopers being hunted down and annihilated in the jungle was too much to contemplate. Those not killed or captured would become separated and starve. In addition, Colonel de Crèvecoeur in Laos did not believe that Lieutenant Colonel Godard's relief units could get to Muong Nha any earlier than 20 May. It was simply too late. Colonel Dominique Bastiani, Cogny's chief of staff, appreciated the garrison was tired, hungry and demoralized, advising that in the face of a strong enemy and difficult terrain there would be only one outcome. Cogny agreed and felt that the garrison should resist until the very last. This would serve France's sense of honour, especially as the garrison had fought so heroically throughout the battle.

Unfortunately, additional help from the French navy was too little too late. In early April, the navy rushed Flottille 14F to Indochina. Leaving their aircraft at their home base in Bizerte, Tunisia, the pilots and ground crew were flown to Saigon. The American carrier USS *Saipan* delivered former U.S. Marine Vought AU-1 Corsairs for them to fly. This unit was not combat ready until 25 April, its contribution to breaking the siege simply too late. Like its carrier-borne cousin the Bearcat, the Corsairs flew all their missions from land bases.

Those pilots supporting Dien Bien Phu were completely exhausted and were nearing physical breakdown. On 30 April, the French carrier *Bois Belleau* arrived to relieve the *Arromanches*. As well as Squadron 14F, she was supposed to take *Arromanches*'s Squadron 11F. Its pilots, though, had been in combat for four months and were grounded on medical grounds the very next day. A total of just twenty-eight fighters were available, plus twenty-six B-26 bombers and five naval Privateer bombers.

Dien Bien Phu

Entrenched Viet Minh at Dien Bien Phu.

By the end of the month, the garrison was down to just three days of rations. Ammunition amounted to 275 rounds for the 155s, 14,000 for the 105s and 5,000 for the 120s. It was clear that Dien Bien Phu could not last much longer. Giap ordered a general offensive to commence at 10.00 pm on 1 May. It was time for the kill.

Isabelle is Taken

French dead and wounded being gathered – 9,000 were captured.

Even at this late stage, Cogny and Navarre were contemplating sending three more paratroop battalions to reinforce the beleaguered garrison. It is not clear what they hoped these units could achieve – perhaps they vainly thought that if the defenders could inflict enough casualties on Giap, he would be compelled to withdraw. Elements of the 1st Colonial Parachute Battalion were dropped on 2 May. However, the newly arrived 3rd Foreign Legion Parachute and 7th Colonial Parachute battalions were held back, in the delusion that they could support Operation Condor, should it ever be restarted.

The fresh paras could do little to help stem the tide. The weakened positions to the northwest and northeast of the main base area began to fall one by one. A steady flow of farewells kept coming into the command bunker over the radio. On 2 May, bombers and fighters few direct support, plus flak- and artillery-suppression missions, but of the 128 tons of supplies dropped, less than 65 tons were received by the garrison. Frustratingly, the worsening weather conditions forced many of the transport aircraft to return home still fully laden.

It was now that fresh Chinese weapons helped crush and terrify the still defiant garrison. Giap unleashed a new kind of hell on the afternoon of 6 May, when his troops began to bombard the remains of the base with a dozen Chinese six-barrelled rocket launchers. At least two batteries of these were firing from the northeast in the area of Gabrielle and Beatrice. Based on the Second World War German Nebelwerfer, these screeching launchers were only silenced when the clouds dropped over the hilltops. By this stage, the French had just eight 105s and one 155 left, plus six 120mm mortars and dwindling ammunition stocks.

By dawn on 7 May, the garrison had been reduced to an area about half a mile square. The main base had just a single 105 remaining. Remarkably, Bigeard launched a final counterattack with two companies and the last remaining tank. De Castries and Langlais contacted Cogny and Bodet to update them on their situation. They were told to let the

The defeated Dien Bien Phu garrison marches into captivity.

battle 'die' and that there was to be no hoisting of a white flag. At 5.00 pm, de Castries ordered a ceasefire and the remaining installations and ammunition depots to be destroyed. Just thirty minutes later, the command bunker was captured, along with de Castries and twenty-three of his staff officers.

By 6.00 pm, it was all over. The French did not surrender, they were simply overrun.

To the south, Lalande and the Isabelle garrison were on their own. They had just two 105s and some 1,700 rounds. At 7.00 pm they destroyed the last of their heavy equipment, including a tank. Initially, Lalande thought they might escape northward to Ban Loi and into the jungle, but then opted to go south instead. That night some of his men tried unsuccessfully to break out, but ran into enemy patrols. By the morning of 8 May 1954, Isabelle had also fallen after Lalande surrendered in the early hours. The Battle of Dien Bien Phu was over.

The French garrison suffered 2,200 killed and 6,450 wounded. Several thousand were missing or had deserted. Around 9,000 ragged survivors were rounded up and taken prisoner. Just seventy-eight managed to escape the Viet Minh cordon, not the 3,000 that had been hoped for. Initially, Giap's losses were estimated to be about 20,000 killed and wounded. De Castries, while in captivity, was later informed that Viet Minh casualties had been nearer 30,000. It was a costly victory.

The Armée de l'Air and the Aéronnautique Naval had made a Herculean attempt to break the Viet Minh siege and keep the garrison resupplied. They flew over 10,000 sorties in support of Dien Bien Phu, with 2,650 by the air force's combat aircraft, 1,019 by naval aircraft and 6,700 by the transports. Many of the crews flew upward of 150 combat hours during April, but it was not enough. Some 86 per cent of the aircraft involved in the battle were damaged, with forty-eight shot down and another fourteen destroyed on the ground.

Surprisingly, and despite the superiority of Giap's artillery, his expenditure of ammunition was not greater than that of the French. The latter estimated the Viet Minh had

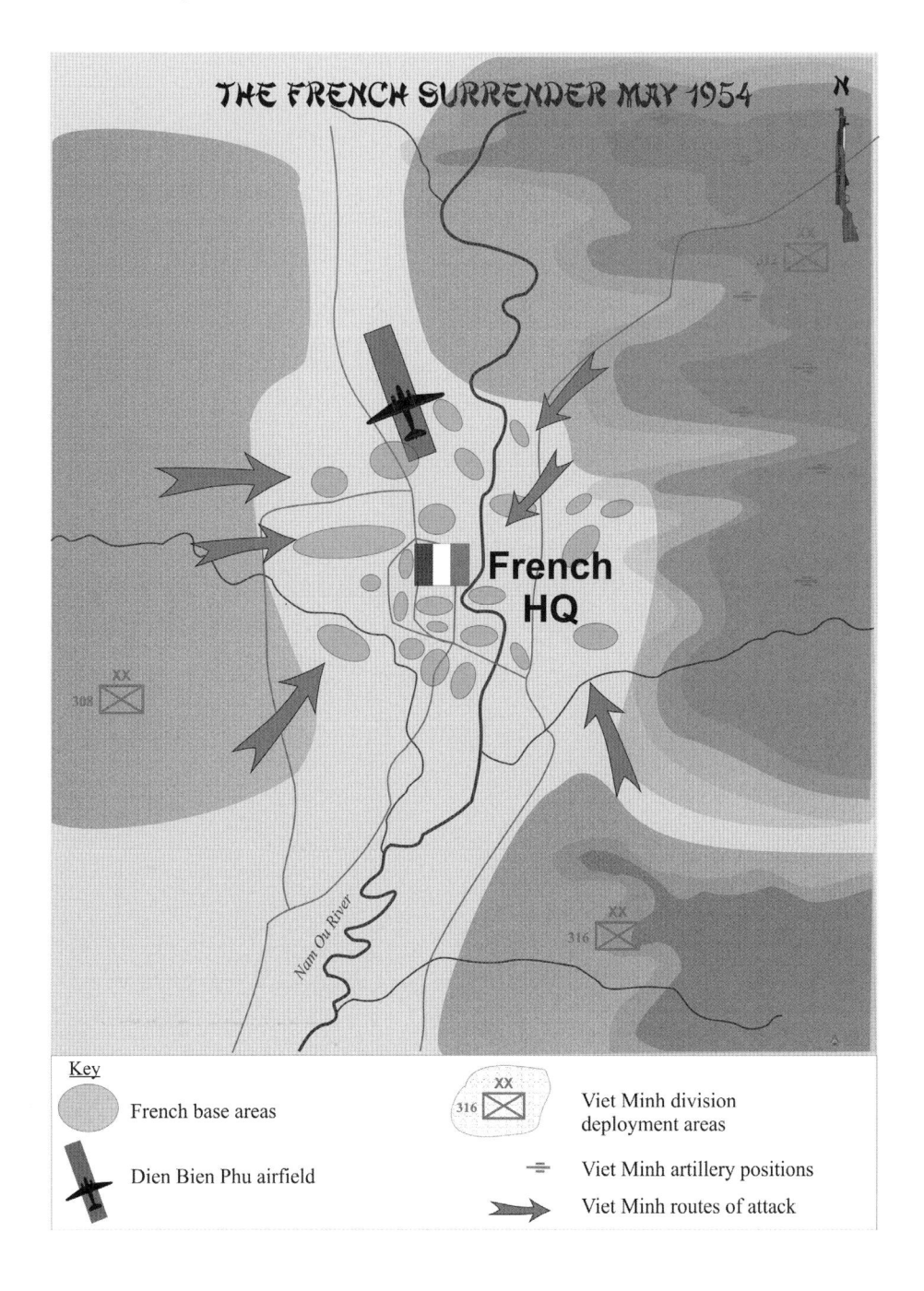

THE FRENCH SURRENDER MAY 1954

Key
- French base areas
- Dien Bien Phu airfield
- Viet Minh division deployment areas
- Viet Minh artillery positions
- Viet Minh routes of attack

expended around 30,000 105mm rounds and around 100,000 other calibres. Much of the old-time, expired Japanese 75mm ammunition proved to be duds and did not explode on impact. French artillery and mortar units fired some 95,000 105mm, 8,500 155mm and 38,000 120mm rounds. Therefore, 130,000 against 141,500. What it meant was that, in terms of calibre and the weight of the round, French firepower had actually been greater. This also does not take into account the tonnage of bombs dropped by the French air force and navy. It makes Giap's victory even more remarkable.

These figures show how French intelligence greatly underestimated Giap's logistical abilities in getting such vast quantities of ammunition to the front. In addition, they illustrate that the French artillery was nowhere near as effective as they had hoped. This was particularly the case with their counter-battery fire, which never silenced even a fraction of Giap's concealed guns.

France's military prestige suffered a shattering blow, equivalent to the loss of Singapore by Britain in 1942. It was now evident to the indigenous peoples that European armies could be defeated. The French military knew that they could not hold on to Indochina any longer – a negotiated withdrawal was the only solution to avoid yet more bloodletting.

Triumphant Viet Minh troops celebrate their stunning but hard-won victory.

USS *Montague* was an Andromeda Class attack cargo ship that assisted with the mass evacuation of Tonkin.

The war cost French Union forces 75,867 dead or missing, including 15,000 North Africans, as well as 65,125 wounded. Around 20,000 of those killed were from metropolitan France, with a large proportion of these officers.

The French Foreign Legion gained particular fame at Dien Bien Phu, where it provided more than half the fighting units – seven out of thirteen – as well as two-thirds of the paratroop contingent. A total of 11,620 legionnaires lost their lives in Indochina. The national armies of the Indochina states fighting for the French suffered a further 31,716 casualties. Giap's Viet Minh lost upwards of 150,000 men while trying to drive the French out. Inevitably, Dien Bien Phu accelerated the peace process.

Just as the news was breaking, French Defence Minister René Pleven found himself attending a dinner party at the British Embassy, which was hosting the Duke of Edinburgh and Field Marshal Montgomery. The despondent Pleven and his wife were an hour late, missing the start of the meal. They were just settling down when Montgomery, never sensitive to others' feelings, exclaimed across the table, 'Well Mister Pleven, what does it feel like to be the most unpopular man in France?'

This was clearly a rhetorical question, but the other dinner guests were stunned. Pleven and the French government had been shamed and he did not need Montgomery or the British revelling in their woes. One diner recalled, 'I shall not forget the moment of ghastly silence which fell on that dinner party!'

Pleven must have gritted his teeth and smiled weakly. His government had asked America and Britain for help in France's moment of need, but it had not been forthcoming. Montgomery should have shown greater tact and, indeed, sympathy for the loss of the French garrison. As an old soldier, he should have known better, but then his jibe had been aimed at a French politician not a French soldier.

17. THE COLD WAR RECKONING

The repercussions of Dien Bien Phu were swiftly felt around the world.

Charles de Gaulle had always been adamant that the loss of Indochina would spell the end of the French empire. He was soon proved right. It spelt not only the beginning of the end for the French Union, but also the Fourth Republic. In Paris, Prime Minister Joseph Laniel's short-lived government fell. He was succeeded by Pierre Mendés-France, who had been a regular opponent of the war in Indochina. He headed for the stalled peace talks in Geneva that were dealing with the troubled issues of Indochina and Korea. The British and Americans tried to support Mendés-France, but there was little to be salvaged from the situation.

Only Ho Chi Minh's powerful allies kept him in check from exploiting his victory even further, but he was prepared to bide his time. China proved a stumbling block to the Viet Minh dominating all of Vietnam, north and south. The Soviets, alarmed at the prospect of the Chinese expanding the war throughout Southeast Asia, applied pressure on Chinese Foreign Secretary Chou En-lai. The Chinese, however, had their own agenda, which had been set well before Dien Bien Phu and the Geneva Conference.

Mendés-France and Chou met on 23 June 1954, without the Vietnamese present, to cut a deal. The terms were not what Ho and his comrades had fought for all those years. When Chou saw the Viet Minh delegation he warned, 'If the Vietnamese continue to fight, they will have to fend for themselves.'

Mao made it clear that if Vietnam's communists continued the war, he would cut off all military support. Pham Vam Dong, Ho Chi Minh's negotiator, was instructed to concede. It was a bitter blow, for it meant the Viet Minh in the south were to give up the struggle.

'I travelled by wagon to the south,' recalled Le Duan, who later became Vietnam's leader. 'Along the way, compatriots came out to greet me, for they thought we had won a victory. It was so painful.'

Nonetheless, Indochina's nationalists achieved almost all their goals with the Geneva Accords of 21 July 1954. Cambodia and Laos had their independence recognized, while Vietnam was divided along the 17th Parallel. This created a formal ceasefire line, which accepted communist control of the north but not the south. Washington was far from happy with this latter concession. To some, it looked like Korea all over again.

British intelligence in March 1954 had accurately forecast the likely scenario if the French were defeated at Dien Bien Phu, stating:

> The Soviet Union and China may be prepared to see an end to the fighting provided that the future of the Viet Minh were assured, either by coalition or partition, but they are unlikely to abandon the Viet Minh in return for any concessions in other fields that we could afford to offer ...

Ho Chi Minh returned triumphant to Hanoi as the leader of the new Democratic Republic of Vietnam, consisting of Tonkin and northern Annam. In Saigon, Ngo Dinh Diem formed the pro-Western Republic of South Vietnam from Cochinchina and southern Annam.

The French agreed to withdraw their forces from the north, while the Viet Minh reluctantly withdrew from the south.

The immediate headache for the French was that the Geneva Accords allowed for a 300-day period of free movement between the two Vietnams. Upwards of a million northerners, including around 200,000 French citizens and troops, wanted to move south, while about 150,000 civilians and Viet Min fighters wanted to go the other way. It was an enormous mass movement, with people travelling by land, air and sea. The French navy and air force shifted the bulk of them, though they were also supported by the U.S. Navy.

After Dien Bien Phu, neither the French had the stomach to continue the fight in South Vietnam, nor were the South Vietnamese keen on them staying. The French defence budget was exhausted. In Paris, there was unease that nationalist unrest might break out in France's other colonies, which had long held aspirations of independence. At the end of the Indochina War, the French Expeditionary Corps, numbering approximately 140,000, faced a swift reduction. It was cut to just 35,000 by mid-1955, with many of those withdrawn sent to Algeria. Tellingly, the French military budget for the following year made no mention of Indochina.

America, which from the start had said it would not support British and French colonialism, had nonetheless assisted the French in Indochina. Washington had committed over a billion dollars, two-thirds of which was on equipment delivered straight to the French Expeditionary Corps. The American armed forces, however, had no say in how it was used or what happened to it. President Eisenhower refused to sign the Geneva Accords and moved to support the South Vietnamese army.

By December 1954, formal agreement had been reached between America, France and the Republic of Vietnam for the U.S. to provide aid through its military assistance programme. This included provision for a drastically reduced South Vietnamese armed forces of 100,000 and a joint Franco-American training mission. At the time of the armistice, the Vietnamese armed forces stood at some 205,000 men. These were largely infantry under French officers and non-commissioned officers. When the troops were redeployed from North to South Vietnam, desertion became a major problem. In addition the Vietnamese had no real experience of military logistics, having been dependent on the French for so long.

Tragically, the French desire to be rid of Indochina as quickly as possible sowed the seeds of the Second Indochina War – better known as the Vietnam War. By this stage, trouble was brewing in French North Africa. The French military, understandably, set about cherry-picking the best equipment from Indochina. American personnel were forbidden access to French bases and depots, which meant that they had no idea what was available to the Vietnamese. The French simply took vast quantities of equipment with them, some of it that had been supplied to the Vietnamese under the military assistance programme.

The intention was to ensure that the South Vietnamese forces had full logistical independence by January 1956, but this never happened, nor was it ever really achievable. As the final French withdrawal approached, they dumped tons of old and poorly maintained military materiel on their former Vietnamese allies who did not know how to handle it properly, and containers were opened and piled randomly out in the open. The last French troops left Vietnam on 28 April 1956, having decided that Indochina was no longer their problem.

Washington soon came to the conclusion that in light of the build-up of the Vietnamese communist forces in the North, the Army of the Republic of Vietnam should be maintained at 150,000 strong. Following the departure of the French and the dissolution of the joint training mission, Washington had no choice but to increase its military advisers and its military commitment to South Vietnam. The Cold War was far from over in Southeast Asia.

U.S. Navy LST *516* loading refugees at Haiphong, 1 October 1954.

Predictably, Ho's government announced in December 1960 that the Viet Minh would resume their operations to liberate South Vietnam. In response, President John F. Kennedy sent 686 military advisers to organize the South Vietnamese army, which was to be expanded by 20,000 with American assistance. Slowly but surely America was dragged into the conflict between the two Vietnams.

Ironically, the presence of the Americans ensured China and the Soviet Union did all they could to support Hanoi's desire for unification. In 1968, the U.S. military found itself facing its own Dien Bien Phu at a place called Khe Sanh. On this occasion, though, it was not the main focus of General Giap's massive Tet Offensive. Although Khe Sanh was not overrun and Tet was defeated, the long-term effect was the same.

Further afield, Dien Bien Phu caused an unwelcome chain reaction throughout the French Union. The impact of the French defeat was immediately felt in France's most prized colonial possession – Algeria. The French had always deluded themselves that it was part of metropolitan France. This was a fiction perpetrated to legitimize France's long-standing colonial presence. On VE day in May 1945, an anti-French Muslim demonstration in the Algerian town of Sétif culminated in over a hundred Europeans being butchered. In the weeks that followed, in an orgy of revenge, 6,000 Muslims were killed. Internationally, these events were largely ignored thanks to more pressing matters in Indochina. The Algerians, though, did not forget.

There was also growing unrest in France's other two North African territories: Morocco and Tunisia. These though were protectorates and France had no right to cling to them. During the Indochina War, French units were deployed in both countries. Between 1952–54 these were drawn from Algeria and, afterwards, from forces returning from Indochina. Algeria and Algerian troops had played a key role in Indochina. In particular, the country had provided an enormous training and transit facility. The French military had some 60,000 troops in Algeria, but less than a third were deployable, while two-thirds of them were Muslim colonial forces. To counter any trouble, the French only had about 3,500 combat troops available. It was not enough.

In November 1954, Algerian nationalists began their first coordinated attacks on French military and police installations. The violence soon spread. France could not, and would not, walk away from Algeria, not when it was home to 1.2 million Europeans. Just as importantly, in 1954 oil was discovered in the Sahara, which convinced the French that Algeria was economically vital. Ironically, even French Communists were largely indifferent to Algerian nationalists. They had no desire to support Algerian independence if it was to the detriment of the prosperity of the French working class.

Two years later, Morocco and Tunisia gained independence and the French garrisons withdrew. The two countries inevitably provided safe havens from which Algerian nationalists could operate. The withdrawal from Indochina, Tunisia and Morocco hardened French resolve over Algérie Française. This time, the politicians had the full backing of the military. The professional army had learned some very important lessons in Indochina about guerrilla and psychological warfare. Many felt guilty about abandoning their Vietnamese allies, seeing Algeria as an opportunity to avenge Dien Bien Phu and preserve the shrinking French Empire.

By early 1955, the French military had rapidly boosted their Algerian garrison to 74,000 troops. By the summer, there were 105,000. The following year, through the use of reservists, they had expanded their presence to 200,000, vastly more than had ever been committed to Indochina. This doubled by the end of 1956, a number that was to be maintained until 1962 and Algerian independence. By the end of the brutal conflict, French forces had suffered around 25,000 fatalities, having killed 155,000 Algerian guerrillas.

The French also gained valuable experience using helicopters in Indochina and did much to develop helicopter warfare. At the time of Dien Bien Phu, the French Army only had a single helicopter in Algeria. Three years later, they had assembled a force of eighty. By the end of the conflict in Algeria, the French had 120 transport helicopters in-country, capable of airlifting 21,000 men a month.

In France's sub-Saharan colonies, because the French were focused on Indochina and North Africa, they had allowed a greater degree of devolution. African nationalist energies were expended on each other as they argued over closer association with Paris, loose federation or no relationship at all. By the spring of 1956, the French Union was clearly disintegrating. The associated states had broken free and the African colonies were moving towards self-government. French sovereignty was reduced to only those territories that were ruled as part of France, the old Colonial West Indies, the territories in the Indian Ocean, and troubled Algeria. In 1956, France tried to prove that it was still a world power by joining Britain in the brief Suez War against Nasser's Egypt. It ended in international humiliation for both.

Britain, with its own colonial problems, watched the French defeat in Indochina with interest. Since 1948, it had been fighting to contain a communist insurgency in Malaya. The opening scenario was very similar to Indochina. Originally armed to fight the Japanese, after the Second World War Malaya's communists decided to resist the returning British administration. They were, however, largely drawn from the local ethnic

Troops of the Foreign Legion's 13th Demi-Brigade, Algeria, 1950s.

Chinese population rather than the Malays and Indians. On 16 June 1948, on two rubber estates near Sungei Siput in Perak, three European managers were murdered. As a result, a state of emergency was declared that would last until 1960.

By 1951, the Malayan Races Liberation Army numbered 8,000, though 90 per cent were Chinese. Until this point they were known as 'bandits', but were subsequently dubbed 'CTs' or communist terrorists. Fortunately for Britain, support for the guerrillas by China and the Soviet Union was limited. Unfortunately for the Malayan Communists, China was distracted by the wars in Korea and Indochina, which were right on its doorstep. China had no mutual border with Malaya, thereby making it difficult to provide supplies.

To isolate the insurgents, the British adopted a policy of detention and resettlement – especially with Malaya's Chinese population, which numbered almost two million. At the same time, the British conducted a protracted pacification campaign in the deep jungles and the central mountains. Britain also made it clear that independence would only be granted once the security situation had been restored, but would not surrender the country to the communists. This stance ensured that much of the population continued to support the British presence. This was a situation that the French were never able to replicate in Indochina.

Having gained the upper hand, British forces were keen to avoid the Malayan communists being reinvigorated by the victory at Dien Bien Phu. Between July and November 1954, the British launched their largest operation to date with Operation Termite in Perak, deep inside the jungle east of Ipoh. Also, Operation Apollo was carried out from mid-1954 until mid-1955 in the Kuala Lipis area of Pahang. It was another five years before the Malayan emergency was declared over, by which time the communists had lost 10,684 killed and captured.

To the outside world, Dien Bien Phu confirmed that France was the victim of weak and chaotic government. The Fourth Republic endured twenty-four governments when Britain had four and Germany just one. France remained polarized between the left and the right. The RPF (Rassemblement pour la France) made considerable gains, and although de Gaulle relinquished the leadership in 1953, it was still a powerful right-wing force. On the left, the communist party continued to garner about a quarter of the vote. Continuous war had strained the economy, causing a devaluation of the franc in 1957.

The fallout from Dien Bien Phu brought France to the brink of military dictatorship. While de Gaulle was an ardent supporter of the Union Française, he had little regard for the pro-Algerian element within the army, as they had backed generals Pétain and Giraud against him in 1943. When in May 1958 it looked as if the government would settle over independence, the military, led by generals Massu and Salan, formed the Committee of Public Safety. It was obvious that France was facing a coup. Through the RPF, de Gaulle brought pressure to bear and was appointed president-premier with dictatorial powers for six months. A new constitution was drafted, giving the president far greater authority.

In October 1958, the Fifth Republic began with a Gaullist Party victory and de Gaulle appointed president for seven years. His period in office until 1969 was essentially one-party rule. The Algerian crisis gave him the opportunity to create riot police and employ secret-service methods that caused widespread condemnation. He also created a new relationship with France's remaining colonies in the French Community. This enabled France to retain close economic links with her former African colonies.

Dien Bien Phu

Men of the Foreign Legion's 13th Demi-Brigade in Algeria in the late 1950s.

In 1954, France was humiliated by its defeat at Dien Bien Phu. Its conventional forces had been defeated by a communist revolutionary war waged by peasant guerrillas backed by Communist China. While the French had striven to defeat the Viet Minh on the battlefield, they had done little to counter their grass-roots ideology. French promises to maintain the French Union, comprising mutually aligned territories, had a hollow appeal to those wanting full independence.

One of the greatest advantages that Giap enjoyed was that, although his men were trained and organized as regulars, with regiments and divisions, they also fought as guerrillas. This meant that they had firm command and control plus the discipline of regular soldiers, rather than being ill-disciplined militia. This discipline was enforced by the iron hand of communist ideology, which insisted on the greater good outweighing the needs of the individual.

In contrast, the French, despite their best efforts with airborne and mobile groups and local militias, never really mastered irregular or counter-insurgency warfare. Thanks to the Second World War and the Cold War, their ethos and doctrine were very much anchored in conventional warfare that was based on fighting set-piece battles. This was what they would have to do if called on to resist the armies of the Warsaw Pact. Ultimately, their lack of adequate off-road mobility and logistical back-up was their undoing in Indochina. It was not until the intervention of the American military, with the concept of air-mobile cavalry using large numbers of helicopters, that the conflict in Vietnam became truly fluid. French adherence to fixed defences at the end of their inadequate logistical lines was never going to be a war-winning formula.

France's persistence in holding ground in Indochina drained its manpower and deprived it of the initiative. Even French mobile units had to rely on vehicles, not aircraft or helicopters, for quick reaction, which had left them constantly vulnerable to ambush. Defeat at Dien Bien Phu destroyed the French Union and the French Empire. Just as importantly, it showed the communist world what was possible. It ensured that, although the Cold War never became hot in Europe, conflict proliferated elsewhere in the world. In France's case it led to the wholly unnecessary war in Algeria and yet more loss of life. Such was the tragedy of Dien Bien Phu. Vietnam, meanwhile, was consigned to yet another war.

EPILOGUE – THE RETURNED

There was no way that General Henri Navarre could survive the disaster of Dien Bien Phu. He and Commissioner General Maurice Dejean were sacked and replaced by General Paul Ely on 3 June 1954. Ely's military deputy was none other than Navarre's predecessor, General Raoul Salan. Navarre retired two years later to write *Agonie de l'Indochine*. General René Cogny held him responsible for what had happened and sued him.

The Geneva agreement secured the release of both sides' prisoners of war by the end of 1954. Cold War and anti-imperialist politics played a part in how this was carried out. Interestingly, the Viet Minh treated those captured differently, depending on where they were recruited. This greatly hampered establishing the precise numbers of those they set free and those unaccounted for.

Only French citizens were handed back directly to the French authorities. The Viet Minh returned a total of about 11,000 captured French troops, of whom 3,900 had been taken at Dien Bien Phu. Discounting the legionnaires, this posed the question of what happened to the rest – some 4,100 men. The French government refrained from causing a fuss, for fear it might impede any future releases.

The legionnaires and African colonial troops were repatriated via China and the Soviet Union to their countries of origin. For example, around 1,000 East European legionnaires were returned to communist-bloc states such as East Germany. Some of them then managed to make their way back to their units. The North and West African recruits, seen as fellow oppressed peoples, were subjected to anti-colonial propaganda and encouraged to support nationalist movements once home. The French were understandably not happy with these arrangements, which deliberately undermined the authority of the French military in Africa.

The Viet Minh viewed the French Indochinese troops as traitors to the cause of nationalism and

Czech native and veteran of the French Foreign Legion, Pavel Knihař fought in French Indochina from April 1949 to April 1953. Here he receives the Médaille Militaire for outstanding military service, 16 July 1955.

independence. Some were later given the chance to fight for communism, some remained incarcerated, some managed to return home, and others died or were killed. In excess of 26,000 Vietnamese and non-Vietnamese (that included Cambodians and Laotians) soldiers remain unaccounted for. This was a stain on French military honour.

Despite overseeing one of France's most shocking military defeats, Christian de Castries's career did not end when he was released. He was quietly sent to West Germany to command the French 5th Armoured Division, before eventually retiring in 1959. Para Pierre Langlais went on to attain the rank of brigadier general, but took his own life in 1986. His comrade, Marcel Bigeard, was sent to Algeria in 1956 to help fight the nationalists. His last military command was in the Central African Republic in the early 1960s. Legionnaire André Lalande fought in Algeria and, likewise, became a brigadier general. Jean Gilles, commander of the airborne troops in Indochina, also survived the scandal and fought during the Suez Crisis and then in Algeria.

The Geneva Accord brought the war in Indochina to an end.

APPENDIX I

FRENCH ORDER OF BATTLE
DIEN BIEN PHU
6 DECEMBER 1953 – 8 MAY 1954

Far East
Command
French Far East Expeditionary Corps: HQ Saigon
Commander-in-Chief Far East: General Henri Navarre
Commander Far East Air Forces: General Henri Lauzin
Commander Far East Maritime Forces: Admiral Auboyneau

Indochina Command
Land Forces North Vietnam: HQ Hanoi
Commander: General René Cogny
Tactical Air Group North
Commander: General Jean Dechaux
Air Transport
Commander: Colonel Nicot
Land Forces Laos
Commander: Colonel Boucher de Crèvecoeur

French Garrison 6 December 1953
Airborne
HQ Airborne Divisional Element
2nd Battalion, 1st Parachute Light Infantry Regiment
1st Colonial Parachute Battalion
1st Foreign Legion Parachute Battalion
5th Vietnamese Parachute Battalion
8th Parachute Shock (Assault) Battalion
17th Airborne Engineers Company
Infantry
3rd T'ai Battalion
Artillery
35th Airborne Artillery Regiment
1st Foreign Legion Heavy Airborne Mortar Company
Laotian Autonomous Artillery Battery

French Garrison 13 March 1954
Commander Operational Group North West: Colonel de Castries
<u>Airborne</u>
1st Foreign Legion Parachute Battalion (HQ Reserve)
8th Parachute Shock Battalion (HQ Reserve)
<u>Infantry</u>
1st Battalion, 13th Foreign Legion Demi-Brigade ('Claudine')
3rd Battalion, 13th Foreign Legion Demi-Brigade ('Beatrice')
1st Battalion, 2nd Foreign Legion Infantry Regiment ('Huguette')
3rd Battalion, 3rd Foreign Legion Infantry Regiment '(Isabelle')
2nd Battalion, 1st Algerian Rifle Regiment ('Isabelle')
3rd Battalion, 3rd Algerian Rifle Regiment ('Dominique')
5th Battalion, 7th Algerian Rifle Regiment ('Gabrielle')
1st Battalion, 4th Moroccan Rifle Regiment ('Elaine')
2nd T'ai Battalion ('Elaine')
3rd T'ai Battalion ('Anne-Marie')
T'ai Partisan Mobile Group No.1 (Francoise and other strongpoints)
<u>Artillery</u>
2nd Group (i.e., 2nd Battalion), 4th Colonial Artillery Regiment ('Claudine' & 'Dominique')
3rd Group (3rd Battalion), 10th Colonial Artillery Regiment ('Claudine' & 'Isabelle')
11th Battery, 4th Group, 4th Colonial Artillery Regiment ('Claudine')
1st Foreign Legion Heavy Airborne Mortar Company ('Claudine')
1st Foreign Legion Composite Heavy Mortar Company ('Gabrielle')
2nd Foreign Legion Composite Heavy Mortar Company ('Anne-Marie')
<u>Tanks</u>
3rd Squadron, 1st Light Horse Regiment

French Airborne Reinforcements 13 March–May 1954
1st Colonial Parachute Battalion (incomplete)
2nd Battalion, 1st Parachute Light Infantry Regiment
2nd Foreign Legion Parachute Battalion
5th Vietnamese Parachute Battalion
6th Colonial Parachute Battalion
3rd, 5th & 6th airborne surgical teams

Note: This orbat does not include the French air force, army aviation, naval aviation, intelligence, and the numerous support units involved in the Battle of Dien Bien Phu.

APPENDIX II

Viet Minh Order of Battle
Vietnam People's Army
Dien Bien Phu
13 March–8 May 1954

Central Command
Commander-in Chief: General Vo Nguyen Giap
Chief of Staff: General Hoang Van Thai

'Nam Dinh'
304th Infantry Division: General Hoang Sam
9th Infantry Regiment:
353rd, 375th & 400th battalions
57th Infantry Regiment:
265th, 346th & 418th battalions
(third regiment not committed)
345th Artillery Battalion

'Viet Bac'
308th Infantry Division: General Vuong Thua Vu
36th Infantry Regiment:
80th, 84th & 89th battalions
88th Infantry Regiment:
23rd, 29th & 322nd battalions
102nd Infantry Regiment:
18th, 54th & 79th battalions

'Ben Tre'
312th Infantry Division: General Hoang Cam
141st Infantry Regiment:
11th, 16th & 428th battalions
165th Infantry Regiment:
115th, 542nd & 564th battalions
209th Infantry Regiment:
130th, 154th & 166th battalions
154th Artillery Battalion

'Bien Hoa'
316th Infantry Division: General Le Quang Ba
98th Infantry Regiment:
215th, 439th & 933rd battalions

174th Infantry Regiment:
249th & 251st battalions
176th Infantry Regiment:
888th, 970th & 999th battalions
980th Artillery Battalion
812th Heavy Weapons Company

Support
351st Heavy Division (Reinforced): General Vu Hien
45th Artillery Regiment:
950th & 954th battalions
675th Artillery Regiment:
83rd, 175th & 275th battalions
367th Anti-aircraft Regiment
237th Heavy Weapons Regiment
151st Engineer Regiment
Field Rocket Unit (unidentified)
148th Independent Infantry Regiment:
910th & 920th battalions, plus 121st Heavy Weapons Company

Lieutenant Colonel Bigeard and Colonel Langlais on release from captivity.

BIBLIOGRAPHY

Bishop, Chris & Chant, Chris., *Aircraft Carriers: The World's Greatest Naval Vessels and Their Aircraft.* (St. Paul: MBI, 2004)
Buszynski, Leszek, *Soviet Foreign Policy and Southeast Asia.* (Croom Helm, Beckham, 1986)
Chalfont, Alun. *Montgomery of Alamein.* (Weidenfeld & Nicolson, London, 1976)
Chang, Jung & Halliday, Jon, *Mao: The Unknown Story.* (Johnathan Cape, London, 2005)
Clayton, Anthony. *Three Marshalls of France: Leadership After Trauma.* (Brassey's, London, 1992)
Collins, Brigadier General James Lawton, Jr., *The Development and Training of the South Vietnamese Army, 1950–1972.* (U.S. Department of the Army, Washington DC, 1975)
Cradock, Percy, *Know Your Enemy: How the Joint Intelligence Committee Saw the World.* (John Murray, London, 2002)
Crawley, Aidan, *De Gaulle.* (Literary Guild, London, 1969)
Dunstan, Simon, *Armour of the Vietnam Wars.* (Osprey, London, 1985)
Fall, Bernard B., *Hell in a Very Small Place: The Siege of Dien Bien Phu.* (Da Capo Press edition, 2002)
Francillon, René J., *Vietnam Air Wars.* (Hamlyn, London, 1987)
French, Patrick, *Liberty or Death: India's Journey to Independence and Division.* (Harper Collins, London, 1997)
Hamilton, Nigel, *Monty: The Field-Marshal 1944–1976.* (Hamish Hamilton, London 1986)
Hastings, Max, *The Korean War.* (Michael Joseph, London, 1987)
Hogg, Ian, *Twentieth-Century Artillery.* (Grange Books, Hoo, 2005)
Jackson, Julian, *Charles de Gaulle.* (Sphere, London, 1990)
Karnow, Stanley, *Vietnam: A History.* (Viking Press, New York 1983 & Penguin, Harmondsworth, 1983)
Lacoutre, Jean, *De Gaulle: The Rebel 1890–1944.* (Harvill, London 1993. First published in France in 1984 as *De Gaulle: Rebelle 1890–1944*, by Editions du Seuil)
Maclear, Michael, *Vietnam: The Ten Thousand Day War.* (Thames/Methuen, London, 1982)
Markham, George, *Japanese Infantry Weapons of World War Two.* (Purnell, London, 1976)
O'Ballance, Edgar, *The Wars in Vietnam 1954–1973.* (Ian Allan, London, 1975)
Pimlot, John, ed., *Guerrilla Warfare.* (Bison, London, 1985)
Ridgway, Matthew B., *The Korean War.* (Barrie & Rockliff, The Cresset Press, London, 1968)
Scurr, John, *The Malayan Campaign 1948–60.* (Osprey, London, 1982)
Spurr, Russel, *Enter the Dragon: China at War in Korea.* (Sidgwick & Jackson, London, 1989)
Suermondt, Jan, *Illustrated Guide to Combat Weapons.* (Grange Books, Hoo, 2004)
Sumner, Ian & Vauvillier, François, *The French Army 1939–45 (1).* (Osprey, London, 1998)
Sumner, Ian & Vauvillier, François, *The French Army 1939–45 (2).* (Osprey, London, 1998)
Thomas, Nigel & Abbott, Peter, *The Korean War 1950–53.* (Osprey, London, 1986)
Thompson, Leroy, illustrated by Chappell, Michael, *et al, Uniforms of the Indo-China and Vietnam Wars.* (Blandford Press, Poole, 1984)

Thompson, Sir Robert, ed., *War in Peace: An Analysis of Warfare Since 1945*. (Orbis, London, 1981)
U.S. Marine Corps Institute, *Operations Against Guerrilla Units*. (MCI, Washington DC, 1984)
White, Dorothy Shipley, *Seeds of Discord: De Gaulle, Free France and the Allies*. (Syracuse University Press, New York, 1964)
Windrow, Martin, *The Last Valley: Dien Bien Phu and the French Defeat in Vietnam*. (Weidenfeld & Nicolson, London, 2004)
Windrow, Martin, *The Algerian War 1954–62*. (Osprey, London, 1997)
Windrow, Martin, colour illustrations by Chappell, Michael, *Uniforms of the French Foreign Legion 1831–1981*. (Blandford Press, Poole, 1986)
Windrow, Martin, *The French Foreign Legion*. (Patrick Stephens, Bar Hill, 1976)
Windrow, Martin, *French Foreign Legion*. (Osprey, Oxford, 1971)
Wintle, Justin. *The Viet Nam Wars*. (Weidenfeld & Nicolson, London, 1991)

ABOUT THE AUTHOR

Anthony Tucker-Jones is a former defence intelligence officer and a widely published expert on regional conflicts, counter-terrorism and armoured and aerial warfare. He is the author of over thirty books including *The Vietnam War: The Tet Offensive 1968*, *The Gulf War: Operation Desert Storm 1990–1991*, *The Afghan War: Operation Enduring Freedom 2001–2014* and *The Iraq War: Operation Iraqi Freedom 2003–2011*. He is security and terrorism correspondent for *intersec – The Journal of International Security*. His website can be found at www.atuckerjones.com.